Breaking Traditions

By

Hannah Carnley

© Hannah Carnley 2025

ISBN: 978-1-918264-29-6

...

1st book in the 'Ashley Morgan' series

...

Although this story is meant to be set in Wales, the landscape featured here is entirely fictitious and not meant to symbolise a real place. Likewise, the characters presented in this story are completely imaginary and any similarities to real people or other stories are purely coincidental.

...

WARNING

This story discusses mental health issues, domestic abuse and animal cruelty

Dedicated to my dad. ☺

I can't thank you enough for all the support and encouragement you've given me over the years. You've always been happy to let me ramble on about my imaginary world and I loved the illustrations you did. You're a huge source of inspiration and I'm very grateful for you reading various drafts of my stories.

Contents

Character List	3
Family Tree	4
Bad Blood	6
Myths & Legends	15
A Familiar Intruder	25
The Broken Aeroplane	32
Abusive Locals	44
Traumatic Memories	52
Attic Adventures	68
Toxic Childhood	80
Hunting for Whistles	88
Shadow	99
Local History	103
A Wild Forest	118
Difficult Discoveries	125
Awkward Family Reunion	146
Time to Grieve	162
A Guiding Beacon	173
Hunted	184
Tunnel Invader	192
The Outcast	201
Painful Revelations	209
Rose	229
Cruel Master	239

The Morgan Gallery	251
Honourable Ancestors	263
Mad Runaway	272
Missing Key	283
Paranormal Assistance	292
The Battle for the Locomotive	298
An Offensive Gift	311

Character List

Ashley Morgan	Main character
Luke Matthews	Ashley's best friend
Robbie & Michael Slater	Ashley's half-brothers
Tom Hayes	Luke's cousin
Bryony & Jenna Taylor	Twin sisters & bandmates of Luke & Ashley
Suzanna Thatcher	Luke & Ashley's friend from primary school
Rose Frost	Ashley's cousin
Dean Morgan	Ashley's father
Heidi Cairns	Ashley, Robbie & Michael's mother
Ethan Slater	Robbie & Michael's father
Enid Morgan	Ashley's aunt & Rose's mother
Glen Morgan	Ashley & Rose's uncle
Pamela Dawson	Ashley, Robbie & Michael's guardian

Family Tree

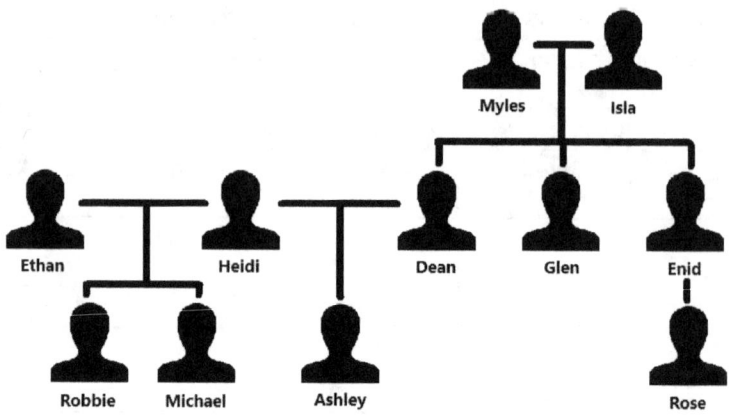

Bad Blood

Ashley Morgan had been dreading this holiday for weeks. He really didn't want to return to the place of his nightmares where he had almost died as a child, so he had been in a bad mood all week as he worried about what the trip might be like.

His friends eyed him quietly as they stepped down onto the platform with their luggage. They'd never seen Ashley like this before, so anxious and fidgety, and they wondered what could have provoked such a reaction. He was usually the strong and confident one, so they weren't entirely sure how to handle his current nerves.

They had arrived at a beautiful little Welsh town nestled in a narrow valley and Ashley looked round critically as he hoisted his rucksack further up his shoulder. Somewhere, hidden within the thick, misty forest that cloaked the landscape, was the Morgan manor, where they were due to stay with his aunt and cousin. As soon as he spotted a set of tall, Gothic chimney stacks rising up out of the trees on the hillside, Ashley felt his blood turn to ice. So, this was it. He was finally here. It was time to confront his demons.

"Come on. There should be a taxi-rank somewhere outside the station. We'll see if we can get a lift." Tom's voice declared, firmly snapping Ashley out of his thoughts and leading the way through the grand old Victorian building.

"I wouldn't bet on it." Ashley muttered, reluctantly traipsing after his friends towards the main road.

Tom gestured for them to wait a moment before he walked up to the nearest taxi. The man obediently rolled his window down and Tom held out his phone to show the address they wanted.

"Hello! Could you take us to this house please?" He asked, politely.

The man considered the address for a few moments before he turned to glare across at Ashley in the background. Then, he firmly shook his head.

"No, thank you. That place means trouble. And your friend is one of *them*. I know he is. He's got bad blood. They all have the same dirty black hair and piercing eyes. I don't know what you're up to, boy, but I want no part of it." He answered, urgently rolling his window back up again before driving away down the street, clearly keen to escape the situation.

Tom frowned, turning to look round at the other taxi-drivers instead, who suddenly appeared to be quite busy and wouldn't meet his gaze.

"What the hell-?" He gasped, shocked by the men's blatant refusal to serve them and looking round awkwardly as Ashley came over to join him.

"Come on, let's just walk." He muttered and Tom raised his eyebrow as he considered his friend's new appearance. Since being recognised as a Morgan a few moments ago and rudely rejected, Ashley had pulled his hood up over his offensive black hair and fastened a face-mask over his mouth and nose to try and hide his identity, leaving only a pair of intense, eyeliner-soaked blue eyes to peer out at Tom.

"What's going on? How do they know who you are? And why did the man say that you have bad blood?" Tom asked and Ashley's eyes scowled darkly.

"You'll find out soon enough." He growled, turning to stalk off down the street and forcefully dragging his suitcase along behind him.

His friends glanced at each other nervously for a few seconds before they turned to follow him, creating a thunderous racket with their cases and wondering why they had to walk all the way to their destination. Why was Ashley so viciously unpopular around here that people would actually refuse to serve him? From what they'd heard, he hadn't been here for twelve years, so the townsfolk shouldn't have any cause to hate him so much. It was all very strange. Ashley obviously understood what was going on since he'd chosen to try and disguise himself and his friends hoped he would explain everything soon.

By the time they arrived at the narrow forest lane that led up to the manor, they were all thoroughly exhausted and paused a moment to rest, with Ashley firmly ripping the mask off his face to breathe in the fresh air. There was little chance of anyone recognising him now since this road only went up to the Morgan manor, so he decided it was safe enough to reveal himself again.

His best friend, Luke Matthews, eyed him curiously for a few moments before he offered out a bottle of juice.

"It would seem that you have a bad reputation around here, Ash. Why are you so unwelcome?" He asked as Ashley reached out to accept the drink.

Ashley said nothing, gesturing for his friends to carry on up the lane ahead of him as he turned to offer the hostile town a final menacing glare.

Luke remained loyally by his side all the way up the long, gloomy forest lane and Ashley turned to nod at him gratefully. Normally, his wealthy best friend would spend his summers lounging on a hot, sunny beach somewhere in the Mediterranean rather than freezing to death here in cloudy old Britain, but Luke had happily agreed to the switch and Ashley was relieved. He'd always known this trip would be quite painful, but Luke's calm presence made him feel a lot better.

Ever since he had received the letter from his aunt earlier that year, which invited him to come and stay at the manor with his friends, Ashley had been on edge. The letter had provoked a lot of unpleasant thoughts about the night his mother had been cruelly stolen from him and Ashley wasn't sure he was ready to deal with that just yet.

The memories of that traumatic night frequently haunted his dreams even now and he would always carry the long scar down the left side of his face. It stretched down from his forehead, split his eyebrow in half and continued down his cheek to finish at his jaw. Thankfully, his left eye had remained perfectly intact and Ashley knew he had been lucky to escape with his life. He had been a mere child when the attack happened, a helpless four-year-old, and to this day he had never told his two younger half-brothers how their parents had died. He was the only one who knew the entire truth about what had happened as he had just about been old enough to remember it.

Now, Ashley was sixteen and wondered why his aunt had chosen this year in particular to invite him up from Cornwall for a holiday. He could only assume that she had been waiting until he and his siblings were old enough to deal with the pain of returning to the place where their lives had been changed forever. His aunt had always written and sent presents, but Ashley had no memory of her so this would be their first proper meeting. At the moment, he only knew that her name was Enid, which he thought was quite a pretty, *safe* sort of name. She had always sounded really nice in her letters so Ashley hoped they would get on well.

"Stop worrying." Luke's voice murmured and Ashley half-flinched as Luke reached out to lay an encouraging hand on his shoulder. "I swear you've had that dark, brooding look in your eyes all day. *Relax,* man. I might not understand why you're so jittery, but I guarantee it won't be as bad as you're expecting. Trust me. I think your aunt sounds lovely. And if you're not happy then we can always go home again. I won't judge you." Luke sighed, gently turning Ashley round to face him and fixing him with a solemn smile.

Ashley rolled his eyes. Of course Luke would figure out what he was thinking about. Nothing ever escaped him. Luke noticed everything. It was like he had superpowers. No matter how hard Ashley tried to hide his emotions and lie that everything was fine, Luke would always see straight through him with a knowing smirk that showed he knew the truth. Ashley really hated that smug little smirk. Even when his face remained blank to all other observers, Luke could still read him perfectly, picking up on the tiniest little twitch of an eyebrow, the mood in his eyes or his body language. He would then add these details to the wealth of information he had about the current events of Ashley's life to draw an expert conclusion on what was bothering him this time and how best to react. His extraordinary mind-reading abilities had always baffled their friends and they were alarmed every time Luke demonstrated that he could read them with ease too and that his peculiar skills were not just reserved for Ashley.

The pair were absolutely inseparable and had become an interesting combination of light and darkness which their friends found quite fascinating. Of course, Ashley was the darkness, with his rich black hair styled into a handsome, spiky pompadour and his love of dark clothes. Over the years, he seemed to have developed a passion for synthetic leather jackets, skinny jeans and biker boots and was now rarely seen in anything else. This, along with his bold, black eyeliner, long facial scar and brooding aura often made him appear quite cold and hostile until you got to know him better.

Luke, on the other hand, was the light, with his playful, optimistic personality, sparkling green eyes and dirty blond hair. Like Ashley, Luke was also a bit of a rule-breaker since he refused to cut his hair short, as was generally expected for boys, and instead wore his thick, wavy mane half tied back out of the way. While Ashley had been firmly cast as the unpopular dark freak by their classmates, Luke was the polar opposite. *Everyone* wanted to be his friend and he was regularly questioned on why he had chosen Ashley for a best friend of all people. Luke was the one you could talk to about anything. He was always happy to listen and his fierce loyalty meant that he would stop at nothing to help resolve a problem. Luke's classmates had learnt the hard way not to speak a bad word about Ashley while Luke was in earshot for fear of igniting his wrath. Ashley might not care what was said about him, but Luke would preach until the offender had given a sincere apology.

Despite their contrasting appearances and personalities, Luke and Ashley had an awful lot in common and their friends often commented that it was like they had been made for each other. They were both quite tall with a headstrong attitude to life and they were both the eldest child in their families, with Ashley having two younger brothers while Luke had two little sisters and a baby brother.

They also shared a deep love of music and had been writing songs together for eight years now. Here again they seemed to complement each other quite well, for Ashley had been gifted a beautiful, silky voice and was a truly phenomenal singer with a talent for crafting haunting lyrics, while Luke was more of a musical genius instead and could always find the perfect tune for Ashley's ideas.

Over the years, Luke's wealthy parents had paid for both his piano and guitar lessons while poorer Ashley had adopted Luke as his own guitar teacher after begging him to pass on what he'd learnt at his lessons. In exchange, he had taught Luke how to sing and the pair had become quite the musical duo, eventually joining up with the equally-gifted twins, Bryony and Jenna Taylor, at secondary school to form a successful band. So, when Ashley's aunt had generously offered that his friends were also welcome to visit, Luke, Bryony and Jenna had been an easy choice.

Luke turned to offer Ashley a friendly nod of encouragement as they followed their friends up the forest lane to the Morgan manor. They usually told each other everything, but Ashley had never told the story of his past. Luke had often wondered what had happened to Ashley during his early childhood to leave him with such a gruesome long scar, but he could see how much those memories hurt him, so he had never asked, out of respect for his friend.

Ashley allowed himself a faint smile as he considered Luke's remarkable optimism and reached out to pat him on the shoulder a few times to show that he appreciated the support. Most of the time, Luke didn't need to *say* anything to cheer up the mood; he brightened a room just by walking into it with a broad grin pasted across his face and a loose, relaxed posture. Ashley didn't know what he'd done to deserve such a devoted and sunny best friend and found Luke's vibrant energy quite addictive.

Up ahead, their friends had now gathered by a pair of tall, intimidating iron gates and peered through to the manor beyond, hidden within the dark forest a world away from the lively market town below in the valley bottom.

Robbie and Michael Slater were Ashley's younger brothers, with Robbie being two years younger than Ashley at fourteen while Michael was the 'baby' at thirteen. They all shared the same mother but Ashley had a different father, so his surname was Morgan instead of Slater and he often felt like the awkward misfit despite being the oldest.

Robbie had the scruffiest appearance of the three brothers, always turning up with ripped jeans, worn-out trainers and messy brown hair as though he never bothered combing it. On the other hand, Michael was always neatly dressed with clean clothes and his blond hair smartly brushed to one side. At home, Robbie loved to reach out and tousle Michael's hair whenever he walked past because it always earned him an exasperated moan and a cold scowl, with his little brother protesting that he didn't want to look like dirty, messy Robbie; people would think he was being led astray. No, Michael preferred to remain neat and tidy and *respectable*, thank-you very much.

Then, there was Tom Hayes, who was the oldest member of the group at seventeen. He was Luke's cousin and had therefore developed quite a close friendship with Ashley too since he and Luke were largely inseparable. Unlike his cousin, Tom's hair was brown and cut quite short and he also did not share Luke's impressive wealth, so his clothes tended to be fairly common while Luke's were more expensive and branded with all kinds of fancy names and logos. As the eldest, Tom's role within the group had always been pretty obvious; he was the silent authority figure who kept them all in line and commanded their respect with his sensible decisions and friendly attitude. If Tom told you to shut up or apologise, then you did without question.

Finally, Ashley had invited three of his closest girl-friends from school, feeling a little bit awkward for inviting so many people even though his aunt had assured him it was okay and that the manor was plenty big enough to house everyone comfortably. His friendship group was a strong one and he wouldn't dream of leaving anyone behind. They'd surely hate him forever.

He and Luke had met Suzanna Thatcher at primary school and been firm friends ever since. She had immediately accepted Luke as a friend, but it had taken a lot longer before she welcomed Ashley because of his reputation as the school freak. It was only because she had a huge crush on Luke that Ashley had eventually become her friend too, since she had once nervously invited Luke to her birthday party and been faced with his usual request to invite Ashley as well. But she had agreed, needing Luke at her party so badly that if Ashley also had to come then so be it. Then, she had discovered Ashley wasn't as mean and scary as everyone made out and they had been great friends ever since, although she wasn't particularly fond of the way he loved to tease her about her affections for his best mate.

Suzy was the sophisticated 'lady' of the group, with her smart clothes, classy make-up, neatly plaited auburn hair and polite language. She wouldn't dream of ever uttering a bad word and Robbie had decided long ago that obviously Suzy must have been born in the wrong era. She was quite small for her age and resented that she only came up to Ashley's chest, often claiming that he had stolen all of her height and she wanted it back. But, despite her small size, she shared the same sensible maturity as Tom and commanded equal respect within the group which pleased her greatly. It was always satisfying to put tall Ashley back in his place.

The twins, Bryony and Jenna, had only joined the group in secondary school, but they fit in really well despite their opposing personalities. Suzy had been absolutely delighted to finally have some female company at last after spending so long with five boys. She had happily declared that it was nice to have someone else to talk to, something Luke and Ashley had found a little offensive.

The elder twin, Bryony, was the tough and feisty one. She was a strong advocate for equality and could be very outspoken and argumentative when she didn't agree with something. Bryony was definitely not one to keep her thoughts to herself and Ashley could never decide if this was a good thing or not. Bryony had long brown hair, which she kept tied up in a practical pony-tail so that she was always ready for an adventure. Her eyes were almost the same colour as her hair and had a rather stern attitude which her friends found quite unnerving at times since Bryony always looked as though she was about to scold them.

Jenna, on the other hand, was the lively, flirty twin who could charm just about anyone and loved to dress up and experiment with different hairstyles, much to Ashley's amusement. Originally, she had shared the same long brown hair as her sister, but had dyed it a magical deep purple instead and found her new appearance very empowering. She was much more relaxed and friendly than her prickly twin and had the same kind of popularity as Luke. She just wanted to make people happy. Like Luke, Jenna was also one of the few people who had managed to earn Ashley's *absolute* trust and the pair had grown really close over the years, to the extent that they were sometimes mistaken for a couple by foolish idiots who refused to accept that a boy and girl could just be friends.

Bryony and Jenna had been really excited when Luke and Ashley suggested they team up and form a band, with Bryony taking great delight in her 'controversial' role as a girl-drummer. Jenna, meanwhile, was in charge of the bass, leaving the two boys to tackle the main guitars, although gifted Luke could also switch onto the keyboards when necessary. Ashley had also learnt to play the drums quite well too, thanks to Bryony, and they enjoyed setting each other complicated challenges to try and improve their skills. Being the more impressive singers, Ashley and Jenna tended to share the lead vocals between them, but they were more than happy to surrender the spotlight to Luke or Bryony from time to time to keep things fair and friendly.

But despite Ashley's usual loud and confident personality, he'd barely spoken since they left Cornwall, keeping his answers short and blunt when someone did coax him into talking and fixing them with a menacing scowl as a punishment. Luke had wisely decided it wasn't worth trying to force Ashley into conversation if he wasn't in the mood and had simply offered him one of his earphones so they could listen to music together and attempted to distract him with various pen-and-paper games, snacks or phone pictures, all without saying a word to him.

Why did this place make Ashley so uneasy? And why did the people in town already seem to know who he was despite him not setting foot in the area for over a decade? His friends were curious to know.

Myths & Legends

Tom eyed the imposing iron gates nervously, reaching out to give one a firm push and frowning when he found it locked.

Ashley calmly padded over to a small box that was fixed at one side of the road and reached out to press a button, waiting a few moments until a woman answered and asked for his name. Ashley introduced himself quietly and the gates immediately creaked open to let them in, revealing a grand and spooky old manor house with ivy growing up the walls and shuttered windows.

"It's the Morgan manor. They're not going to just let you walk straight in. Of course the gates are operational." He remarked, firmly shooing his friends inside and taking great care to plant himself at the back.

Suzy turned to eye him curiously as the front door of the house was thrown open to reveal a woman and young adolescent girl, both of whom shared the same rich black hair as Ashley.

"Your family is most peculiar." She commented and Ashley half-nodded in agreement.

"Welcome! My name is Enid and this is my daughter, Rose, who is eleven. This is the Morgan manor, which dates back to the sixteenth century. I hope you will find it comfortable. We've prepared the west wing for your stay, which has lovely views down over the lake in the valley bottom. Now, which one of you boys is my nephew?" The woman smiled, first turning to gesture round at her daughter and the house before peering round at the boys critically.

Tom frowned, reaching out to place a hand on Ashley's back before giving him a firm push forwards.

"He's here, skulking at the back." He announced and Enid nodded, taking a moment to appraise her young nephew before she cautiously reached out to hug him.

"Ah yes. Now I see the black hair. I wasn't sure if you would have chosen to dye it or not since it's so offensive around here. Let me look at you, my boy. You were only a child the last time

I saw you so it's quite a shock to find you all grown up and handsome! Has it really been so long? Now I do feel old! Wow, Ashley, you look a lot like your father. I wasn't expecting that." Enid began and Ashley flinched.

"*Don't* mention that backstabbing piece of trash. Please. I may be cursed to look like Dean but you don't have to mention it. He's dead to me. I'll be glad never to see his ugly face again." He scowled, shrugging away from his aunt's touch and offering her a pleading look.

"Quite. Well, if it's any consolation, at least you have your mother's beauty and her lovely blue eyes. And from what I've heard off your guardian, you've also inherited Heidi's kind heart and her musical talents which pleases me enormously. I was worried you might be swallowed up by your dark Morgan blood so I'm glad to see that you take more after your dear mother instead. I'm really sorry that you lost her. I know how that feels seeing as my own mum was taken by cancer a whole decade before you were born. It's not easy to watch someone die before their time." Enid agreed, eyeing her nephew sadly.

Somewhat stiffly and guarded, Ashley turned to introduce his crowd of loyal friends, starting with his younger brothers since Enid was already familiar with their names.

When her name was called, Suzy stepped forwards to shake Enid's hand politely and offered her a warm smile.

"Enid. It's so nice to meet you. It's very kind of you to invite us, Ashley's friends, to stay here as well. I can't wait to see the inside of this fascinating old house." She said, instantly making the nervous woman feel more at ease and turning to offer young Rose a friendly smile as well.

Now that all the introductions were taken care of, Enid turned to lead the way inside, beneath the worn family crest over the front door that showed a wolf padding under a pair of crossed swords.

Luke turned to consider his best friend critically as he thought back on Ashley's words. In all the years they'd known each other, Ashley had always described himself as an orphan, which implied that *both* of his parents were dead. And yet now, hearing the way Ashley spoke to his aunt, it sounded like his father was very much alive and Luke was confused. Ashley,

Robbie and Michael had been raised by a guardian and Luke couldn't understand why that would be the case if Ashley still had a living parent. And why would he go to such great lengths to imply otherwise? It was all very bizarre. Would Ashley really prefer that his father was dead and he an orphan? Surely not. Luke decided he would have to ask Ashley to explain himself later when he could catch his friend in a fairly amicable mood. What had Dean done to deserve so much hatred? Had he run away when Ashley was a baby or something? What was going on?

Ashley rolled his eyes as he caught Luke staring at him with that familiar soul-searching gaze and raised one hand up to cover his face so Luke couldn't try to probe his brain before he was ready. He loved Luke more than anything but his best friend could certainly be quite irritating at times with his super-observant gaze as he tried to figure out what Ashley was thinking. Sometimes Ashley wished that Luke would worry about him less and leave him alone. It was like having a permanent babysitter.

He looked round curiously as Enid led them into the main reception room of the manor, a large banquet hall that appeared quite reminiscent of a rustic hunting lodge with a huge antler chandelier suspended from the rafters. In keeping with this theme, the walls were decorated with old tapestries and various mounted heads of woodland creatures, including a majestic stag and a wild boar, while a snarling wolf seemed to take pride of place above a beautiful marble fireplace. There were two of these, one at each end of the room, except one of the fireplaces was more accessible than the other, which had been partially obscured behind a grand piano and so clearly was no longer in use. The rest of the room was taken up by a long pine table and twenty matching chairs upholstered with green leather; nine on each side of the table plus an extra one at the top and bottom end for the more important diners. Two suits of armour guarded the stairs while three enormous bevelled windows dominated the opposite wall, offering a panoramic view out across the surrounding forest and moorland down to the glittering lake far below in the valley bottom.

"Wow." Ashley muttered, staring round the room in shock and padding over to abandon his luggage by the wall along with everyone else's.

Enid and her daughter had clearly been busy for a feast awaited them on the grand banquet table. Ashley cringed as his stomach gave a loud rumble of approval before he obediently sauntered over to claim his rightful place beside Luke and set about examining what was on offer.

Suzy glanced at him nervously before turning back to Enid.

"Excuse-me, Enid, but what's the story of this old building? It's very rare these days that you encounter families still in possession of manor houses like this. Now they tend to be open to the public and used as museums rather than remaining as private homes." She asked, curiously.

Enid smiled to herself, peering round the hall thoughtfully for a few moments as she considered that the townsfolk would probably just burn the place down in disgust if they tried to offer it for public use. It was certainly a magnificent, beautiful old building, but its residents had caused a great deal of grief and outrage amongst the local population over the years and the manor still guarded a large number of family secrets to this day.

"Well, this house has always belonged to us. Prior to the construction of this building, the family occupied an ancient castle, the ruins of which can still be found in the Morgan lands if you know where to look, so our name is an old one. My ancestors built the manor house to give themselves a more comfortable life as the castle had become inadequate for their needs and very old fashioned. Many of the stones used to build the manor were taken from the Morgan castle and recycled, both to keep costs down and preserve the spirit of their old lodgings…" Enid began, pausing as Robbie gave a snort of disbelief and turned to stare at Ashley across the table.

"Wait, there's a castle too? Bloody hell, Ash! Why didn't you tell us that you're filthy rich? Lucky you, sitting pretty on top of all this while Mitch and I get nothing just because we had a different dad. What other secrets have you been brooding over all these years, I wonder? Next you'll be telling us that you're royalty or something." He exclaimed, incredulously.

"I'm not rich, Rob. In case you hadn't noticed, this is *Enid's* home not mine, so I have to make my own way in life just like you and Mitch. Don't be so rude." Ashley growled, glaring across at his angry little brother.

Michael frowned as he considered the mysterious smile that had suddenly appeared on Enid's face. What was that supposed to mean? Did Ashley have some kind of secret inheritance he didn't know about? How very odd.

Luke eyed Ashley and Robbie awkwardly as he listened to their grumpy little argument. They were always bickering about something and regularly declared that they *despised* each other, with Robbie taking great delight in making Ashley's life a complete hell. In return, Ashley seemed to spend half his time at home angrily shouting abuse at his younger brother as he triggered another one of Robbie's pranks, or 'punishments', before going to clean himself up again and furiously slamming everything he touched. Robbie had always insisted that he was also a first-born since he was his father's first child and felt that Ashley had no authority over him whatsoever. With his different surname and profoundly different looks, Ashley was the one who didn't belong, so Robbie argued, and he absolutely refused to do as Ashley instructed. He would not be bossed around by his big brother, something which caused their guardian an enormous amount of grief. Luke privately thought that Pamela deserved a medal or something for dealing with such troublesome siblings. It was no wonder that she had begun to turn grey before her time.

"Come on, Robbie. Don't be mean. Money doesn't always bring you happiness. You should know that well enough by now with all the ingenious pranks you keep dreaming up from free stuff you find in the bin, you strange boy." He muttered, turning to fix them both with a hard stare.

"You're one to talk, Matthews, you wealthy git." Robbie grumbled, sourly.

Luke merely rolled his eyes and turned to address their host politely.

"I'm so sorry, Enid. These two are always at each other's throats. What were you saying-?" He apologised and she nodded.

"Yes, so I've heard. Well, you can see that the manor is vast, but it was constructed from other people's wealth as the Morgans were always notorious as smugglers, highwaymen, thieves, pirates and so on. The men were infamous warriors and very powerful and were known as 'wolves' since they usually worked as a team, like wolf packs. They were a dark force and ruled over these lands with threats and blackmail, simply terrorising the local towns and villages into submission. This estate was constructed from the stolen wealth of others as the Morgans would do as they pleased and refused to conform to society's rules, with one very important exception. I'm sure you've learnt from your history lessons at school that men were widely regarded as the dominant sex and this was something the Morgans always treated as gospel. It was the one rule they never broke. The men were trained to become dangerous criminals and honour the cruel family traditions while the women were expected to stay behind and look after the children." She continued, pausing again as Bryony turned to gesture round at the fancy hall.

"But surely things must be better now, right? I mean, *you're* in charge of the manor and yet you're a woman." She asked, hopefully.

Enid shook her head.

"I'm afraid not. I am not the true owner of the manor, merely the guardian. Nowadays, the manor is more of an heirloom rather than a functional building, so my job is to ensure that it is kept in good condition ready to be passed on to the next generation. This *used* to be the headquarters for my family's criminal activities, back when they ruled over this land. In those days, the manor was a symbol of their dominance and power. But with the rise of the police and the loss of six of our men to world wars, now the focus is more on survival. There aren't many of us left these days and Ashley is the last one to bear the Morgan name since my daughter has her father's name instead. Therefore, since this is the first place the police would visit following a suspicious crime, my relatives prefer to live elsewhere and operate from the shadows rather than stay here at the manor and risk being arrested." She explained and Ashley's moody little scowl darkened considerably.

"Oh please. 'Survival' my ass. Maybe you should try telling that to your dear brother." He huffed and Enid half-nodded in agreement. Ashley's friends turned to each other curiously. This was now the second time Ashley had bad-mouthed his father since their arrival at the manor and they couldn't help wondering why he felt that way.

Bryony sighed.

"I'm sorry, Enid. Do you mind if I call you that? I can't believe, in this day and age, that you're not given more respect. Why shouldn't you be allowed to own the manor? Seriously, why do men get all the privileges? Why does your anatomy make you so important? It's not fair. People should be judged based on their actions, not by their gender. Women have always had to fight for what should rightfully be theirs whereas you men just get life handed to you on a silver plate. I'm shocked to hear that so many of your ancestors were treated badly, Ashley, just because they had the misfortune of being born female." Bryony frowned, turning to offer her bandmate a cold scowl across the table that he promptly returned.

"Don't give me that look. Don't you dare. You have no right to blame me for what my ancestors did just because I'm a guy. How is *that* fair? I'm not like them! I've always treated my girlfriends with respect. You should know that perfectly well since we share out the band's profits in equal amounts. I won't let you attack me like this about my ancestors' behaviour. Just like the Morgan girls never asked to be female, I also never asked to be a boy. That's just how I was made. And in this family at least, I would say that it is more of a curse than a blessing to be born a boy. You heard Enid. All of the men are trained to become dangerous criminals, so of course that was also expected of me when I was born. Do you remember how the taxi driver reacted to me back at the station? Just because I'm a Morgan boy everyone automatically thinks I'm evil and destined to follow a dark path. I have been treated that way all my life and I'm sick of it. I am bombarded by dirty looks wherever I go, so don't think you can go accusing me of 'having it easy'. I've had to fight for everything in my life, including my own survival. Look at me. I almost died the night

I got this." Ashley snapped, glowering back at her irritably and reaching up to gesture at his scarred face.

There was an awkward silence for a few moments as Ashley and Bryony continued to glare at each other before Jenna gave a quiet little cough and turned to fix them both with a pleading look.

Enid eyed them thoughtfully for a while before she nodded.

"I'd say you're both right. In this family, neither the men nor the women have it easy. We are all expected to fall in line and do as we are told. If you don't, the punishment can be severe. People have even been murdered for their disobedience. It would take someone of great character and courage to shatter the dark Morgan legacy. Many have tried, but so far none have succeeded. It's not easy, trying to challenge a thousand years of history." She told them, sadly.

Luke considered her words quietly as he peered round at the nearby suits of armour. Originally, he'd thought they were just placed there for decoration, but now he couldn't help wondering if they were in fact family heirlooms and had once been worn by somebody.

"So, what else can you tell us about this place, Enid? Are there any hidden passages we should look out for, or secret carvings and stuff like that? I love that kind of thing. And is there anywhere in the manor that you'd rather we didn't go? I don't want to be disrespectful since you've been so kind in accommodating all of us." He asked, absolutely thrilled that he was allowed to stay in such a fascinating old building. That was something most people could only dream of. Was this really Ashley's heritage? Why had he never spoken of it before?

"Yes, there are. Most old manor houses tend to have one or two secret doors or priest holes or whatever but this place is absolutely full of them. Their locations were passed down through instruction, but over the years the hidden entrances to these tunnels have been forgotten and lost along with their destinations. Now we only have the stories of what the Morgan villains got up to, such as tales of great caverns filled with glittering treasure and scandalous reports of a stolen steam locomotive. Some of these stories may be true but the treasure hoards are so well hidden beneath the wild growth of plants and trees that they have never been found. It is hard to tell sometimes which stories are true and which are myth. But *something* must have paid for this enormous building and the castle that came before. They can't have been funded purely from the adventures of a few petty thieves. As for your other question, Luke, I would say that there's not really anywhere I consider 'off-limits'. There's perhaps one room on the top floor that Ashley may not want you going in, but I'll leave that up to him. It's normally locked but I've told him where the key is. Otherwise, you are free to wander where you like. Just make sure you don't get lost in any of the secret passages." Enid finished, smiling at her captivated audience. Even Ashley had turned to listen, showing a little interest despite his reluctance to return to this place.

Jenna beamed.

"Wow! Imagine finding a hoard of glittering jewels! That's the kind of thing you only read about in books. It's amazing to think it might actually be possible." She exclaimed and Tom smiled to himself in amusement.

"I wouldn't get your hopes up. It's probably just a story. I highly doubt there'd be anything left for us to find." He warned, eyeing the dreamy look on Jenna's face.

Enid studied Ashley thoughtfully for a moment before she offered him a cautious nod of encouragement.

"To this day, the name of Morgan is still stained and dirty amongst the townsfolk down in the valley and you have to earn their respect before they will do anything for you. I am now welcomed and accepted, but it has taken years for me to earn that friendship and trust. I've worked hard with the community to prove that I am not cruel and heartless like my ancestors. I care about the people down in the town and I now have good friends there. Over the years, I've donated my share of the Morgan wealth to support all kinds of projects, from helping to restore the church tower and establishing the community garden to providing the local primary school with new sports equipment. I may have dirty blood but I wanted to show that it doesn't control my actions. It won't be easy, Ashley, but you must try and improve your reputation." Enid explained and he sighed.

"Yeah, I know." He replied, idly twirling his fork through his fingers as he glanced up at the overhead beams nervously. Tomorrow, he would find the room of his nightmares and confront his past. He just hoped that he'd be able to get some rest first. He'd barely slept all week for worrying.

A Familiar Intruder

Luke lay awake in bed, frowning as he listened to Ashley toss and turn in the bunk above him with the occasional whine of tortured memories. It was now two in the morning and Luke had laid there for almost three hours, unable to rest while Ashley was sleeping fitfully above him and feeling the need to watch over his best friend. It was *that* old nightmare again, he could tell. But this time, the memory seemed a lot more vivid. Ashley wasn't usually this restless when he was having that dream; he normally just froze solid and had been known to scream occasionally, which had been very awkward and embarrassing for him over the years on school trips.

When Ashley was very small, shortly after Luke had met him, he had become quite ill, so scared of falling asleep and being forced to relive the same haunting memories each night. It was always the same dream and told the story of the attack that had given Ashley his ugly scar.

Whenever he had experienced one of these horrific nightmares, little Ashley had become quite dangerous, violently thrashing around in bed and screaming in terror as he savagely fought against whoever was trying to calm him down. Luke had received a lot of cuts and bruises over the years from trying to soothe Ashley during sleepovers and had developed a deep hatred for whoever had caused Ashley's suffering. Even now, Luke still bore a faint scar of his own across his neck from one particularly bad night during a school residential when Ashley had scratched him like a feral cat as he wriggled around desperately in his sleep.

In those early years, Ashley had tried everything to stop himself falling asleep. He had thrown tantrums, screamed and cried as he begged his guardian to let him stay up a bit longer. Soon after, of course, young Michael would burst into tears too, scared by his brother's terrified screaming and reacting the only way he knew how to back then.

Once, Ashley had even fallen asleep over his desk at school from pure exhaustion, something his bullies had found highly entertaining. His teacher, however, had been less amused and had angrily lectured him on his behaviour, warning that he shouldn't stay up all night playing video games before sending him off to visit the headmistress.

Ashley had become so distressed and ill from the mental anguish and lack of sleep that his guardian had dragged him to the doctors, desperate for something that would help him rest peacefully. He had been diagnosed with post-traumatic stress disorder and referred to a children's mental health clinic for a while which young Luke had found very upsetting since he didn't understand what had caused Ashley's misery.

Over time, Ashley had learned to live with the painful memories and was no longer scared of falling asleep, instead merely looking ruffled and grumpy in the morning if he woke up after experiencing his old nightmare. But since he still suffered these horrible dreams, it was obvious that the memories really tortured him and had made his personality very private and defensive as a result. Eventually, with Luke's help, Ashley had learnt how to deal with his cruel bullies and absolutely refused to change himself just to fit in with their idea of perfection. They could give him as many insulting nicknames and unpleasant gifts as they liked; Ashley didn't care anymore. Now, at sixteen, he had the most remarkable self-confidence and willpower, but his friends and family all understood that it had taken a long time and a lot of hurt before that became his identity.

Everyone had seen how Ashley didn't want to come here and Luke couldn't help wondering if Ashley's old nightmare was somehow connected to this place and that the atmosphere of the manor was making the dream worse.

The boys had been given a large room to share on the ground floor that had the same rustic style as the banquet hall and offered a marvellous view out over the surrounding forest and moorland. It was decorated with ugly, dark green wallpaper that Luke found very old-fashioned, but the bunk-beds were quite modern, so it felt as though the room had once been a study or something instead. A beautifully-carved stone fireplace was tucked away in the far corner and housed a few lonely old toys from bygone eras on the mantelpiece underneath a fabulous antique mirror.

When Enid had first shown them the room a few hours ago, she had nervously commented that she hoped they didn't mind sharing it despite being growing teenagers. The manor may have plenty of unoccupied rooms, but Enid was the only housekeeper left, so it was much easier for her to prepare two bedrooms for their visit than eight. Ashley had politely told her that it was no problem at all and he was grateful for the accommodation. Thankfully, they'd managed to sort out the sleeping arrangements quite easily and Luke thought it was no different than staying in a bunkhouse somewhere on a school residential; it was quite fun.

Tom had taken the single bed underneath the large bay-window since he was the oldest, leaving Luke and Ashley to share one bunk-bed while Robbie and Michael took the other. The only downside of Tom's bed was that he constantly had the moonlight shining down on his face since the curtains were so delicate they hadn't dared touch them. But Tom had been so tired from their long journey up from Cornwall that the lack of darkness hadn't bothered him in the slightest and he'd fallen asleep almost immediately, curling up under the duvet with a contented little sigh that quickly morphed into a soft snore.

Luke and Ashley, meanwhile, had claimed the bunk-bed next to Tom since they were a close trio and pretty much the same age. Their bunks were pushed up tight against the wall beside a ghostly set of white handprints that had been left behind by a mischievous small child. Ashley had insisted on taking the top bunk, grumbling that Luke liked to go for random midnight wanderings when he couldn't sleep and having Luke forever climbing up and down the ladder would surely drive him insane.

Robbie and Michael's bunk was located on the other side of the room, which suited Robbie just fine since it meant he didn't have to sleep near 'irritating' Ashley. They were partly obscured from the door by a large wardrobe, the top of which Robbie had claimed for a bedside table since he had the higher bed. Normally, Michael hated being fenced in at the bottom, but Robbie was very unpleasant to argue with and so Michael had quietly accepted his place without making a fuss. However, he'd since discovered that because Robbie wriggled around so much in his sleep, his covers had slid off and formed a nice, cosy little den that felt very safe and private, so Michael supposed it wasn't too terrible to be stuck at the bottom.

Luke had spent the past few hours lazily reading a book by torchlight and gazing around their room quietly, admiring the many crystal sun-catchers hung down at various lengths in the window above Tom's bed. Occasionally, some of them sparkled as they were caught in the moonlight, watching over the boys like tiny spirits, and Luke thought they were quite magical.

As a lover of history, Luke particularly liked the impressive old wooden trunk beside his and Ashley's bunk-bed, the iron frame dark and rusty from years of neglect and the initials 'L.M.' carved onto the top. Luke had taken great pride in this when they arrived, claiming the trunk for himself since he had the same initials and leaving the others to share the wardrobe. But Luke's surname was Matthews, not Morgan, and he wondered about the original owner of the trunk and where they fitted in with Enid's tales of treasure hoards.

Their room was quite a contrast to that of the girls, who'd been given a more modern and sunny room further down the corridor with two proper beds and a sofa-bed as well as a window-seat, Alpine cabinet and numerous bookshelves. Suzy had generously claimed the sofa-bed for herself, leaving the twins with a bed each. There was no sound from the girls' room, so Luke assumed they were all asleep too and he was the only one still up. Young Rose had her own bedroom in a different part of the manor.

He suddenly looked up from his book as Ashley moaned loudly above him, squirming beneath his blankets and breathing heavily.

Luke sighed, sitting up and swearing softly as he smacked his head on the bottom of Ashley's bunk. He quietly slid out of bed and clambered up the ladder to study his best friend, finally perching on the side-rail and leaning over to grip Ashley's wrist. His pulse was strong beneath Luke's fingers and, almost immediately, Ashley was calm, soothed by Luke's touch even in his sleep.

Luke had learnt this little calm-down trick years ago and had once explained that gripping Ashley's wrist and feeling his pulse seemed to pull him back to peaceful reality away from the nasty, scary dreams as he realised that he was in the presence of a trusted friend and was therefore safe. Trying to subdue Ashley's violent and dangerous reaction to a nightmare by grabbing his arms and legs and attempting to pin him to the bed or forcefully hug him never worked because it just scared him more as he believed the aggressive touches were ones made by the enemies in his sleep rather than by a worried friend. But one simple touch around the wrist soothed him really well.

Over the years, Ashley had learnt to identify Luke's touch in his sleep as Luke always gripped his wrist in a particular way, like a unique signature, so he calmed down much faster from Luke's touch, simply because Luke was his best friend and Ashley trusted him the most.

Luke and Ashley had such a deep bond and Ashley's guardian had frequently said that if it weren't for the event that had given Ashley his scar, then he and Luke may never have met. So, even though Ashley had lost his mother and stepfather, almost died himself and been haunted by the memories of that night ever since, he had gained a devoted best friend, as big-hearted Luke had been there for him when Ashley needed someone the most.

Luke watched over Ashley a few moments longer before he turned to face the ladder again, thinking he should probably return to his own bed now that Ashley was calm. However, he was distracted by the sight of their bedroom door quietly swinging open and instinctively flopped down beside Ashley, horrified by the idea that there was an intruder in the house. Ashley grunted slightly in surprise at the sudden invasion of his bed but thankfully remained fast asleep.

"Shhhh, it's okay...." Luke whispered, quickly burying himself underneath Ashley's blankets and laying a gentle hand on his shoulder. He really needed his best friend to keep quiet right now and hoped Ashley's sleepy brain would somehow figure that out.

Ashley gave a faint mumble of acknowledgement and helpfully rolled over to give Luke more space. Unfortunately, his head fell off the pillow in the process and Luke cringed at the soft moan of pain Ashley made as he head-butted the wall.

Alarmed, Luke turned to peer out at their shadowy intruder through a tiny hole in the blankets as he wondered whether they had heard Ashley's misfortune as well. Apparently they had, for the dark figure had paused in the open doorway, obviously confused at finding the room occupied and silently debating their next move.

For the time being, Luke could only see the man's eyes glinting in the moonlight and frowned uncomfortably at this creepy midnight invasion of their bedroom. Who was this weird guy and what did he want?

The stranger peered round the room critically for a few moments as he tried to assess whether anyone was still awake. Eventually, his gaze fell on Luke's empty bed and he twitched slightly before turning to stare back out into the corridor, clearly wondering if someone might suddenly pad out from the nearby bathroom and catch him sneaking around.

Once he was satisfied that the coast was clear, the mysterious figure stalked over to open the wardrobe, carelessly dumping all of Robbie, Michael, Ashley and Tom's clothes on the floor as he reached in to examine the back panels.

Robbie gave a loud huff of contempt, disturbed by the sound of the stranger searching through the wardrobe beside his head and grumbling to himself faintly as he roughly pulled the covers over his head to block out whoever was making such an inconsiderate noise.

Startled by the sudden movement, the man froze, staring up at Robbie's bunk anxiously for a few seconds before he continued with his peculiar examination of the wardrobe, taking great care to keep his movements as quiet as possible now that he'd learnt Robbie was a fairly light-sleeper.

After a while, the stranger turned to investigate the rest of the room, leaving the boys' clothes abandoned on the floor and all mixed up together.

Tom was left undisturbed by the window as the figure slowly tiptoed over to examine the trunk below Luke and Ashley, this time leaving Luke's clothes scattered across the floor as he reached in to the bottom.

Finally, the figure straightened up in the moonlight beside Luke and he gasped in shock. The man had the same jet-black hair as Ashley, along with the same sharp jawline, slim build and piercing eyes, except Ashley's were a bright blue whereas the stranger's were a cruel amber. Therefore, Luke concluded that the intruder must be Ashley's mysterious father, Dean Morgan, who had somehow earned such a passionate sense of loathing from his teenage son that Ashley would much rather describe himself as an orphan.

Luke didn't understand it at all. Why did Ashley have such a negative opinion of his father? And what on earth was the man doing now, sneaking around their bedroom in the middle of the night?

As though sensing Dean's presence, Ashley squirmed and stiffened up beside Luke, growling slightly in discomfort. Luke slowly reached out to grip Ashley's wrist again, feeling his best friend relax at his touch as he continued to monitor their creepy intruder from underneath the blankets.

Dean glanced around the room in obvious frustration at not being able to find whatever it was that he was looking for before he padded over to the door and vanished back into the shadows of the hallway beyond.

Luke frowned, cautiously poking his head out from under the covers and looking down at the abandoned mess of their clothes that had been chucked across the carpet. Robbie would likely become very difficult if he knew his clothes had been mixed in with *half*-brother Ashley's, complaining that all his clothes had been contaminated and that he would have to wear his pyjamas for the rest of the holiday, so Luke decided it was better for everyone's sanity that he never found out.

It was almost half-three by the time he finally got to sleep. Ashley had slipped into a deep and peaceful slumber in the bunk above and Tom's soft, purr-like snoring had also ceased when he rolled over to face the window, leaving the room in a tranquil silence.

The Broken Aeroplane

The room was bathed in rainbows the next morning when Ashley woke, as the sun shone brightly through the windows and hit the various crystals that hung there. It was a really beautiful sight and Ashley smiled to himself faintly, feeling a little more optimistic about the difficult day ahead. Surely, it wouldn't be as bad as he imagined?

He quietly dressed in the bathroom, cringing at the squeaky floorboard outside the girls' room as he set off to explore the old manor. The early morning was peaceful and private and he wanted some time alone to consider the memories of his past which had made him so reluctant to return to this place.

He'd been half-inclined to refuse Enid's invitation, but his guardian had suggested that it might be quite beneficial and therapeutic to revisit the manor again after all this time. They had sat down one day for a serious chat about things, with Ashley nervously admitting that the idea of going back just made him feel sick. He'd nearly died the last time he visited the manor and he was worried that coming back would just finish him off. But Pamela thought that perhaps Ashley *needed* to go back. After all, he'd never really had the opportunity to say goodbye to his mother and stepfather so it might help him to visit the manor and get some closure at last.

Everything had been so hasty and complicated back then, with Ashley and Robbie needing hospital treatment for their injuries while social workers rushed to organise the paperwork that would allow Pamela to take the three brothers safely away down to their new home in Cornwall. Since the boys had almost been murder-victims as well, the authorities were concerned that their attacker might come back to finish the job and therefore everyone was quite keen for the children to be removed from the area as fast as possible to help guarantee their safety.

However, that had meant that Ashley and his brothers had never been given the chance to attend Heidi and Ethan's funeral, something Pamela thought was really sad. She had tried to help the boys deal with their grief as best she could but the lack of a proper funeral seemed to have left them with a painful hole in their hearts. Therefore, Pamela thought that Enid's invitation for the boys to come and visit the manor again was a wonderful idea. She hoped that it would finally give them some peace and allow them to move on from the horrific attack. She didn't want to send them off into adulthood still damaged from that night and so had firmly insisted they give Enid and the manor a chance.

Ashley scowled to himself irritably as he padded down the corridor and out into the banquet hall. He couldn't remember where exactly the offensive room was, but Enid had mentioned over dinner that it was somewhere on the top floor, so that was where he went to begin his search. Enid had explained when she bid them goodnight that the room was usually locked but the key was hidden behind a nearby painting and that Ashley was welcome to visit the room if he wished.

Most of the manor's grand old rooms were abandoned now and Ashley peered round curiously into the various open doorways that he passed, wondering what the rooms had once been. The furniture had been covered up with dust-sheets and most of the decorative ornaments and paintings had been taken away into storage elsewhere. It was easy to see that the building had once housed a much larger family and Ashley thought it was quite sad that Enid and Rose lived here alone. That must feel quite suffocating and lonely at times. Enid had written in her letter that she and Rose lived in the old servant quarters above the kitchen these days, because that area was smaller and more manageable. Ashley privately felt that it also allowed them to disassociate themselves from their shameful criminal family too, by refusing to live in the main house where they rightly belonged.

Eventually, he arrived on the top floor and looked round anxiously, hearing the ghostly laughter of children echo around his mind from a distant memory. Taking a deep breath to calm his nerves, he quietly padded down the wood-panelled corridor to look for the floral painting that Enid had described. It didn't take him long to find it, hung on the gloomy wall beside the second door and he gulped. He knew exactly what was waiting for him behind that door.

Ashley considered the small painting for a few moments before he gently reached out to lift it off the wall. Sure enough, taped to the back, was an old key. He carefully prised it free and spun it through his fingers a few times as he turned to study the offensive door.

He cautiously reached up to trace one finger down his long facial scar before he gave a firm nod of decision and crouched down to push the key into the lock. He'd barely inserted it halfway in when the door swung open with a faint creak, revealing an old bedroom with the same dark wood panelling as the corridor outside.

Ashley frowned, raising the key up in front of his eyes to examine it before he leaned back to peer up and down the corridor. Enid had definitely said that the door would be locked, so why had it swung open without him even having to turn the key? Was there someone else in the house?

He raised his eyebrow suspiciously as he straightened back up to his full height, slipping the key in his pocket as he did so. Then, he quickly stepped into the room away from prying eyes and turned to silently push the door shut again. He closed his eyes for a few moments and leaned forwards to rest his head against the door, trying to calm himself down enough to turn around for a proper look at his surroundings.

When he did eventually summon up the courage to turn around, he was surprised to find the old murder scene exactly the way he remembered it from twelve years ago. Everything was just the same as it had been that night, as though Enid had simply abandoned the room once the police investigations were over. Now, the only differences were the layers of dust that had accumulated over the years and a dried-up bouquet of flowers that had been placed on top of the ripped bedsheets.

Ashley's gaze was immediately drawn to the faint bloodstains on the floorboards and he wrinkled his nose in disgust. There was one large stain at his feet, halfway between the door and the edge of the bed, with the broken remains of a toy aeroplane scattered nearby after it had been violently stamped on. The other large floor-stain was over by the window and stretched down out of sight in-between the old tester-bed and the window-seat. This stain was also accompanied by other ones splattered across the wall and Ashley frowned, remembering from his recurring nightmare that the first stain, by the door, had belonged to his stepfather, Ethan, while the messier ones by the window had been left by his mother, Heidi.

Ashley quietly sunk down onto his knees beside Ethan's death-spot, feeling like he might pass out if he remained standing for much longer and crawling over to sit back against the wall instead, opposite the enormous bed.

He couldn't believe everything was still here after all this time. Even the cot remained, pushed up into the far corner with an animal-themed mobile suspended over it. This was the only piece of furniture that seemed to have escaped the bloody horrors that consumed the rest of the room and Ashley smiled to himself faintly. That had once been Michael's cot and Ashley was glad that his youngest brother had at least survived the attack unscathed. Robbie, however, had gained an ugly gash across his right forearm that had turned into a permanent scar, just like Ashley's injury. Except Robbie's wound could be safely hidden underneath a long-sleeved top whereas Ashley's past was carved across his face for all to see.

Various items of clothing and old toys had also been left scattered across the floor and Ashley crawled over to pick up one of the dusty teddy bears curiously. This had once belonged to him. He had seen it before on old photographs, but no child would want it now. The bear was splattered with blood and slashed open with his stuffing falling out and missing an eye. Ashley stared down at the bear for a while before he casually tossed it aside onto the window-seat with a sigh.

It was Tom who found him a little while later, having been sent up by the others to bring Ashley down for breakfast. Tom had already searched the rest of the manor, getting lost a few times in the maze of identical wood-panelled corridors, before finally climbing up to investigate the top floor.

Ashley heard him coming long before he arrived since Tom had decided to make his presence known by calling Ashley's name at the top of his voice, hoping that Ashley would shout back and save him from having to look in every damn room he passed. But Ashley knew better than that. He wouldn't give his position away that easily. No, Tom would just have to look for him. This was the Morgan manor, after all. You never knew who might be lurking in the shadows. It paid to keep your mouth shut sometimes.

Eventually, Tom pushed open the door to the old murder scene, finding Ashley to be laid out on his front across the floor, his tongue between his teeth as he carefully stuck the fragments of a broken toy aeroplane back together with strong glue that he'd found in a drawer on the landing.

"Oh, finally! There you are. Do you want some breakfast? The others sent me to find you and I've been looking for ages. What are you doing up here, all alone?" Tom exclaimed, relieved to have located his friend at last. He was really hoping there'd be something good left to eat by the time he got back to the banquet hall and not just the blackened toast Jenna had cremated.

Ashley scowled up at him, firmly crossing his feet over in the air behind him as a silent message that he wasn't planning on moving anytime soon.

Tom frowned, crouching down beside Ashley and taking a few moments to examine the room. It had the same sort of gloomy, mournful atmosphere as a funeral ceremony, with the furniture caked in layers of dust from the many years of neglect and Ashley dressed entirely in black as usual. Tom studied Ashley curiously as the younger boy returned to his task of sticking broken toy fragments back together again, wondering what had happened in Ashley's past to make him so moody and fiercely protective of the people he loved.

"Ash?" Tom asked as his stomach gave a loud rumble, demanding that it be fed immediately or it would make him very anti-social as a punishment.

Ashley gave a heavy sigh.

"I'm not hungry." He mumbled.

Tom considered him for a few moments, sitting cross legged on the floorboards beside Ashley and eyeing the shredded bedsheets nervously. Ashley knew this place; that much was obvious. He knew what terrible things had taken place in this room.

"What happened here?" Tom asked, gently.

"This is where I nearly died." Ashley said, carefully sticking the final piece back onto the toy aeroplane and raising it up to examine his handiwork. When he discovered that he'd accidentally stuck his thumb to it as well, he gave a soft curse and set about trying to free himself again without undoing all his hard work in the process. "This was Robbie's once." He muttered, flicking his eyes up briefly to fix Tom with a hard stare.

"Robbie's?" Tom asked, smiling in amusement as he reached out to help separate Ashley and the little plane.

"Mmm. This used to be his favourite toy, back when we were still friends. Now he bloody hates me. We don't have much family left these days, so I wish he'd just accept me and stop trying to torture me every day with his stupid pranks." Ashley replied, finally prising his thumb free and gently setting the toy down on the floorboards.

Then, he straightened up and turned to leave the room with Tom quietly trailing a few paces behind. Ashley paused a moment to lock the room properly, the way it should have been when he arrived, and fastened the key back onto the painting before hanging it up on the wall again. But, as he turned to walk towards the stairs, Tom suddenly reached out to grab hold of his arm and twisted round to stare further down the dingy corridor.

"Did you hear that?" He asked and Ashley frowned.

"Hear what?" He muttered, cocking his head to one side slightly as he listened for whatever noise Tom was on about.

"Something smashed." Tom declared.

Ashley considered the old corridor thoughtfully for a few seconds before he shook his head.

"Nah. You're hearing things. Look, everything's fine. Come on; let's just go join the others before they start panicking. You know what Luke's like whenever I'm late." He said, deciding to keep the fact about finding the room unlocked a secret for now. If there *was* someone up here with them, then he didn't think it very wise to go looking for them.

"Do you think this place is haunted?" Tom asked, peering round at the nearby ornaments suspiciously as though expecting an invisible ghost to suddenly throw one at his head.

"Probably." Ashley answered, calmly tugging his arm free from Tom's grip and turning to head downstairs away from this creepy, dark floor.

By the time they arrived back in the banquet hall, their friends had already scoffed most of the breakfast and Tom sighed, staring across at the empty plates longingly. How rude. First they sent him off to look for Ashley alone and then they didn't even bother to save him any food.

Enid smiled at them cheerfully.

"Ah, there you are. Good morning, Ashley. I hope you slept well. I was just telling your friends that I thought you might like to look round the town this morning. I don't think you'd appreciate me hanging round you all the time since you're teenagers and you like your independence, so I'll let Rose give you the guided tour while I get some work done here. Is that alright?" She offered and her daughter nodded, a little intimidated at being surrounded by so many older teens.

Suzy patted her on the arm gently.

"So, where do you recommend visiting in the town, Rose? I thought it was a really beautiful place yesterday when we arrived at the station so I can't wait to have a good look round now that we've settled in." She asked with a warm, friendly smile.

"Well, there are lots of rocky streams and waterfalls around here and the scenery is amazing. But my favourite place is the community gardens because it brings people together to create something special and my mum helped to establish it." Rose answered, shyly.

"That sounds lovely. You're so lucky to live in such a pretty place." Suzy told her, deciding to try and take the nervous girl under her wing a bit. She didn't want Rose to feel uncomfortable in her own home. It couldn't be easy to suddenly have a bunch of strangers invade your private sanctuary like this. Ashley may be Rose's cousin, but it was clear that the pair had never met before so he was just as unfamiliar to her as anyone else. Judging by the cautious look in Rose's eyes, it seemed that she wasn't entirely sure what to make of Ashley yet since he had been in a bad mood the previous evening and also towered over her quite a lot with his tall height. Therefore, being the smallest female of the group, Suzy decided to make it her mission to try and befriend Rose.

The girl offered her an uncertain little smile before turning to look back down the table as Robbie cleared his throat.

"So where did you go this morning, Ash? You'd already gone when we woke up." He asked, casually leaning back in his chair and grinning mischievously as he wondered if there was some way to land his brother in trouble for his peculiar disappearance.

Ashley shrugged.

"What-? I just wanted a look round." He replied, glancing over at Enid with a sad little smile. She nodded back at him respectfully, understanding that he had been to find the old murder scene and thinking that he had been quite brave to tackle it on his own.

Seeing as he was the only one properly dressed and ready to leave, Ashley was kept waiting while the others all dashed back into their private corridor to fight over the bathroom, tripping over each other in their haste and shouting playful insults back and forth as they went. Rose eyed them critically for a while before she turned to wander off in a different direction towards her own part of the manor.

Ashley decided that he would wait for them outside, wanting some fresh air after spending so long in the dusty little crime scene. The weather was sunny and dry and he sat down against a tree, reaching round to dig his trusty leather journal out of his bag and opening it on a clean page before he set about sketching the old manor and surrounding forest.

This journal went everywhere with him and contained quite a lot of private thoughts so he didn't like anyone other than Luke seeing what was inside it. Most of the pages were filled with neat drawings of places he had visited along with little pictures of his friends that he liked to do whenever they thought he wasn't looking. There were also a lot of scribbled ideas for song lyrics, some of which might eventually be used while others were discarded but Ashley liked to write them all down anyway, just in case. It was very handy to have them recorded nearby and saved a lot of brain power in trying to remember stuff. Who knew when a random idea would turn into something exciting?

Music had always been a big part of his life for as long as he could remember. His mother had also loved to sing and Ashley was proud to have inherited her talent. Heidi may only have sung privately at home but Ashley wanted to be a professional musician and share his skills with the world. He loved performing his songs for people and found that writing music was a good way to focus his thoughts. It encouraged you to be concise and he'd often felt that singing about something helped to expel the problem from his system. Music was his life; he didn't want to do anything else. It was in his blood.

He sat there for a good twenty minutes, quietly sketching out the spooky manor and jotting down various words around the edge as they popped into his head. Eventually, a shadow passed over his face and he looked up to find Luke standing in front of him with his hand outstretched.

"May I-?" Luke asked, politely.

Ashley glanced down at his journal for a moment before handing it over. There was no point in keeping secrets from his best friend. Luke would only get upset and he could usually mind-read Ashley pretty well anyway. It was borderline creepy. Luke eyed the last few additions thoughtfully for a while before he handed the journal back.

Ashley sighed.

"I think it's time I told you about the night I got my scar." He muttered, nervously.

"Are you sure?" Luke asked and Ashley nodded.

"Yeah. I've suffered on my own for too long and it hurts. You all saw me yesterday. I hate this place. This is where I was attacked as a child and it's haunted my dreams ever since so I really didn't want to come back. I know you're all curious about my scar and I think it's only fair to tell you the truth now, so you'll understand why I didn't want to accept Enid's invitation." He said, picking himself up off the floor and dusting himself off.

Luke considered him silently for a few seconds, a look of solemn scolding on his face as he studied Ashley's long scar.

"You never had to suffer on your own. You can tell me anything, Ash; I promise. I'd never think badly of you. I'm your best friend! You shouldn't feel that you have to suffer in silence. How are you supposed to heal if you don't address the problem? Maybe that's why you still experience that same recurring nightmare all the time? It's a sign that you have unfinished business from your past that you need to resolve." He suggested and Ashley scowled.

"Yeah, that's what my guardian says." He grumbled as Suzy and Rose emerged from the manor and came over to join them.

"Hello." Rose muttered, shyly.

"What were you talking about?" Suzy asked, eyeing the nervous, insecure look on Ashley's face and reaching out to lay a friendly hand on his back.

"When we return from looking around town, I've decided to tell you the truth about my past." Ashley answered, peering down at her anxiously for a few moments before he turned to glare at the others as they noisily spilled out of the front door and frightened all the birds away.

Suzy nodded.

"Okay. I'd like that. You know I wouldn't want to push you into telling your story before you're ready, but after watching you sulk all day yesterday, I think it might help to get it out of your system. Then you can relax and enjoy the rest of the holiday. Whatever it is that you have to tell us, I *promise* it won't affect our friendship. We've known each other a long time so I'd say our relationship is pretty solid by now." She smiled and Ashley shuddered, glancing up at the manor awkwardly.

"Maybe. But I know Robbie is going to be angry with me when he hears the truth. Well, more angry than usual anyway. Would you believe, I nearly ended up painting my eyes with a red marker pen this morning instead of my usual black eyeliner because the slimy git had swapped them over. I still haven't found where he dumped the real pen so I had to borrow some of Jenna's stuff instead. They looked almost identical so he must have been planning that trick for a while. Now I'll have to buy a new one in town. Ugh, how can one person be so irritating? I *swear* Robbie must be a damn changeling. There is absolutely no way my mother and stepfather could have a child that evil. They were the nicest, most charitable people you could meet." He sighed, staring across at his younger brother sadly before he turned to follow Rose down the lane.

Jenna skipped over to join them, looping her arm through Ashley's and playfully bumping him out of step with her hip.

"So, where did you sneak off to this morning, mister? You're not usually the first one up. You're more of a night-owl, so I was quite surprised when the guys reported that you'd already left. I was expecting to find you at breakfast with Enid and Rose but you weren't there either!" She asked and Ashley shrugged.

"Yeah, I just wanted some time alone. I went up to visit the locked room on the top floor that Enid mentioned last night over dinner. Except it wasn't actually locked, which was weird. The door just swung open when I pushed the key into the lock. Tom was wondering if the place might be haunted because he thought he heard a loud crash or something from further down the hall." He explained and Jenna frowned.

"I'm not sure I believe in ghosts. Most of the time there's a perfectly rational explanation for so-called 'hauntings'. Sometimes, I think the stories are just invented tales to help boost local tourism. What about you? Do you believe in ghosts?" She asked, curiously.

Beside them, Luke suddenly stopped and half-turned to stare back at the manor. He was just in time to see a dark figure step back into the shadows from a top-floor window and frowned to himself suspiciously. For the past five minutes he'd been consumed with an unpleasant feeling that someone was spying on them and he wasn't very happy to learn that his senses were right. Surely Ashley's creepy father couldn't still be sneaking around? Didn't the guy ever sleep, or eat, or anything? What was he, a vampire?

"What are you looking at?" Michael asked as he and Robbie caught up with Luke and turned to stare back at the manor as well.

"Nothing. Something just spooked me." Luke muttered and Robbie rolled his eyes.

"Yeah, it's a spooky house. It makes sense that Ashley would be descended from all this, the bloody freak." He shrugged, casting a final glance over the big house before he turned to sprint down the lane after the others. "Hey, wait for me!" He yelled, giving Ashley a violent shove into a nearby bush on his way past to join Suzy and Rose at the front.

"Leave me alone!" Ashley shouted back, angrily hurling a pinecone at his brother's head as a punishment for getting him covered in leaves.

Luke stared up at the manor for a few moments longer before he shook his head and turned to follow the others into town.

Michael studied the house a bit more as he wondered what Luke had seen. Eventually, he tried jumping up and down a few times to check whether Luke's extra height had revealed something that he himself couldn't see. When that proved fruitless as well, he sighed and turned to follow his friends down the hill. Why did he have to be so short? He'd give anything to have the same tall genes as Ashley. He was sick of having to burrow through crowds all the time and getting endlessly whacked in the face by various shoulder-bags.

Abusive Locals

Enid may have been wrong about the locked door, but she was definitely right about the townsfolk being hostile towards anyone of Morgan blood. The rude behaviour of the taxi-driver made perfect sense now after hearing Enid's tales of her criminal ancestry.

They were quietly exploring the ancient church opposite the manor's private lane when Ashley realised his mistake. He'd been so preoccupied with thoughts about the murder scene that he had completely forgotten to try and disguise himself. With his hoodie and face masks packed away back at the manor, he would now have to walk around town with his offensive Morgan black hair on display for all to see. Ashley sighed. This was not going to go well.

It didn't take long before his actions began to provoke a few unpleasant consequences and Ashley felt quite embarrassed that his friends had to witness them. He was used to receiving dirty looks and insulting comments since he'd been endlessly bullied and ostracised throughout his school years, so he held his head high as they walked through town, which his friends found very admirable. Ashley just decided it was his own stupid fault for forgetting to wear a hat or something, so he handled the abuse quite well.

The first incident came from a woman who rudely spat at Ashley's feet as he passed, which in turn provoked another family to divert down a side-street when they realised who he was. Then there was a man who threw a glass of water in Ashley's face as they walked past an outdoor café while the waiter promptly turned the sign over to read 'CLOSED' and locked the door.

However, the worst attack happened while they were gathered at the edge of the community gardens, listening to Rose give a nervous explanation about the project since her mother had helped to fund it.

Ashley was idly gazing round at the colourful summer flowers when a sudden movement in his peripheral vision caught his attention and he turned to see what was going on. He was alarmed to find an angry old woman marching towards him with her walking cane raised in the air as she prepared to strike him. She was muttering under her breath as she approached and Ashley frowned, reaching out to take a rough hold of Jenna beside him before he yanked her downwards out of the way as well, causing the woman's stick to sail harmlessly over their heads.

However, a moment later there was a loud crack and a violent cry of pain before Luke collapsed down beside them on the ground, clutching his nose with both hands.

"Owwww...." He moaned, cautiously trying to push himself up onto his knees without much success. His fingers were already stained red with blood from his nose and Ashley stared at him in horror. He may have protected himself and Jenna from the woman's enraged attack, but Luke had been hurt instead and Ashley felt terrible.

Thankfully, Suzy was quick to react, dropping to her knees beside Luke and thrusting a handkerchief into his palm to help deal with the blood flow. Then she set about rummaging through her bag for more tissues and some wipes while Tom gently helped his wounded cousin back to his feet.

Without a word, he solemnly marched Luke and Ashley into the gardens and sat them down on a bench at the far end, away from the abusive old lady. Suzy trailed after them obediently and the three of them set about tending to Luke's raging nosebleed while the others stayed behind to try and calm the woman down.

When they eventually caught up a few minutes later, Luke had almost stopped bleeding and Bryony was relieved.

"Wow, are you okay?" She asked, eyeing the bloody state of Luke's top and fingers and the wet tissues in Ashley's hand.

"I'm fine." Luke insisted, his voice a little muffled from behind another red handkerchief that he had pressed to his face.

Suzy frowned.

"Are you sure you don't want to go to hospital? You should really get checked over after a nasty assault like that!" She worried and Tom nodded in agreement.

"No." Luke snapped, removing the handkerchief from his face and gesturing at himself. "Look. I said I'm *fine*. I would tell you if I wasn't. You know that. I don't need the hospital. Trust me. My siblings are always whacking me in the face with various toys or punching me when they're having a stroppy little tantrum. I'm used to it." He answered, looking round as Ashley leaned closer to examine his nose.

"Well, it doesn't look broken. I guess you'd probably feel if it was. I'm really sorry. That attack was meant for me, like the other ones. It's only because I ducked that you got hurt. I should have just taken it." He mumbled, eyeing the bloody state of Luke's face and scowling darkly.

"Why would you say that? It's not *your* fault that I got hurt. No, this one's on me for not paying attention. I was too busy gazing round at the scenery. Don't blame yourself, Ash. Please. I don't know what happened in your past, but I know that you don't deserve to be assaulted. You've one too many scars already and I'm sure you didn't deserve that first attack either. People around here just take one look at you and assume that you're dangerous. It's not fair." He protested, indignantly.

Ashley merely sighed.

"Watch out, someone else is coming." Jenna muttered as a teenage girl cautiously approached them.

"Um...hello." She began, offering them a nervous little wave.

"Hello." Bryony replied, politely. After all, the girl hadn't done anything to offend them yet, so there was no point in assuming the worst. That would make her no better than the hostile townsfolk.

"I'm Erin." The girl continued, anxiously fiddling with her sleeve. "I saw what happened over there. Are you okay?" She asked, staring at Luke's sticky red fingers and bloodstained top and shuddering.

Luke smiled.

"Yeah, I'll be fine. I'm pretty tough." He answered, bravely.

Erin considered his blotchy face thoughtfully for a few seconds before she turned her gaze on Ashley instead.

"You're Ashley Morgan." She announced, slowly trailing her eyes down the length of his scar.

"Yeah, I know." He muttered, frowning slightly at this strange comment.

Behind him, Michael sat up a little straighter and offered Erin a suspicious look over Ashley's shoulder.

"Wait, how do you know the *Ashley* part of his name? It's obvious that he's a Morgan from his black hair; everyone can see that. But how did you know his first name? I can't imagine he's that much of a celebrity around here already. We only just arrived yesterday and he hasn't done anything wrong." He demanded and the others turned to him curiously.

"Good point." Luke agreed. Normally, it was his job as the observant one to pick up on suspicious comments or shady behaviour, but he was still a bit preoccupied with blood at the moment so he was glad that someone else had noticed Erin's odd remark.

"Oh, everyone knows the name *Ashley Morgan* around here. Everyone knows the stories about Ashley's criminal father and of course they all expect Ashley to turn bad too. They think he'll be just the same as the rest of his Morgan ancestors. 'Like father, like son' kind of thing, you know?" Erin explained, calmly.

Ashley considered her quietly for a few moments before he offered her a hopeful little smile.

"And you don't?" He asked, curiously. Maybe this town wasn't *all* bad.

"No, of course not. It would be unfair to judge you before I know anything about you. After all, they say that you should never judge a book by its cover so why should it be any different for humans? You have to give people a chance to prove themselves. And I have to say, you seem completely normal." Erin shrugged, looking round in surprise when Robbie gave a loud snort of disagreement.

Ashley rolled his eyes briefly at his brother's rudeness before he offered out his hand towards Erin politely.

"Thank-you. I really appreciate that. It means a lot." He mumbled, relieved to hear that someone in this stupid town still had their head screwed on properly.

Erin nodded, obediently reaching out to shake his hand and pressing a scribbled phone number into his fingers before gesturing back towards the park gates.

"I'm sorry, I have to go. I'm supposed to be babysitting and I'm already a little late. But I hope we meet again sometime. If you ever need help in befriending the rest of the town, you can count on me." She smiled, giving them an awkward wave of farewell before rushing off down the path.

Luke stared after her thoughtfully for a few seconds before he turned to fix Ashley with a curious look.

"I thought the townsfolk were just hostile towards you because you're a Morgan male. But Erin claims that they know exactly who you are and think that you are *particularly* dangerous. Why would that be? What did your father do in the past that makes everyone really suspicious of you?" He asked and Ashley sighed.

"That's probably because my father is a murderer." He confessed, staring round at his friends nervously as he waited for their reaction. He'd never admitted this painful truth before and he was a little afraid of what they might say.

Luke's eyes widened and he stared at his best friend in horror.

"So it was your *father* who hurt you?" He asked, reaching out to point at Ashley's gruesome scar.

"Yeah, it was. He tried to kill me when I was little. Now, wherever I go, people take one look at my ugly scar and assume that I'm dangerous. And it's all because of him. If what Erin says is true and the townsfolk already know about my past, that means I have been branded 'the son of a killer' and therefore I'm not just threatening as a Morgan man but also because my blood is especially toxic. I know I have quite a mean, black temper sometimes, which I must have inherited from Dean, but otherwise I generally take after my mother." Ashley complained, bitterly.

Jenna shook her head, shocked by what her bandmate had just confessed and wondering how you were supposed to deal with that.

"That's awful! I'm so sorry, Ashley. I can't believe you had to go through that." She gasped, reaching out to give him a cautious little hug.

Robbie eyed his brother darkly for a few moments before he strode around the bench and planted himself directly in front of Ashley.

"When you say that your father is a murderer, does that mean he killed our parents?" He demanded, gesturing between himself and Michael.

"Yes." Ashley answered, bluntly.

Robbie glared back at him angrily and slowly clenched his hands up into fists.

"Why didn't you tell me?" He demanded and Jenna blinked in surprise.

"Wait, you didn't know?" She asked and he shook his head.

"No. I was just told that they *died* when I was very small. I didn't know it was because of *him*." He snarled, pointing an accusing finger in Ashley's face.

"How dare you? I never said it was *my* fault! I almost died that night too!" Ashley protested, jumping to his feet and glaring back at his little brother furiously.

Luke decided it was about time he took charge of the situation before things got out of hand. He'd been breaking up Ashley and Robbie's hostile arguments for years and had learnt that if he didn't step in quick, they would eventually start fighting for real.

"Alright, that's *enough*. Ashley promised he would tell his story back at the manor, so how about you listen to what he has to say first before you tear him to shreds? Maybe there was a reason why he never told you the truth." He suggested, walking over to plant himself in-between the angry siblings and gently pushing Robbie back a few paces.

"Oh, sod off, Luke. You always take his side." Robbie grumbled, but obediently flopped back onto the bench nonetheless. He didn't like to argue with Luke; the older boy could be really scary at times.

Ashley considered him nervously for a few seconds before he turned his gaze on Michael instead. So far, he'd not spoken a word since Ashley confessed the truth about his father and the silence was beginning to feel really uncomfortable.

"Mitch-?" Ashley asked, fearfully.

"What? It's like Luke said. I want to hear the whole truth before I decide how I feel. But I'm pretty sure none of it was your fault, regardless of what Robbie says. How could it be? You were just a child! I know that I don't have the same kind of familial bond towards my parents that you and Rob cherish because I was only a baby when they died, but I'd still like to know what happened to them." Michael answered, taking great care to choose his words and glancing between his older brothers awkwardly.

Ashley nodded, reaching out to pat him on the shoulder gratefully before he turned to lead them back towards the park gates.

"Come on, then. I shouldn't put this off any longer." He sighed, striding ahead of his friends through the colourful gardens and looking like he'd rather be anywhere else in the world.

Jenna turned to study Luke in quiet concern for a few seconds as they obediently tagged along at the back.

"How are you feeling now?" She asked and he shrugged.

"I'll live." He answered.

"What are you going to do about the woman who assaulted you? Do you want to report her to the police?" Jenna persisted, anxiously.

"No. I don't. She may have hit me pretty hard, but I'd much rather she hit me by accident instead of assaulting Ashley as she'd intended. He's dealt with enough! Besides, pressing charges against her would solve nothing. It would only push the townsfolk further away and they'd hate Ashley all the more. No, the best option is to forget this incident and instead work on befriending the townsfolk. We just need to show them that Ashley's no villain and then things should improve. At least we've got one friend in town now; Erin." Luke replied, calmly and diplomatically.

Thankfully, they managed to avoid any more unpleasant encounters on their walk back through town, although Ashley really did not appreciate having Luke, Tom, Michael, Bryony and Jenna form a protective circle around him. He could take care of himself just fine; he didn't need their silly little human-shield. But whenever he tried to step out of line, speed up or slow down to try and shake them off, they would all dutifully adjust their pace or direction to keep him firmly imprisoned in the middle.

Michael decided that he wouldn't have been at all surprised if Robbie walked beside Ashley with a large sign pointing at him, since he'd just learnt that he could get equal pleasure from watching other people attack his brother and it saved him the hassle of having to plan out more tricks. But Robbie followed them in silence, too scared of the threatening 'don't even try it...' vibe that Luke was giving off.

There was a brief pause when Ashley sent Suzy over to buy some flowers from a nearby shop, arguing that it was something he really wanted but clearly the townsfolk refused to serve him so he would have to send someone in his place. Judging by the delighted look on his face when she returned, she had chosen wisely and seemed quite pleased with herself as she handed over his wallet.

Eventually, they arrived back at the manor in a much more sombre mood than they had left it, with Robbie and Michael glancing round at each other uncomfortably as they followed their brother inside. Now that they had returned, they weren't entirely sure they wanted to hear the truth about their parents' deaths. If Ashley's long scar was anything to go by, the attack must have been really vicious and the idea of it made Michael feel quite nauseous.

Traumatic Memories

Ashley was silent as he led the way through the maze of dark corridors up to the top floor, clutching his precious bouquet of flowers close against his chest and seeming absolutely terrified. When he finally stopped beside a closed door, Luke was alarmed to see that Ashley was shaking and reached out to lay a gentle hand on his shoulder.

"I don't know if I can do this…" Ashley muttered.

"Just take your time. There's no rush. We know this is hard for you. But think how much better you'll feel once it's done." Luke answered and Ashley nodded, taking a few deep breaths to try and calm his pounding heart. He shouldn't be this nervous. He'd visited the room once already. It shouldn't be that hard. But this time he was accompanied by a crowd of nosy people and it made him feel sick. He took a few moments to compose himself before he reached out to snatch a key from the back of a nearby painting. Then he firmly slotted it into the lock and turned it, muttering to himself irritably when he found the door properly sealed, just as he'd left it.

"I know this room. I've seen it a thousand times in my sleep." He announced, pushing the door open and stepping back to let his friends file inside.

Robbie peered round curiously.

"So, this is it?" He asked and Ashley nodded.

"This is it." He confirmed, finally stepping inside and crouching down to pick up the toy aeroplane that he'd mended earlier that morning. "You probably won't remember, but this used to belong to you." He said, offering Robbie the toy with a faint smile on his face.

Robbie accepted it quietly, running his fingers over the little plane with a soft tenderness that his friends had never seen before. He raised his arm up to make the toy fly through the air for a few moments, smiling happily as he did so. Then he realised that everyone was staring at him and he stopped, feeling childish and silly as he placed the treasured object down on the bed.

"Thank you." He muttered and Ashley blinked, surprised by the unexpected gratitude. Normally, Robbie only ever thanked him for something when he was prompted to, not of his own free will. But Robbie was obviously delighted to have his favourite childhood toy back and it had made him unusually friendly.

"This, however, once belonged to Michael." Ashley continued, padding over to reach into the dusty cot and pulling out a small dummy. He'd found it earlier when he first visited the room and had thought it quite cute with a little picture of a lion still visible on the back.

"Great." Michael answered, obediently holding out his hands to accept the dummy and eyeing it in disgust.

Robbie smirked, reaching out to reclaim his beloved plane off the bed now that it seemed more grown-up.

Tom watched them quietly for a few seconds before he turned to scan the rest of the room.

"What about you? If Robbie had a toy plane and Michael had a dummy, is there anything in here that once belonged to you?" He asked and Ashley pointed to where Luke was perched on the old wooden window-seat.

"Yeah. That used to be my teddy." He replied and Luke promptly twisted round to look for the discarded toy. He eventually found it lying in the dust behind him and picked it up gently.

"Ugh. What happened to him?" He asked, raising his eyebrow slightly as he considered the bear's miserable state.

Robbie huffed.

"I remember that. His name was Paws and Ashley would never let me play with him." He explained, frowning as he realised what he'd just said. "Don't ask me how I remembered that. Or why." He added, surprised to learn that he'd clung onto such a random piece of information from his early childhood.

"Paws. Good name." Luke declared, gently sitting the distressed bear on his lap and patting him on the head.

Ashley smiled to himself and padded over to join his best friend on the window-seat while Bryony flopped down onto the bed, taking great care not to disturb the old flower bouquet that lay there. One by one, the others crouched down to sit back against the wall, with Michael dropping his embarrassing dummy into the dirt before giving it a violent kick across the room.

"So, what happened here?" He asked, brushing his hands together in disapproval.

Ashley squirmed.

"Yes, I know. I'm really sorry I never told you about this before, but it hurt too much to remember what happened and I didn't want you to suffer the same nightmares that have always haunted me. I was only four when Mum and Ethan died and it took me years to deal with the trauma, so Pam and I thought it best to wait until you were older before we told you the truth. Even now I'm still a little damaged, mentally, but I do feel a lot stronger and able to talk about it more. As I said, I'm sorry it's taken so long but I hope soon you'll understand and forgive me." He began, peering round at his younger brothers uncomfortably.

Michael nodded, accepting the apology easily. But Robbie's eyes narrowed darkly, suggesting that he might never forgive Ashley for this heinous betrayal.

Luke gently wrapped one arm around Ashley's shoulders.

"It's okay to cry if you need to. Don't feel ashamed. We won't judge you." He murmured, watching the glistening tear that was dancing in the corner of Ashley's eye.

Ashley sighed, hesitating a few moments as he stared down at the space around his feet. In his mind, he could clearly see his mother's body sprawled out across the floorboards and frowned as he felt his throat dry up with nerves. He had never spoken about the terrible things he'd seen that night, keeping the complicated mix of pain, sadness and anger tightly locked away deep inside him and only allowing himself to grieve when he was alone. He'd always felt that he must be the strong one of the family and that he must be there for his brothers when they needed him and do whatever he had to in order to keep them safe and protect them from hurt. That was his duty as the first-born. But now he had to talk about those painful memories and confront the grief he'd kept locked away all these years. This was not going to be easy.

"It's probably best if I start from the beginning so bear with me." Ashley continued. "You need the backstory in order to understand the murders. Some bits will be my own memories while other parts come from things I've read in my mother's old diaries or discussions I've had with my guardian." He explained and Suzy cringed, wondering why Ashley didn't think it was remotely invasive or inappropriate to read his late mother's diaries. Surely, the only respectful thing to do when Heidi passed away would be to dispose of her diaries somehow so that her private thoughts were kept entirely her own. Suzy certainly hoped that would be the case with *her* journals. She couldn't bear the thought of anyone else reading her diaries but decided that perhaps Ashley's guardian just didn't like the idea of 'deleting' her best friend's life.

Jenna nodded, offering Ashley a faint smile of understanding across the room.

"It's your story, so tell it however you like." She replied, quietly shifting into a more comfortable position on the floorboards as Ashley opened his mouth to share the painful tale of his past.

It began in London.

His mother, Heidi Cairns, had just completed an apprenticeship in floristry and was working at a prestigious shop in Covent Garden when she stumbled across the man who would later become his father, Dean Morgan. Heidi hadn't been looking for romance at all, but Dean had totally charmed her and so Heidi had nervously agreed to be his girlfriend. Then, a couple of months later, they moved into a small flat together.

That was when things started to go wrong.

Dean had initially told Heidi that he worked 'night shifts' but she had grown suspicious when he began to give her all kinds of expensive presents and eventually discovered that it was all stolen. Dean had been surprisingly calm when she confronted him about the gifts, simply explaining that he came from a long line of Welsh criminals and had been trained to continue the family tradition.

Realising that she had fallen in with the wrong crowd, Heidi had tried to break up with Dean but he had become quite violent and abusive, insisting that she *belonged* to him now and had to do as she was told. It hadn't taken Heidi long to realise that since she and Dean were a couple, he had access to a lot of personal information that he could use against her to make sure she remained obedient. Heidi was further dismayed to discover that Dean was more than happy to hit her whenever she dared to speak her mind or criticise his decisions.

Upset, she had ended up absent-mindedly discussing the situation with a regular client, Ethan Slater, at the flower shop one day and had been really surprised when the military pilot offered out his phone number afterwards, admitting that he only came in to order flowers so that he could spend time with her. Now, on hearing about the poor state of her relationship, Ethan wanted Heidi to know that she had people who cared about her deeply and that he was always happy to chat whenever she needed to. Heidi had been really touched and had begun to meet up with Ethan twice a week on her lunchbreak at a popular café nearby.

They had fallen madly in love and were busy making plans to free Heidi from Dean's cruelty when she discovered that she was pregnant. This had left Heidi feeling very conflicted as she had always wanted to be a mother but she knew without a doubt that the baby's father was Dean, not Ethan. She hadn't wanted to risk getting too friendly with Ethan in case Dean found out and therefore knew that her unborn child was a Morgan.

When she gave Dean the news a few days later, he was absolutely delighted, although Heidi was quite offended at the way Dean insisted that the child had to be male and had sharply replied that she didn't have any control over that. Dean would just have to be satisfied with whatever he got.

Ethan was a little disappointed to be sidelined but understood that Heidi wanted to give Dean a chance to prove himself now that she was expecting his child. Even so, Ethan couldn't help wishing that the baby was his instead and continued to visit Heidi at the flower shop to see how she was doing.

As the months progressed, Heidi found that she kept having to remind Ethan of his place. She had made the mistake, one day, of excitedly confessing that she was having a little boy and that the child was due to be called Ashley, which had prompted

Ethan to wrinkle his nose slightly in disapproval. Heidi had ended up having to sternly remind Ethan that it wasn't his baby and therefore he didn't get to choose the kid's name.

She had hotly protested that she really liked the name 'Ashley'. Her partner had spent ages thinking of ideas and it made her quite hopeful that Dean had finally put his abusive ways behind him. Originally, Dean had wanted to name their son 'Ash' as he was quite inspired by the way the name referenced his criminal family with its violent volcanic links whilst also making sense for Heidi's floristry career too thanks to the ash tree. But Heidi had thought that 'Ash Morgan' sounded quite cold and blunt on her tongue so they had agreed to use 'Ashley Morgan' as the child's official name instead.

Eventually, Ashley had arrived on the 18th November and Heidi had known that her life would never be the same again. She absolutely adored her son and vowed that she would do anything to keep him safe. It didn't take her long to realise that Ashley had inherited her love of music and she really liked picking out noisy toys for him to play with. Dean, however, had argued that Ashley's musical interests weren't appropriate for a Morgan son and would regularly yell at Ashley to be quiet which Heidi found very stressful.

Young Ashley clearly didn't like his father much either for he would give a loud scream of protest whenever Dean tried to pick him up. The first time Heidi introduced her baby son to Ethan, however, Ashley was totally silent, and Heidi found the comparison quite fascinating.

Ashley had just turned ten months old the first time Heidi found a suspicious set of bruises across his body and wasn't at all convinced when Dean angrily claimed that the little boy had hurt himself playing with one of Heidi's 'dangerous' musical toys. Of course, Ethan didn't think this was very plausible either when Heidi told him what had happened and had boldly taken it upon himself to go and speak to Dean, claiming that he and Heidi were old friends from school.

But Dean wasn't stupid. He'd realised that Ethan was actually Heidi's secret lover and the pair had ended up yelling at each other furiously, with Dean shouting that Ethan had no business telling him how to raise his own kid while Ethan snapped back that Dean was *lucky* to have a child and that he should support Ashley's musical interests. That was his duty as a parent. Ashley wasn't a piece of clay to be moulded however Dean saw fit. He was a person in his own right and Dean had to respect that Ashley's mindset wouldn't always line up with his own.

Ashley was a little over a year old when Heidi finally made the painful decision to cut Dean out of their lives. She had come back from buying the groceries to find Dean angrily smacking their young son and yelling at him furiously while Ashley was just sobbing in fear. Horrified, Heidi simply abandoned the groceries by the door before dashing over to rescue her little boy, hugging and kissing him soothingly for a few minutes. When questioned, Dean merely shrugged and answered that he'd been trying to watch a football match but Ashley wouldn't stop playing with his favourite musical toy.

So, that night, Heidi waited until Dean was fast asleep before packing a bag full of clothes, important documents and Ashley's most-treasured toys before scooping her small son out of his cot and disappearing out into the city. She had first tried calling upon one of her close friends from work but the woman never came to answer the doorbell and so Heidi had been forced to rethink.

Fortunately, Ethan was still up when Heidi arrived at his flat and his warm welcome had caused her to burst into noisy tears at the realisation that she and Ashley were finally safe. They spent the rest of the night discussing the situation and reporting Dean's abuse to the police before fleeing down to Heidi's homeland of Cornwall a few days later to start a new life together.

Ethan had been more than happy to run away as he'd spent almost two years waiting for an opportunity to become Heidi's partner and had also been made redundant a while back, so the idea of a fresh start was very appealing. He'd had enough of the big city.

Now that the pair were finally allowed to be together, they wasted no time in getting married, although Heidi absolutely refused to let Ethan change Ashley's surname to Slater, claiming that she still wanted her tiny son to have some kind of link to his paternal heritage, as dirty as it was. She may have taken Ethan's name but that didn't mean her son had to as well. Ethan had also bought Heidi her very own grand piano as a wedding gift and loved to watch her play various tunes in an evening, with little Ashley happily perched on her lap and stabbing at nearby keys as he tried to join in. Shortly after, Ashley had gained his first sibling, a little boy named Robbie, and took his 'big brother' duties very seriously. Then, when Ashley was three, Heidi gave birth to another child, Michael, and Ethan was delighted.

Heidi, meanwhile, was wracked with guilt. Every time she turned to watch her husband playing with the three boys, she was overcome with a horrible feeling that it had been really cruel and unfair of her to just cut Ashley's biological father out of his life and wondered if they could make some kind of arrangement that would allow Dean to safely interact with his son.

When she mentioned her concerns to Ethan though, he was rather dismissive, simply replying that Heidi had left Dean for a reason. Besides, it wasn't like Ashley was missing out on a male role model. Ethan may only be a father-figure but he liked to think that he did a good job and had always taken great care not to treat Ashley any differently. In Ethan's eyes, Ashley was just as much his son as Robbie and Michael, even if the boy did have quite a silly, unconventional name.

But Heidi was insistent. She wanted Dean to be part of Ashley's life. So, the family had nervously travelled back up to London a few days after Christmas when Ashley was four years old, Robbie was almost two and Michael was a precious seven months. Heidi had discovered, via Dean's sister, that he still lived in their old flat, alone, which she thought was rather sad.

Unfortunately, it seemed that Ethan's fears had been well-founded, for Dean was not at all pleased to see them. The man wouldn't even let him get a word in, merely branding him a 'selfish, girlfriend-stealing ape' whenever Ethan tried to voice his thoughts and seeming totally repulsed by the sight of the younger children.

The meeting turned out to be such a monumental disaster that Heidi and Ethan found themselves having to flee again.

Except this time, they chose to hide at the Morgan manor instead, thinking that was the last place Dean would expect to find them.

But, somehow, he had managed to follow them and took the family by surprise when he suddenly burst into their room and plunged a knife deep into Ethan's back as poetic justice for what the man had done to him by stealing Heidi away.

The scream that had left Heidi's mouth as Ethan slowly crumpled to the floor was one that would be forever carved into Ashley's memory. He had been sitting on her lap with Robbie while Ethan entertained them with a silly miming game when Dean stormed into the room and so had witnessed his stepfather's murder first-hand.

As Dean crouched down to butcher Ethan's body a little more, Heidi had roughly thrust Robbie into Ashley's chest and snapped at him to look after his little brother before gesturing for them to hide under the large oak tester bed that dominated the room.

Ashley vaguely recalled Heidi planting a final, teary kiss on his cheek and mumbling that she loved them but he didn't have any visual memories of her murder, thankfully, since he had obediently dragged Robbie under the bed to do as his mother directed. He just remembered Heidi crying as Dean spoke to her in a low, cold-hearted voice in the corner and the fact that his name had been mentioned a few times. Then, following a blood-chilling set of screams, Heidi had collapsed onto the floorboards beside the bed, peering across at her older sons forlornly for a couple of seconds before Dean crouched down over her body to investigate where Ashley and Robbie were hiding.

The dark, predatory look in Dean's eyes as he stared at them under the bed and the sinister glint of the bloody kitchen knife in his hand was another image that had always haunted Ashley's dreams and he remembers feeling absolutely terrified. Robbie was squirming around insistently in his arms as he tried to free himself, having always disliked hugs, so Ashley was totally unable to defend himself which just made his fear worse.

Despite being seconds away from death, Heidi had reached out to clamp her fingers around Dean's arm as she tried to protect her sons and this memory always fills Ashley with a sense of pride and warmth. Even when his mother had finally passed away in a pool of her own blood, her hand had remained tightly fixed in place for a few moments until Dean roughly yanked his arm back with a low snarl of disgust.

Then, seeing as he was too big to fit under the bed and Heidi and Ethan's dead bodies were blocking the way, Dean had simply inserted one arm underneath the frame and swiped the long knife back and forth. The weapon had found Ashley first, quickly carving a deep wound across the left-hand side of his face and causing him to give a violent scream of pain. A moment later, when the knife was on the returning swipe, it caught Robbie's right arm too since he'd been reaching up to angrily tug on Ashley's hair as he tried to free himself from his brother's iron grip.

Ashley remembers hearing Robbie give an agonised yell of his own and Michael's terrified wailing from where he was still imprisoned in his cot and found these memories particularly stressful to experience in his recurring nightmares. But his last recollection of the murder night was hearing footsteps thundering up the stairs from Enid calling the police in a wild panic before Dean hastily straightened up and turned to face the wall, so he presumed his father must have escaped via a secret passage somehow in order to avoid being arrested. After that, his memory just went black so Ashley imagined he must have passed out at that point from shock and the violence of his life-changing injury.

Unfortunately, Dean had escaped. He had just disappeared into the night and so had never been charged for the murders of Heidi and Ethan and the attempted murders of Ashley and Robbie because the police never found him. Even now, twelve years later, Dean remained at large and the thought just made Ashley's blood boil. The police would have told them if Dean had been caught but no-one had ever come knocking on their door. Ashley was certain of it. His guardian would never keep that secret from him.

He peered round at his friends sadly as he waited for their reactions, the bouquet of white lilies still clutched tightly in one hand.

Luke squirmed. He was the only one who knew that Dean was sneaking around the manor again and he was suddenly quite scared for Ashley as he remembered how close Dean had come to Ashley the night before and Ashley's fear as he sensed his father in his sleep.

"Thank you for sharing your story with us. I know it wasn't an easy thing to do but I hope you feel a little better now. I'm so sorry you had to go through that." Luke murmured and Ashley gave a defensive little shrug.

"I'm sorry I never told you before. It was just too painful and too personal to share and I needed to know that I could trust you with it. I know you've always wondered where my scar came from but thank you so much for not badgering me about it, all of you. That really helped. Having to deal with people asking nosy questions about my scar or rudely staring at it in morbid curiosity and disgust was one of the reasons why I started wearing eyeliner in the first place. I wanted to force people to look me in the eye, so I decided to draw attention to them by painting them black. I saw it as a silent statement, like 'Hey, my eyes are up here; stop being rude' or something like that. Plus, my decision to start wearing eyeliner proved to be really good therapy since it forced me to look in the mirror every morning in order to put it on, so it helped me to get used to my ugly long scar. I first started using it when I was six and now I've been wearing it for so long that it's just become part of my identity. I love the way it makes me look and it gives me a lot of confidence too so I guess it's like my armour. Without it, I just feel exposed and vulnerable and my face looks weird. I've gotten into a *lot* of trouble over the years for wearing it at school but I don't care about that. It's not my fault that the rest of society doesn't like the way I look." He explained, sourly.

Luke pouted.

"I'm so sorry." He muttered, completely shocked that Ashley had almost been murdered by his own father and wishing he could take away all the hurt that Ashley had suffered over the years as a result. Since he couldn't, he settled for just enveloping his best friend in a crushing hug instead, not caring in the slightest if he got Ashley's precious eye make-up smeared all over his chest.

"Um..." Ashley muttered, a little startled by the intimate, smothering hug and reaching out to awkwardly pat Luke on the back a few times.

"*Thank you* for telling us." Luke repeated, peering round curiously as Tom, Bryony, Jenna and Suzy all came over to hug Ashley as well, leaving him almost invisible underneath his devoted friends.

"Please...stop..." Ashley gasped, feeling a little too crowded and cautiously pushing against the various bodies that surrounded him until they released him.

Jenna planted a friendly kiss on Ashley's cheek as she pulled back, hovering in front of him sadly as she studied his long scar.

"To tell you the truth, when we met back in Year Seven, your scar *wasn't* the first thing I noticed. You might think that everyone is drawn to it but I'm sure that's not the case. The first thing I noticed was your eyes. I'd never seen anyone with such intense blue eyes before and I was mesmerised. I thought it was like gazing into a tropical ocean. So don't feel like everyone is judging you all the time. It was ages before I noticed your injury." She told him and he smiled, recalling that Jenna *had* spent most of that first lesson staring at him across the room.

As Luke considered Ashley's dark past a little more, he suddenly realised that Ashley had never once tried to cover up his long scar beneath make-up and wondered why that thought had never occurred to him before. Ashley had also chosen to keep his split eyebrow exactly the way it was rather than trying to fill it in so that it looked normal and Luke smiled to himself. Obviously, Ashley was quite proud of being a survivor. He might not like people rudely staring at his scar all the time but he wouldn't dream of covering it up. The attack was part of Ashley's history and Luke thought it very admirable that his friend had learnt to accept his appearance. That was something a lot of people struggled with. The pressure to try and fit in could be unbearable so Luke was glad to see that Ashley at least was comfortable with himself.

Meanwhile, Robbie was busy rolling up his shirt sleeve to examine his own gruesome scar that climbed up the outside of his forearm. He'd always wondered where it came from. But since it had been there for as long as he could remember, he'd just assumed it must be an old playground injury or something since he was known to be a reckless wild child. Now, after learning that Ashley's demonic father had been the one to wound him, Robbie just felt numb with shock.

"Let me see." Michael muttered, crawling over to examine Robbie's arm in quiet curiosity.

"I don't remember that..." Robbie declared, staring down at his arm in disgust and shuddering as Michael reached out to trail one finger over it.

"I think you do." Ashley replied, sliding forwards off his perch and crouching down beside them.

Robbie shook his head insistently.

"No, I *don't*." He argued, glancing round as the others came over to investigate his arm as well.

Ashley offered him a sad little smile.

"Hear me out. I know you don't *consciously* remember the attack because you were too young. But I do think it had an impact on your behaviour. I reckon that's why you've always been really mean to me. You just remember that you were with me when you got hurt so you've never trusted me since. And seeing my scarred face all the time reminds you of that pain. After all, *I* was the one who wouldn't let you go, so I think you've always blamed me for your injury." He explained and Luke nodded.

"That makes sense." He agreed, staring down at Robbie thoughtfully.

"No it doesn't! Maybe I just think Ashley is super irritating? Stop trying to psycho-analyse me all the time, the pair of you. It's weird." Robbie protested, roughly tugging his sleeve back into place before he folded his arms across his chest.

Bryony eyed him critically for a few seconds before she turned her gaze on Ashley instead.

"I'm quite amazed that *you* remember so much about the attack, Ashley, to say you were so young! I don't remember anything from my early childhood at all." She remarked and he frowned.

"Well, to be honest I don't remember *everything* since I was only four. I just have a timeline of flashbacks, so my nightmares are a bit like a jerky, stop-motion horror film. I've pieced together the bits in-between. Sometimes, I just see the images in my sleep, while other days I just hear the sounds, but mostly they tend to come together. It's weird getting one without the other; it makes the whole thing twice as creepy." He admitted, as Tom lay down across the floorboards to peer under the bed.

"Wow, Ash, it's really dark under there! I'm surprised that Dean even spotted you hiding in the shadows with your thick black hair. You would have blended in quite well, I imagine." He exclaimed as Luke turned to Ashley curiously.

"Do you remember anything else?" He asked and Ashley shrugged.

"No, the next thing I remember is waking up in hospital with a splitting headache and Mum's best friend, Aunty Pamela, sitting at my bedside with Robbie and Michael cradled on her lap. I was wearing different clothes, my face was covered in plasters and there were lots of people staring at me. I just remember feeling really scared and wanting my mum back. Robbie had his wounded arm bandaged up too and I found that quite frightening. I didn't really understand what was going on and I felt so small and lonely." He confessed, awkwardly.

Luke considered his words for a while before he offered out Ashley's childhood teddy-bear, Paws, who'd been lovingly stitched back together.

He'd been really upset to watch the tortured expressions of heartbreak and grief pass over Ashley's face as he explained about the murders and had decided that he wanted to do something nice to try and cheer him up a bit. It had been Robbie who gave him the idea to try and repair Ashley's old teddy bear as he watched the younger boy idly play with his mended toy aeroplane and so he had quietly asked to borrow Suzy's emergency sewing kit and spent the rest of Ashley's story sewing up the bear's grizzly injuries.

He was quite pleased with the results. Sure, the stitches may not be perfect, but his mother had insisted that he learn to repair his own clothes as she would not be buying new ones every time they ripped from his reckless adventures. It didn't matter that the Matthews were wealthy and could easily afford new things, that wasn't the point. No, it was more about learning the value of things and trying to think ahead about the consequences of your actions. Clothes were not meant to be readily-disposable, they were made to last and you had to look after them.

Ashley stared at Luke for a few seconds, amazed that he had managed to repair 'Paws' and suddenly feeling quite emotional. Of course, he'd vaguely noticed that Luke was busy sewing things as he explained about his past but the painful memories had prevented him from seeing what Luke was actually doing. Now, as he considered the mended teddy Luke was holding, Ashley felt really happy. Just as he'd taken the time to repair Robbie's toy aeroplane, Luke had made the effort to fix his teddy and Ashley understood the gesture perfectly. This was Luke silently telling him that no matter how broken and lost Ashley may feel, Luke would always be there to help make things better.

"Thank you." He muttered hoarsely as he reached out to accept the little bear and examined it curiously. He particularly liked the rich black fabric that Luke had used to make the bear's eye-patch, having found a few scraps of loose fabric at the back of Suzy's repair kit. He'd even stitched a tiny letter 'A' onto the fabric in silver thread and Ashley thought that was quite cute. He reached down to sit the bear on top of his rucksack before giving it a fond tap on the head.

Luke smiled.

"There! All mended! Poor teddy. He's been sitting here in the dust for twelve years, waiting patiently for you to come back! Now he just needs a good wash to get rid of all the dust and the blood but then he should be okay." He explained, pleased that Ashley was going to keep the bear and thinking that he seemed a bit happier now.

Suzy frowned, staring up at Ashley mournfully for a while as she reflected on everything he had told them.

"It's so sad to think that you never made it back home." She mumbled and Ashley nodded.

"No. And that's why I wanted these flowers. This is where my mother and stepfather died, so I wanted to buy something to help commemorate their passing. I never got to attend their funeral and I don't know where they were laid to rest either, so this room is important to me. It's the last place I associate with my family." He explained, miserably.

Jenna smiled.

"Let me help. I'm sure there must be a nice vase around here somewhere. If your mother was a florist then we should take care to display your flowers properly." She said, picking herself up off the floor and padding out into the corridor to look for one. She was only gone a couple of minutes before she returned with a beautiful glass vase half-filled with water and offered it out to Ashley proudly.

"Thank you. That's a really nice idea." He muttered as she gently set the vase down on the window-seat beside him. He was silent for a while as he unpacked his bouquet of flowers and set about arranging them neatly into the vase. Eventually, he decided that his work was done and stepped back to admire the result, his eyes slowly drifting downwards again to consider where his mother had taken her final breath.

Attic Adventures

Ashley was silent for a few minutes as he surrendered himself to his memories before he reached down into his bag and pulled a small, square photograph from the front of his journal.

"Here. My guardian took this just after I'd been released from hospital. It might give you a better idea of what happened that night." He muttered, offering out the image to Luke, who was still perched beside him on the narrow window-seat. Luke obediently accepted the photograph and his eyes widened in horror as he considered the subject.

"Bloody hell." He gasped, staring at the faded little picture for a while before he passed it down to Robbie at his feet. The younger boy merely pulled a face and quickly handed the snap to Suzy beside him, obviously not wanting to be reminded of that terrible day any more than was necessary.

Suzy eyed the old photograph sadly, which was a close-up of four-year-old Ashley taken shortly after the attack. He was standing in front of a hospital wall with a look of blank shock in his eyes as he stared into the camera. Ashley's long facial scar was still quite raw on the left-hand side of his face and he had a neat trail of stitches holding it together that somehow made his appearance even worse. In addition to all of this, Ashley had a nasty black eye on the right-hand side of his face and looked properly miserable. He was nervously sucking his thumb and had a brand new teddy bear loosely clutched in his spare hand, which Suzy presumed must have been a get-well present from Pamela since his own teddy had been left behind at the murder scene.

Suzy decided that it was no wonder he had been outcast first at playgroup and then primary school if this is what he had looked like back then. Even she had been quite scared of him. But Luke had always been Ashley's friend right from the start and Suzy felt that this photograph obviously showed the strength of Luke's character too if his own four-year-old self hadn't been put off by Ashley's gruesome, stitched-up face.

Ashley gestured across at the photograph with a curious look in his eyes that seemed to suggest he was quite fond of the image.

"My guardian said that she took that picture as a record of what Dean had done to me. There's also one of Robbie with his arm all bandaged up somewhere back home. Now, my image lives in my journal because I think it's good motivation for when I feel like I'm having a bad day. It reminds me that no matter how tough things might seem, nothing can ever be *that* bad, so it helps to put things in perspective." He explained as the photograph was passed onwards to Jenna and Michael before ending up in Bryony's hands.

She eyed the image thoughtfully for a few moments before she turned it over to see if there was anything written on the back. When she found herself staring down at a confident sketch of a phoenix, she couldn't help but give a wide smile, thinking that the mythical creature suited Ashley very well and wondering what had caused him to add it to the back of the picture.

"How did you get the black eye?" She asked seeing as Ashley hadn't said anything about Dean causing that particular injury.

"That was a gift from Robbie. I told you he doesn't like to be held. So he socked me in the eye while I was trying to restrain him under the bed." Ashley replied and Robbie frowned. He was really shocked to hear about the murder of his parents and was half-wishing Ashley had told him and Michael the truth first in private before letting all of their nosy friends in on their family history.

"Ashley, you should have told me how Mum and Dad died and where my arm-scar came from too. You had *no right* to keep that from me." He growled, staring up at his big brother coldly.

Ashley peered back at him sadly.

"Rob, I couldn't deal with it myself. I was only little when my dad cut my face open and murdered Mum and Ethan. Then, years later, when you started asking how they died, Pam wouldn't say. So you asked me instead and I didn't know what to do. I'd only recently discovered that it was *my* dad who was

69

the killer and I didn't want you to know that. You already hated me enough without adding that damning piece of information. So, whenever you came to ask, I'd find a way to distract you or act like I was really busy. I know it was wrong, but I was terrified of what you might do if you learnt the truth." Ashley argued bitterly.

Robbie shook his head.

"No, you should have told me. Is it any wonder I don't trust you anymore if you never answered my questions? Pushing me away all the time just made me feel really angry and unimportant." He snapped and Ashley cringed.

"I knew I'd have to tell you the truth sometime. That's why I was so anxious at returning here after all these years. I knew this was where the murders had happened and I didn't want to come back to the place of my nightmares. But I also knew that I'd have to tell you and Michael the truth and I didn't feel ready for that. I'm really sorry. At least it's done now. I've told you what happened." He murmured, biting his lip awkwardly.

Rose frowned, one part of the story still not quite making sense in her head as she stared up at his wounded face.

"How *did* you know that Dean was the killer? After all, you left him when you were only a baby. So how did you find that out?" She asked, nervously.

Ashley smiled at her encouragingly.

"That's true. I may have lived with Dean for a year after I was born, but I didn't recognise him as the killer because I hadn't known him long enough. Back then, it was usually Heidi who looked after me so I formed a much stronger bond with her. It was only later that I worked out my father had tried to kill me that night. I already told you that I will never forget Dean's eyes as he was peering under the bed at me. Well, I was reading another one of my mum's diaries one weekend when I was eight and I came across some old photographs of Dean and Heidi together before I was born. I recognised Dean's eyes instantly and I could see that we looked really similar, plus Heidi had written a label on the back explaining that this man was her boyfriend. So, I took the picture to show my guardian and she gently told me what had happened. That day, I learnt that my *father* had tried to kill me and my heart broke. I'd grown up reading lots of stories about happy families and so I found it really hard trying to understand that mine wasn't." Ashley explained and Luke's face crumpled as he relived his own memories.

"I remember that too. You just locked yourself away in your bedroom for days and wouldn't talk to anyone. You wouldn't eat much and it didn't seem like you could sleep either. I didn't know what had happened to try and help you and I've never felt so useless. You wouldn't tell me what had upset you and I was so worried that I just camped outside your bedroom door for three days and kept accidentally tripping Robbie up. I wanted to help but I couldn't." He frowned, hugging his knees tightly and resting his chin on them sadly.

Ashley nodded, offering Luke a faint smile of friendship.

"I don't know what happened to Dean after the attack though. I only know that he was never caught. So I can't say anything more. I don't know if he still lives in London or whether he moved back up here. Maybe he even has a new family. I wonder if I've got any more half-siblings somewhere that I don't know about. A little sister would be nice." He commented and Luke frowned to himself. He knew exactly where Dean was.

Suzy eyed him curiously. What was that look supposed to mean? Did he know something about Dean's whereabouts? Why hadn't he said anything? Normally, he hated keeping secrets from Ashley.

"Are you alright, Luke? You look worried." She asked and he shrugged.

"I was just thinking about Ashley's idea that Dean escaped down a secret passage. I reckon that sounds pretty accurate especially if Ashley remembers him turning to face the wall instead of the door. Why would he choose to flee out into the corridor and risk being collared by the police if he knew another way out?" He lied, smoothly.

Bryony nodded.

"Well, if there is a secret passage here somewhere, I'm going to find it." She declared, bending over to peer at the wooden panelling intently.

Rose smiled, stepping forwards to help.

"Let me see. I've lived here all my life so I'm quite good at finding hidden passages." She said, carefully tracing her fingers over the wall and biting her lip in concentration. The others crowded round to watch her expectantly for a few minutes before Rose gave a sudden cry of victory. "There. See? The wood panelling changes colour slightly and it feels different too." She said, looking round at them proudly. She may be the smallest and youngest, but she was still determined to fit in and pull her weight.

"Wow. Look at that! Well spotted, Rose." Bryony exclaimed, eyeing the younger girl admiringly.

Michael smiled to himself eagerly as he watched their progress. He loved solving puzzles and found the idea of a secret passage really exciting. He'd never stayed anywhere like the Morgan manor before and couldn't believe his oldest brother was connected to this extraordinary place. He was almost jealous.

Rose frowned, pushing against the wall as she tried to force the door open.

"Ugh, why won't it move? They're not usually this stiff. Most of the time, they just swing open if you push on them. I know some operate from a secret lever too, but I can't see anything here that looks like one." She complained, giving the wall a frustrated little smack.

Tom stepped forwards to join her, scanning the wall critically.

"Here, let me help. I'm stronger than you are." He offered and Michael obediently stepped back out of the way.

He watched them for a few seconds before he idly turned his gaze up towards the ceiling as he wondered whether it was decorated with any fancy carvings.

"Errr, guys? Look up." He called, frowning when they ignored him as usual. Rolling his eyes slightly in exasperation, he reached out to place one hand under Robbie's chin before gently tipping his head back. His brother was really good at making himself heard, so Michael decided to let him attract everyone's attention instead

"Oh." Robbie muttered, staring up at the trapdoor in confusion. Then he looked back down at the others still crowded around the wall and sighed. He reached up to place a few fingers in his mouth before he gave a loud, piercing whistle that caused Jenna to cry out in protest.

"Thanks." Michael nodded and Robbie reached out to give him a fond pat on the back. "Look. There's no secret passage but instead a trapdoor. That's why the wall panel feels different. There would have been a lot of people abusing it as they climbed up through the trapdoor, so eventually it got replaced." He explained and the others nodded, looking a bit sheepish at not working this out for themselves.

Luke stepped forwards to run his fingers over the wall thoughtfully. The old tester bed had damage too when you looked closer, from people quickly clambering up the frame instead of patiently looking for a ladder.

"As much as I would love a peek up there, I'd rather not try and climb up the way everyone else did. We'd only end up damaging the old wood even more." He sighed, startled when Michael suddenly jumped up astride his back.

"Of course we can take a look up there. See? There are plenty of us here so we can use each other to climb up. For goodness sake, Luke, stand still! What's wrong with you?" He argued, clinging to Luke tightly for a few moments until the older boy found his balance.

"Well, I was hardly expecting that you were gonna jump on me! Of course I moved; you startled me! At least give me some warning next time before you go climbing up my spine like a monkey…" Luke protested, peering round at him indignantly. He doubled over to let Michael wriggle forwards and sit astride his shoulders before he straightened up again, gripping his friend's legs tightly as Michael reached up to tug on the trapdoor bolts.

"Ugh, they're really stiff!" He grumbled, feeling a little embarrassed that he wasn't strong enough to open them.

Below, Ashley looked round as Bryony tugged on his sleeve gently.

"Do you mind-?" She asked, pointing up at the trapdoor to signal that she wanted a look too.

"Sure." He answered, crouching down to let her climb onto his shoulders before he lifted her up to join Michael in the air.

Bryony settled herself quietly, grateful for Ashley's tall height as she reached up to tug on the trapdoor bolts, pulling them back with ease and causing Michael to scowl at her in shame.

"Show-off." He grumbled.

Bryony pushed against the trapdoor a few times before it opened, exposing a black and dusty world above her head. Intrigued, she reached out to carefully pull herself up into the attic before she turned to offer her hand out to Michael below. He accepted it gratefully and she hauled him up into the gloom, smiling to herself at his clumsy entrance.

Michael peered round curiously for a moment at his new surroundings before he reached down to dig his phone out of his pocket and switched the torch on. He couldn't wait to see what was stored up here and wondered where Ashley's father had disappeared to after reaching this point. Surely Dean couldn't have just hidden away up here while the police investigations took place in the room below? If *they'd* found the trapdoor, a group of nosy teenagers, then the police must have found it too. But Dean had never been caught, so where had he gone? And who would put an important trapdoor like this in a bedroom anyway? Had the room once been something else in days gone by? It was all very weird. Intrigued, Michael set off to explore the forgotten treasures quietly, pleased that his small height was an advantage for once since it meant he wasn't at risk of smacking his head on any of the low beams.

Bryony glanced round at him briefly before she gestured down at the rest of her friends in the old murder room.

"Anyone else want a look?" She asked, smiling when Luke and Rose both nodded.

"Yes, please! I never knew this place was here!" Rose said, eagerly.

Jenna smiled at her encouragingly and padded over to help lift her up.

Then, with Rose safely out of the way, Luke set about making his ascent, walking over to place one foot in Ashley's cupped hands and gripping his shoulder gently as Ashley firmly hoisted him up off the floor. Rose stared at them in amazement as Bryony reached out to help pull her nosy bandmate up through the trapdoor.

"Wow, you're really strong!" Rose gasped, surprised to learn that Ashley had such an impressive hidden strength when he was so skinny. Ashley smiled to himself in quiet satisfaction before he turned to stare round at the rest of his friends.

"Anyone else need me for a human ladder?" He asked and they all shook their heads.

Luke peered down at him critically.

"What about you? Don't you want to see what's up here?" He asked and Ashley shook his head.

"Nah, I'll stay down here. I want some time to think. It's been quite a stressful morning." He answered and Luke nodded.

"Right. We shouldn't be long. And for God's sake, don't you and Robbie start fighting again while I'm gone." He warned, fixing them both with a hard stare.

"They won't. I'll see to that." Tom promised with a reassuring smile.

Robbie scowled, shaking his head firmly.

"Don't you *dare* try to babysit me, Thomas. Do I look like a damn baby? Mind your own business." He growled, glaring at his friend indignantly.

Luke smiled to himself in amusement.

"Yeah, good luck with that." He muttered, smirking as he turned his attention to exploring the attic.

Up ahead, Rose and Michael were busy examining a pile of broken furniture while Bryony was staring across at a collection of old travelling cases. She was so fascinated that she never noticed the large box that was stored somewhat haphazardly at the side of the walkway and cried out in surprise as she stumbled into it.

"Be careful." Michael called.

"You okay?" Luke asked, as he finally caught up to Bryony, bent over slightly against the beams since he was a good deal taller than the others.

"I'm fine. I just stubbed my toe, that's all. Stupid box." Bryony answered, limping over to catch up with Michael. This time, however, she took care to shine her phone-light down at the floor instead to check for any other hidden hazards that might trip her up. She hadn't expected the attic would be quite so dangerous.

"There must be an easier way of getting up here, surely. I can't imagine they'd haul all this furniture up through that tiny little trapdoor we found." Michael frowned, peering round at her critically as he gestured at the dusty items.

Luke nodded in ready agreement, thinking it *would* be quite difficult to haul something big through the small entrance they'd used to access the place. It was only as he considered Michael's words a little more while they explored that he realised something else and straightened up in shock.

Bryony cringed at the violent thud that echoed around the attic as Luke's skull made contact with an overhead beam and promptly rushed over to help look after him.

Luke doubled over, swearing bitterly and dropping to his knees for a few moments as he waited for the pain to subside.

"Oh my God, that hurt like hell." He groaned as Michael and Rose padded over to crowd around him too, staring at him anxiously.

"What did you do that for, you idiot?" Bryony demanded as she reached out to gently poke through Luke's long hair to check if he'd really hurt himself. "Well, your head looks okay. I don't think you've cut yourself. Just sit here for a few minutes until you feel better. You'll have to be more careful on the way back." She scolded.

"Michael, you're amazing." Luke grunted, cautiously uncurling himself and reaching up with one hand to gently examine the place where his head felt to be on fire. "Is the room spinning or is it just me?" He added, looking round at the piles of boxes and old furniture warily.

"Why? What did I say?" Michael asked, bewildered.

"Of course there are other trapdoors up here! That's how Dean escaped, don't you see? He climbed up the one we found and then vanished down another into a different room. From there, I'd imagine he escaped through another secret passage, so the police never caught him because Dean knows this place better than they do." Luke told them, perching on an old trunk to avoid smacking his head again.

Rose hugged him gently.

"That makes sense. There are secret passages everywhere, but I don't know where most of them go and I don't want to get lost trying to explore them." She agreed.

They gave Luke a few minutes to compose himself before they split up to see if they could find any more trapdoors hidden away up here that would support his theory. It didn't take long before Rose spotted one half buried beneath a framed photograph that had been left face-down in the dirt.

Michael lifted the picture up and turned it over to study it while Luke firmly hauled the trapdoor open.

"Glen Morgan. What did he do wrong to be disgraced and cast away up here?" Michael muttered, turning the frame round to show them a fairly modern portrait of another black-haired Morgan child. He'd found the name written on the back of the frame and wondered what had happened to this sad-looking boy.

Rose smiled, obviously recognising the name and reaching out for the photograph.

"Oh, that's my uncle! I've never met him but Mum has mentioned his name a few times. Apparently, she was one of three children. Dean was the oldest, then Glen was the middle child and my mum was the youngest. I know that Glen was kicked out of the family a long time ago but I'm not sure why." She explained and the others nodded curiously.

Luke eyed the photograph briefly before he stretched out across the floorboards and peered down into the room below.

"Please, someone watch me to make sure I don't hurt myself again. It's only the first day and already I've been hit in the face with a walking stick and smacked my head on a roof beam. I don't want anything else to happen, you hear me? I'm quite fond of my head the way it is." He growled and Michael smiled to himself.

"The first time was your own fault when that woman hit you back in town. You were too busy daydreaming." He pointed out.

From what Luke could make out, the room below had once been a small study, except the bookshelves were empty now and the old desk bare and abandoned. A thick layer of dust covered every surface, but the layer across the floor had recently been disturbed, with a faint trail of footprints following the skirting board around the room. Suspicious, Luke leaned forwards slightly for a better look and Bryony immediately reached out to grab hold of him, fearful that he might fall.

Now half-suspended through the trapdoor, Luke could see fragments of broken glass scattered across the floor beside the desk. Judging by a particularly large fragment, the glass had once formed a beautiful vase. This must have been the room Dean was searching when Luke saw him from the road that morning, so he presumed it must also have been Dean who caused the loud smash that Tom heard when he accidentally knocked the vase over.

Then there was Ashley's claim that the murder scene was supposed to be locked and yet when he'd first come to find the room, the door had already been loose and swung open without him having to unlock it. Luke assumed that must have been left behind by Dean as well, as he picked the lock to search the bedroom for whatever it was that he needed.

Luke's blood slowly turned to ice as he remembered sitting in the banquet hall at breakfast, listening to Tom yelling Ashley's name as he searched the manor. The large empty building had caused Tom's voice to echo slightly, so Luke had been able to hear his cousin wherever he went. Thankfully, Ashley had remained silent and Luke hardly dared to imagine what might have happened if Ashley *had* shouted back to Tom and given his position away. Luke shuddered to think that Dean and Ashley must have been mere metres away from each other at that point.

He also theorised that Dean had probably spotted Ashley from this window too as Ashley waited patiently by the gates for his friends to get dressed ready for their trip into town. As a trained Morgan criminal, Dean must surely have the perfect aim with a gun, so he could easily have shot Ashley from this room and finished the job he started twelve years before. But Ashley was still alive and well, so Dean must obviously have more important things on his mind than chasing after his teenage son.

Robbie and Michael had also made their presence quite obvious and Luke was sure that Dean must have recognised them too. Ashley had often said that Robbie looked a lot like Ethan while Michael reminded him more of Heidi since they shared the same soft blond hair. With Michael jumping up and down beside Luke to see what he was staring at and Robbie harassing Ashley further down the lane, Luke knew that Dean's gaze would definitely have been drawn to them.

Luke liked to think that he had protected Ashley a bit when he walked over and stood in front of him to ask what Ashley was writing in his journal. But there was no way of proving that, so he would just have to be on his guard and hope there hadn't been a gun pointing at the back of his head earlier that day. That disturbing little thought would certainly keep him up at night if he let himself dwell on it for too long.

He sighed, hauling himself back up through the trapdoor again and thinking he'd have to keep a close eye on the three brothers from now on.

Toxic Childhood

They were on their way back to join their friends in the old murder scene and explain what they'd found when Bryony tripped over the same box that had caught her out the first time. Except this time she brought Michael crashing to the ground with her since he'd had the unfortunate position of being right in front of her.

"Oh, for pity's sake, it's this stupid box again! That's the second time it's got me. It's almost like it *wants* to be found!" Bryony moaned.

"Help!" Michael squeaked, from where he was still trapped underneath her with an old broom digging painfully hard into his chest.

"Alright, alright, I'm coming. Don't panic." Luke muttered, carefully stepping over them and pulling Bryony back to her feet while Rose crouched down to examine the offending box.

"Look at this! It's got Ashley's name on it!" She called, pointing to the word scrawled on the side in bold marker pen. The others turned to each other curiously and Luke padded over to shout down through the trapdoor to where their friends were still waiting.

"Hey, Ash? You should probably see this." He called, the serious tone of his voice making his best friend look round at him anxiously.

"What-?" Ashley asked, bewildered.

"Just get up here. There's a box with your name on it." Luke replied, reaching down to help pull Ashley through the hole as Tom pushed him up from below.

Of course, the news of a mystery box sparked everyone's interest and they all wanted to see what was inside it too, so Luke ended up having to pull Tom, Jenna, Suzy and Robbie up through the trapdoor as well, leaving the old murder scene below completely empty.

Ashley crouched down beside the strange box, looking round uncertainly as his friends all crowded round him, eagerly peering over his shoulder as they waited for him to open it.

"Hey, back off! This stuff might be private!" He protested, glaring round at them furiously in the dim torchlight. They all cringed and obediently turned to stare in different directions while he carefully unpicked all the parcel tape that held the box together. "Ugh. It's fine, you can look. It's just some of my old baby stuff. How embarrassing." He muttered after a few seconds.

Jenna promptly gave a loud squeal of excitement and turned round to roughly delve through the box while Bryony turned to eye her moody bandmate curiously.

"Why would your baby things be up here at the Morgan manor? Didn't your guardian want them? That seems a bit sad." She asked and he chuckled.

"Nah, Pam could never bring herself to get rid of anything. Back home, our attic is absolutely crammed with boxes of old toys, clothes, photo albums, school reports and childish craft projects. I reckon my mum must have taken at least a million photographs of me before she died. But we don't have much from when I lived in London with Dean, which makes sense when you consider that Heidi was trying to cut him out of my life at that point. When she ran away, she must have just grabbed whatever we *needed* and the photographs she treasured the most and left everything else behind. Then, when my father decided I wasn't worthy of existing, the items Heidi left behind must have come to Enid for safekeeping if Dean didn't want to be reminded of us." He reasoned, awkwardly ducking away from Jenna as she reached out to try and place a fleecy white baby hat on his head.

"Awwww, Ashley! These are adorable! I bet you were the *cutest* baby." Jenna cooed, finally succeeding in capturing Ashley in a firm headlock and giggling hysterically as Robbie and Suzy reached out to cover him in the embarrassing outfits. Tom couldn't resist snapping a photo of his friend's misery and Ashley glared at him sourly.

"You post that anywhere on the internet, Tom, and you're a dead man." He warned as Luke pulled out a large photo album that he'd found at the bottom of the box.

"Oooh, let me see!" Rose begged, urgently scooting over to sit beside Luke while Bryony also shuffled over for a curious nosey.

The first photograph had been taken in a hospital, judging by the medical equipment in the background, and showed a young man with rich black hair carefully cradling a new-born baby in his arms as he grinned excitedly at the camera.

Despite having only seen Dean properly once, when he came snooping around their bedroom during the night, Luke recognised him immediately and eyed the photo critically. He hadn't thought Dean's face would be capable of *smiling*, but the man in the photo looked absolutely delighted by the birth of his son and was cuddling young Ashley with such care and love that it seemed strange when you considered that this was the same man who had tried to murder Ashley only four years later.

"Oh my gosh, look at this one!" Rose gasped as she pointed at the opposite photograph that showed Dean sitting on the floor with baby Ashley as he tried to introduce his little boy to the world of guns. There were three different types laid out on the table in front of the pair while Dean had a fourth in one hand, although he had wisely kept it out of Ashley's reach.

Bryony wrinkled her nose.

"That's disgusting. What sort of parent does that?" She asked, horrified to see that her bandmate had suffered such an abusive infancy.

"Look at the one in Dean's hand." Luke muttered as he leaned closer to examine the photo in more detail. He'd spotted that the weapon in Dean's hand had the Morgan crest proudly emblazoned on one side which was unsettling enough to begin with on an instrument of death. But then Luke had noticed the initials 'A.M.' underneath. Clearly, the gun was meant to be Ashley's once he was old enough and Luke couldn't help wondering what had happened to it after the murders.

Rose shuddered.

"I really hope that thing never got used." She muttered, thinking it would be especially cruel to use a gun decorated with Ashley's initials when he didn't like to associate himself with his criminal relatives.

"The next picture's not much better." Bryony warned as she turned the page over to reveal a photograph of Dean and his criminal friends smoking, drinking and playing poker at the dining table while Ashley lay in his pram beside Dean, happily chewing on his teddy bear's ear and seeming totally disinterested in the game. Dean had a beer bottle loosely dangling from his fingers over Ashley's head as he used his son's pram as an armrest while three empty bottles lay discarded on the table in front of him. Dean was apparently quite good at poker for he had an impressive pile of money laid out before him and had even placed a few chips on the table in front of Ashley to make it seem like he was involved in the game too. Judging by the bump on Ashley's head, it seemed that Dean had accidentally dropped the bottle on him once already, but he didn't appear to have learned his lesson. Instead, Dean had just carelessly stuck a plaster over Ashley's injury in a vague attempt to make up for his mistake.

Bryony shook her head in disgust. She could easily understand why Ashley's mother had chosen to leave this photo album behind when she ran away. From what she'd heard, Heidi had loved her son very much so there was absolutely no way she would have put Ashley in these situations, let alone photographing the moments. Therefore, this abusive album must have been compiled by Dean instead and served as a record of what he got up to while Heidi was out.

Ashley held out one hand towards them.

"Let me see." He insisted, waiting as the photo album was passed around the circle before flicking through it to investigate what other secrets it held. "I don't want you to see anything else." He declared, pressing the book close against his chest and frowning to himself uncomfortably.

"Sorry. I didn't mean to pry." Luke mumbled, awkwardly fiddling with the strings of his hoodie as he watched Ashley take a few deep breaths to compose himself before he slunk away into the shadows to examine the album in more detail, finally settling himself against a timber post and digging out his phone to help illuminate the pictures.

Robbie scoffed.

"What's new? You're always poking through Ashley's thoughts and snooping at his things. I'm surprised he doesn't scold you more often." He replied, shaking his head at Luke in disapproval.

Suzy, meanwhile, was anxiously biting her lip as she laid Ashley's old baby clothes out across a nearby trunk.

"Look at them. I think there was a reason these got left behind. It's not a case that Heidi just forgot about them or ran out of space the night she ran away. It seems to me that Heidi found these outfits offensive and therefore chose to leave them with Dean as another way of distancing Ashley from his wicked criminal ancestry. See? This one is a little pirate suit while that stripy one is reminiscent of cartoon thieves. Then, you have this matching grey set which would have made Ashley look like a mini gangster, albeit a very cute one. I've also found a skeleton onesie, here, while this red hoodie has devil horns and a pointy tail printed on the back. I can't imagine that Heidi would have chosen these outfits for Ashley since they all reference his Morgan heritage, so I believe they got left behind on purpose." She explained as Michael reached out to examine the satanic hoodie critically.

"It's a good job Mum never saw some of Ashley's Halloween costumes then. He loves winding people up." He muttered, turning to shoot his big brother a judgemental look through the gloom while Robbie leaned over to dig a crumpled sheet of paper out of the box.

"Hey, isn't this Ashley's birth certificate? Why would Mum leave that behind? I'd say that was pretty important." He asked, holding it out to show everyone.

Tom's eyes widened.

"Nah. Look at the first column." He replied, pointing to where Ashley's middle names had been crossed out. "I reckon Heidi probably ordered a new one." He muttered before falling silent as Ashley padded back towards them and perched on top of an old stool.

"What did I miss?" He asked, peering round at them expectantly and leaning forwards to dump the thick photo album back in the box.

"Why have your middle names been crossed out on your birth certificate?" Suzy demanded and Ashley shrugged.

"I don't know. My guardian once said that, throughout Heidi's pregnancy, she'd been told I was going to be named Ashley Edward Morgan after Heidi's beloved father. So she was really surprised when she got a card announcing the birth of Ashley Hunter Seth Morgan instead. Apparently, when Dean and Heidi went down to register my birth, Heidi took charge of the paperwork while Dean was instructed to look after me. Heidi hadn't mentioned anything about wanting to give me a different name so when it was Dean's turn to sign the form, he didn't bother to check it first. It was only when they got home that Dean realised Heidi had chosen something else and he was absolutely furious. I don't know why. I always thought that 'Hunter' and 'Seth' were great names. But, according to my guardian, Dean just kept whining that Heidi had betrayed him and that I'd been cursed. Pamela never understood it. Robbie was the one who ended up with 'Edward' for a middle name." He replied as Luke crawled around the circle to investigate the document for himself.

"Yeah, it certainly looks as though your name has been scratched out with venom." He agreed, raising one eyebrow as he considered the way the document had been violently destroyed.

Rose turned to eye her cousin thoughtfully.

"How do you feel about the fact it was Dean who picked your name? You mentioned it downstairs while you were explaining about the murders." She asked and he sighed.

"Honestly? I don't like it. When I first learnt that he was the one who chose the name 'Ashley', it made me feel absolutely sick. I spent a few weeks thinking quite seriously about changing my name. My guardian even got me a book on baby names from a charity shop. She pointed out that it would involve a lot of paperwork, but she was happy to do it. But then I realised that I'd have to tell everyone *why* I wanted a new identity, and I wasn't ready for that. In the end, I decided that it was simpler to just stick with 'Ashley' and threw the baby name book out." He explained, looking round as Jenna laid a concerned hand on his arm.

"What would you like to be known as going forward? I mean, you've told us the story of your past now, so I'd understand if you want to use something else." She asked and he smiled.

"Nah, it's okay. You can still call me 'Ashley'; don't worry. I've come to terms with it. I realised that while Dean may have picked it out, I'm the one who gave it a personality. I've always liked being an 'Ashley'. I think it sounds quite bold and edgy and it seems to suit me really well. My dad can sod off." He replied, grunting slightly as Luke leaned over to give him a hard thump.

"That's my boy! I don't know where you get that impressive mental strength from, but I want some!" He exclaimed and Ashley rolled his eyes.

"Still not *your* boy, pal. How many times?" He scolded, annoyed that Luke seemed to view him as some kind of pet. "I'm sorry I've been so difficult lately. I'm not usually like this, Rose. Ask anyone. I'm just having quite a hard time dealing with my heritage at the moment and figuring out what it means for my future. You can look me up on social media if you want. That will show you what I'm really like." He added, having noticed that Rose seemed to acquire a rather uncertain look in her eye whenever she turned to face him.

"Oh, don't worry about it! Honestly! I appreciate it must have been hard for you to come back here. We've plenty of time to get to know each other properly." Rose answered, flashing her cousin a warm smile through the gloom.

"Here. See? He's actually pretty cool once you learn to look past his dark exterior." Luke urged, offering out his phone to show Rose some photographs of how Ashley was back home in Cornwall. "As for you, mister, I'm just glad that you're finally opening up to us." He added, turning to raise one eyebrow at Ashley suggestively.

He just hoped that Ashley wouldn't find out he had *also* been withholding information. They didn't normally keep secrets from each other so it had been very hard, but Luke suspected that Ashley wouldn't react well to the news that Dean had been sneaking around the manor. He worried that Ashley might go out looking for his wicked father and end up getting badly hurt again, or worse, so he had decided it was better for Ashley's sanity and safety that he remain ignorant. His best friend could be pretty reckless at times. But that was something for Future Luke to deal with. Right now, food was calling.

Hunting for Whistles

Luke stayed up late again that night, keeping a watchful eye over Ashley, Robbie and Michael in case Dean came snooping again.

At least Ashley seemed calm tonight. Returning to this place and finally confronting the issues of his past must have brought him some much-needed peace so that he could sleep without being forever tortured by his memories.

Thankfully, Dean made no appearance, so he must either be resting at last or searching a different part of the manor for his elusive secret passage. Luke couldn't imagine what he was looking for. What could be so important for Dean to risk sneaking around the building and being caught? Was he looking for one of the lost treasure hoards Enid had told them about?

With these thoughts floating round his weary brain, Luke slowly drifted off to sleep, falling into such a deep world of dreams that he never noticed Tom tugging at his arm soon after midnight.

Tom gave a low growl and quietly clambered up the ladder to tug at Ashley instead, wanting proof that he wasn't going completely crazy and the ghostly whistles he kept hearing were real.

Tom firmly shook Ashley awake and pointed out the window.

"Can you hear that too?" Tom hissed as Ashley sat up and rubbed his eyes sleepily.

"Huh-?" Ashley mumbled, yawning.

"Listen....." Tom whispered, still knelt over Ashley somewhat haphazardly.

They waited in silence for a few minutes and Tom scowled. Surely the whistles weren't just in his head? Were they a left-over sound from a scary dream or something? What was going on?

Ashley huffed, fixing Tom with a dirty look before snuggling back down under the covers again and giving him a firm kick to get off his bed.

Grumbling to himself, Tom quietly jumped off the ladder and flopped down on his own bed again, scowling out at the forest irritably. He had just begun to relax when another ghostly whistle pierced the silence of the night, sounding almost like the whistle of a train. But there hadn't been any grand old steam trains in these parts for decades, so what on earth was making that loud wailing noise?

Tom sat up, squinting round at Ashley's bunk through the darkness.

"Did you hear that?" He hissed, urgently.

"Yeah, I heard it." Ashley's voice growled from the shadows, obviously not very happy at being so rudely woken from a rare night of peaceful sleep. He cautiously sat up, giving a heavy sigh as he clambered down the ladder to join Tom at the window.

They peered out at the wild forest for a few moments before another loud whistle startled them, a mournful scream for help across the misty mountains.

Across the room, Robbie gave a sharp sniff of annoyance in his sleep that caused a pained look to spread across Ashley's face. He quietly walked over to pick up the mended toy plane that his brother had left on the fireplace mantel before climbing up the ladder to lay it on Robbie's chest instead. Then, he reached out to gently stroke Robbie's head a few times as Robbie moved his hand to investigate the unexpected weight on his chest. When he realised what the object was, he gave a happy little sigh and rolled over to face Ashley, cuddling the plane close to him as though it were a teddy bear.

Ashley smiled at him affectionately for a while before he climbed back down to join Tom.

"We should see what's going on." He muttered and Tom nodded in agreement, surprised that the peculiar whistles hadn't disturbed anyone else's sleep. After all, Ashley had only woken up because Tom made him while Robbie, who was famed for being a light-sleeper, had only been mildly disturbed.

They quietly pulled on their boots and trekked through the house, staying close together since Ashley had the only torch and the house was so dark and hostile at night. Eventually, they reached the front door and Tom firmly tugged it open before peering round at the forest critically.

"Anything?" Ashley asked, stepping forwards to join him and swinging the torch round the driveway. A few bats were flying around overhead, silhouetted against the moon, and a cool fog was slowly creeping across the road as it crawled out from the depths of the black forest. It was a very spooky, mysterious sight and Ashley was quite inspired by the beauty of it all.

Another sudden, piercing whistle made them both jump and Tom frowned.

"It really does sound as though someone's being tortured out there." He muttered and Ashley bit his lip anxiously.

"Well, come on then. Let's go find out what's going on, just so we can sleep easy without thinking someone *else* is being murdered in this godforsaken place." He insisted, pulling his jacket tighter around himself and setting off into the night without another word.

Tom quickly rushed after him and they tracked the whistles for a while, lured deeper into the gloomy trees and sticking close together to make sure they didn't lose each other in the dark. It was obvious that this part of the forest was rarely explored as the leaves lay undisturbed with no evidence of footprints. Tom didn't like it one bit. The creepy, uncivilised forest and cold summer fog just made him really uncomfortable and he was very glad that he had hauled Ashley out of bed to join him on this strange mission. There was no way in hell he would have set off into the forest all by himself in these conditions. That was just asking for trouble.

Eventually, they emerged into a large clearing and both stopped to gaze round in astonishment, for the area was clearly a derelict old mining complex. There were numerous brick buildings dotted around and some even still had paper advertisements stuck to the windows, which Tom thought was fascinating. In addition, there were also the remains of rusty iron rails curving around the site and sometimes the old mine carts were there too, abandoned on the tracks and silently waiting for the day when they would carry goods once more.

It was a sad scene, for the area had clearly been long deserted and seemingly in a great hurry. The buildings were mostly all overgrown and in a serious state of disrepair and Tom wondered what could have caused the place to be abandoned like this. Had there been some kind of terrible accident down the mine or had it just been overtaken by modern technology? It didn't resolve the matter of the strange whistles though, but for the time being, neither of them cared.

Tom and Ashley gazed down on the mine from atop a steep railway embankment which flanked the bottom end of the site. As they watched, they could make out ghostly figures dashing about, their bodies shimmering with a strange kind of transparent silver glow. Their clothes were clearly old-fashioned and some of them hurried from one building to another, carrying various papers and shouting silent orders round the clearing. Others were wearily plodding back and forth along the rails, pushing phantom wagons into the undergrowth, which Tom assumed must be the entrance to the old tunnels. When these figures came to one of the solid wagons on the track, they would carry on straight through them as though unable to see them at all.

Mesmerised, the two boys stared out across the scene, amazed at being able to view the past as it once was in the main heyday of the mine's operation. Neither of them had ever *really* believed in ghosts, but that had all changed now. These supernatural figures weren't the traditional horrifying spectres that were described in books and films; they were instead just the shadowy visions of people going about their lives as though they had never died.

It was a sorry scene to watch, but captivating too and so both boys had entirely given up on their mission to find the strange noises that had lured them out of the manor. They watched the site for a while until another piercing, ghostly whistle echoed through the dark forest and caused Tom to blink himself back to reality.

He half-turned to see where the noise had come from and his eyes widened at seeing a train speeding down the old track-way towards them. With only a second or two to react, Tom reached forwards to grab Ashley by the collar and firmly yanked him backwards out of the train's path. The torch automatically flew out of Ashley's hand from the sudden movement and sailed through the air before it hit a tree and went out altogether.

Still with Tom's arms wrapped around his shoulders, Ashley stared up at the train in shock as it rumbled past, just in front of his nose. Tom was now leant back against a tree with Ashley pulled close against him out of harm's way and they turned to each other critically when they noticed that the train had the same kind of ghostly transparency as the figures wandering about in the clearing below.

When Tom had first glanced round, neither the silvery glow nor the fact it was an old steam train had crossed his mind. His only thoughts had been to get out of the way and save Ashley from its path.

Now, whilst they were flattened back against the tree, they could clearly see this was a ghost train of days gone by, with phantom smoke billowing from the funnel and countless old wagons creaking along behind. It was a magnificent sight to witness the past come to life right before their eyes.

Finally, the train rumbled past and they turned to stare after it in disbelief for a few seconds, totally shocked by their unexpected discovery.

Tom firmly pushed Ashley off him and tried to hoist himself up from the awkward position he'd been forced to adopt, leaning back against the tree when the ground sloped down from the track-way.

Ashley reached out to help pull Tom back to his feet before he turned to run after the ghost-train excitedly.

"Well, don't just stand there; let's see where it goes, eh?" He yelled.

Tom quickly sprinted after him, soon catching up to Ashley and easily keeping pace as they chased the ghost train through the dark forest.

It was a hidden branch that brought Tom down, hooking over his foot and tripping him up face-first into a muddy puddle on the track-bed.

Ashley leapt over him and carried on running, needing to know where the train went and vowing to come back for Tom once he'd found out.

Tom mumbled some indecipherable profanity under his breath at being left behind and glared at Ashley furiously from where he was still sprawled out in the dirt.

Thankfully, the train was travelling fairly slowly at the moment, winding through the trees past old signs and huts, so Ashley could just about keep up with it. But after a while, the train suddenly vanished into thin air, just as it passed the battered and overgrown remains of a small signal box.

Ashley skidded down the track-way, trying to come to a halt as he looked round wildly to see where the train had gone. But since he'd been running so fast, his momentum carried him further down the path and he tripped over a small rock, rolling head over heels down the hill and finally knocking himself out as he smacked his head on a tree.

Nearby, up on the old track-way, Tom was looking round in confusion as he tried to work out where Ashley and the train had gone. How could they have disappeared so quickly? He hadn't been that far behind them. It had only taken a minute to pick himself up out of the muddy puddle before he chased after them in the dark. But now, there was nothing and no-one in sight. He was really starting to wish they had brought their phones out with them instead of leaving them behind at the manor. That would have made it much easier to find each other again. But they hadn't been expecting to be outside for this long, so their phones hadn't seemed very important.

"ASHLEY-? WHERE ARE YOU?" He shouted, pausing by the old signal box to catch his breath and looking round at the spooky trees fearfully. Eventually, he spotted a dark figure sprawled out amongst the leaves halfway down the banking and frowned to himself suspiciously as he set about slithering down to investigate.

As he got closer, he realised that the strange figure was actually Ashley and dropped down beside his friend anxiously, concerned that Ashley's eyes were closed and he looked to be asleep. What on earth had happened in the few short minutes they were apart? Why was Ashley suddenly unconscious?

"What happened to you?" He muttered, carefully leaning over Ashley to check for any injuries that might explain his peculiar sleepiness. From what he could see, Ashley didn't seem to be bleeding anywhere and Tom gave a faint sigh of relief. "Come on, mate. Wake up. I don't know what to do..." He begged, shifting himself further over to sit back against a nearby tree before he gently lifted Ashley up out of the wet leaves to cradle him protectively against his chest like a baby.

Ashley didn't react at all and Tom bit his lip as he stared down at his friend's blank expression. Clearly, he would just have to wait for Ashley to wake up and see what he remembered. Tom spent the next few minutes idly picking sticks out of Ashley's messy bed-hair and peering round at the forest thoughtfully as he wondered what their friends would make of their strange adventure.

Eventually, a soft moan of 'ughhhh' alerted him to the fact that Ashley was coming to and he looked down at him in concern.

Ashley groaned, his eyelids fluttering slightly as he weakly reached up with one hand to clutch at his throbbing head. When he opened his eyes properly a few moments later, everything was just a dark blur and he frowned in confusion.

"Hey, are you okay?" A voice asked from somewhere above him.

"Huh-?" Ashley muttered, blinking slowly as he turned to look for the source of the noise. He could just make out a blurry figure sitting next to him and stared up at them curiously.

"It's okay. It's me. It's Tom." The voice announced and Ashley smiled to himself faintly, clawing at Tom's chest as he tried to sit up.

"Tommmmy..." He mumbled, a little delirious from being knocked out and thinking the name sounded really funny.

"That's right. Now, can you remember your own name?" The voice asked and Ashley nodded weakly.

"I'm *Ashhhhley*. Hello!" He answered, a silly little grin on his face as he reached up to pat himself a few times.

Tom smiled, pleased that Ashley still knew his identity. That must be a good sign he wasn't *seriously* hurt. He gently reached down to help lift Ashley back to his feet before he gestured round at their location.

"So, what happened to you?" He asked and Ashley turned to squint round at the forest critically.

He was silent for a few moments as he tried to make sense of what he was seeing. His vision was still quite blurry from his accident and he was confused by the way that everything seemed to have multiplied. Even the ground looked to be on three different levels and it made him feel very nauseous. Eventually, he reached up to point at what he thought was the old track-way as memories of their thrilling adventure began to return, floating across his mind like dreams.

"It vanished." He muttered, staggering slightly against his spinning vision.

Tom quickly reached out to grab hold of him, supporting Ashley carefully as he tried to understand what he was talking about.

"It vanished? What do you mean? Like, the train went into a siding or something?" He asked and Ashley grunted in disagreement.

"*No.* It vanished. Poof!" He explained, sounding a little immature as the dizziness of his head made it quite hard to put sentences together. He gestured wildly with his hands for a moment before he turned to peer round at Tom expectantly.

"Okay." Tom frowned, deciding that Ashley obviously meant the train just disappeared like magic. "What happened then?" He asked, gently reaching up to re-examine Ashley's head since his friend was behaving very strangely.

"I fell. Then 'ouch'. Sleepy-time." Ashley explained, staring up at Tom blankly.

Tom eyed him nervously, wondering how he was supposed to take care of Ashley now. Clearly, Ashley had hurt himself quite badly and was a bit spaced-out, but Tom was notorious for getting lost so he really didn't like their current situation one bit. Without Ashley's sense of direction, he feared they might end up aimlessly wandering around the forest all night.

He turned to survey the surrounding landscape critically, reaching out to take a firm hold of Ashley's hand to make sure he didn't suddenly wander off. He didn't know what Ashley might do in this vacant state and decided it was probably best to hang onto him tight.

Ashley blinked back at him innocently and Tom sighed. He was glad to have found Ashley again amidst the spooky trees, but now he didn't have a clue which direction they needed to go in order to return to the Morgan manor. It certainly didn't help that they had lost Ashley's torch back at the old mine because now they had to try and navigate the forest in complete darkness. They didn't even have their phones to try and call for help. Yes, things were definitely looking rather bleak at the moment; there was no doubt about that.

"Come on. Let's try this way." Tom decided, pointing further down the hill. He knew that the hostile town lay in the valley bottom, so he hoped that by walking downhill they might eventually find it. Then, they would be able to climb back up to the manor and go to bed.

"Okay!" Ashley replied, obediently stumbling after Tom like a child.

They plodded through the forest undergrowth for a good thirty minutes, with Tom keeping a firm hold of Ashley all the while since it was clear he was still a bit fuzzy. Ashley kept staggering off to one side from time to time or tripping over stupid things and he also kept reaching out in front of him with his spare hand to try and work out where things were, so Tom got the impression that Ashley must be seeing two of everything at the moment and therefore his spatial awareness wasn't very good.

At one point, Tom had to roughly haul Ashley to one side before he walked straight into a tree and Ashley had peered round at him with big, wide eyes like a toddler that were absolutely adorable and made you want to hold him close and protect him from all the bad things in the world. Tom decided that it was no wonder Luke was so utterly devoted to Ashley if he was constantly on the receiving end of that innocent expression.

Finally, Tom stopped under a large pine tree and shook his head. Even without knowledge of a ghostly mine, the forest was still very spooky with the hooting of owls and nearby twigs snapping as nocturnal animals went about their business.

"Hmmm, I don't think we've a hope in hell of finding the manor in the dark tonight, so I vote that we settle down here and try to sort things out in the morning when it's light." Tom sighed, looking completely worn out. He hadn't expected that looking after Ashley would be so draining and found himself slightly in awe of Ashley's guardian. He couldn't imagine how she'd managed to raise the three brothers all by herself, especially since Ashley and Robbie were so difficult.

"Fine, whatever. It's just my bad luck to be stuck out here with you, isn't it, when my head hurts and I can't see anything. Why couldn't it have been one of the other guys who woke me up instead? At least they know where they're bloody going." Ashley grumbled, roughly tugging his hand out of Tom's grip and crouching down to examine whether the ground was good enough to sleep on.

Tom looked round at him curiously, thinking that Ashley must be feeling a bit better now if he was able to use proper sentences again. That was promising.

"How are you feeling?" He asked, hopefully.

"Lousy." Ashley answered. "I am *never* coming out with you again." He added, sourly recalling that he was only in this mess because Tom had dragged him out of bed at the manor to listen for strange whistles.

Tom smiled, noticing that Ashley had stared at him directly that time so his vision must have returned to normal at last.

"Yeah, I know. I'm sorry. Here, use my coat for a pillow since you hurt your head." He sighed, nobly taking it off and handing it over.

"Thanks..." Ashley muttered, curling up on his side amongst the pine needles and shivering slightly against the cool fog that was still drifting through the trees. "Night..." He added, closing his eyes to try and get some rest.

"Sleep well." Tom replied, laying down behind Ashley and frowning to himself in awkward embarrassment at not being able to find the way home. He felt like the worst friend in the world. He considered their situation quietly for a few minutes before he wriggled further back to press his spine against Ashley's, hoping they might be able to keep each other warm during the long night. "Hey, Ash-? I hope you feel better in the morning. Let me know, okay? Otherwise we might have to find you a doctor. I've never seen you so dizzy and vacant; you really scared me! Ashley-? Are you listening?" He muttered, twisting his head round to try and peer at Ashley over his shoulder.

Judging by his friend's slow, deep breaths, it seemed that Ashley was already fast asleep despite the chilly night air and Tom sighed. He really hoped that Ashley would be alright. He didn't want to be responsible for the boy getting a serious, lasting head injury because he'd woken Ashley up and dragged him out on this supernatural midnight adventure.

He knew that Ashley was quite tough since he'd survived a knife-attack to the face, but he couldn't help worrying anyway. He didn't think he'd ever forget the feeling of cold dread that had washed over him when he found Ashley unconscious amongst the wet leaves. It was awful.

Shadow

It was early morning, with beautiful shafts of sunlight piercing through the trees as a great black hound slowly padded through the forest. There was a new scent in the air, a new intruder into this territory. Tracking this strange scent, the dog was led into a spacious clearing where two boys lay sleeping. One looked familiar but the other was a complete stranger.

The dog padded round the clearing cautiously before approaching Ashley and sniffing him. This boy looked like Master, but he was much younger and the dog was curious. Where had this stray Morgan pup come from? Was it lost?

Ashley stirred as the dog licked his face and laid a heavy paw on his chest. He slowly opened his eyes, finding himself to be laid beneath a giant black dog with an almost satanic appearance. He jumped back slightly in alarm and this sudden movement seemed to startle the beast as much as its devilish appearance had frightened Ashley. They eyed each other critically for a few moments and Ashley's heart-rate gradually calmed down as he realised the creature wasn't going to hurt him.

The dog licked his face again and Ashley groaned.

"Hey. Stop it." He growled, wiping his face dry and reaching over to gently shake Tom awake.

"What? Where am I?" Tom yawned, peering round at his surroundings vacantly for a few moments before he remembered why they had slept in the forest. "Oh. Right." He muttered, wrinkling his nose in disgust as he peered down at the damp leaves on his clothes. He and Ashley must smell absolutely terrible.

Ashley smiled to himself and stretched, gently examining his head with one hand where he'd knocked himself out during their night-time adventures.

"Look, I made a new friend." Ashley announced, gesturing to the black hound beside him.

The dog whined, stretching out across Ashley's legs and nuzzling into his chest gently. This boy was a Morgan like

Master and that was all that the dog needed to know. The pup's black hair stated his identity and the dog was the latest in a long line of dark beasts trained to serve the Morgan criminals.

Ashley frowned, reaching down to stroke the dog as Tom yawned and stretched.

"Well, that dog certainly loves you, Ash. Where did he come from?" Tom asked, shuffling over and reaching out to pat the dog too. It promptly turned its head and growled at him dangerously, baring its teeth and pressing closer to Ashley. "Okay, whoa. Don't be like that. I wanted to be your friend as well!" He protested as Ashley laid a calming hand on the dog's head.

"I don't know where he came from. I only woke up when he started licking my face. Hey, maybe he knows the way back to the manor?" Ashley said as the dog nuzzled into his hand happily.

He stood up, looking around slowly and squinting against the shaft of sunlight on his face. The dog rubbed against his hip affectionately as Tom straightened up too, brushing the leaves and mud off his clothes.

"Just tell me, Ash; how exactly do you plan on *asking* this dog if he knows the way back to the manor? He doesn't know where we came from and he speaks a different language." Tom asked, scathingly.

"Shut up." Ashley scowled, annoyed that Tom had found an obvious flaw in his plan.

"So, what are you going to name your new friend?" Tom continued, looking round at Ashley and keeping a few safe metres away from the dog.

Ashley looked down at the beast beside him, which obediently turned to gaze up at him, wagging its tail gently.

"I think 'Shadow' would be a good name for you. I'm sure your owner misses you greatly. But there's no name or address on your collar, so I'm going to call you 'Shadow'. Is that alright?" Ashley murmured, lazily scratching behind the dog's ears.

"Good name." Tom nodded.

Shadow barked in approval too and padded across the clearing before turning to look back at Ashley.

"He wants us to follow him. What do you think? Should we?" Ashley asked, looking round at Tom expectantly.

"I don't know. Maybe he'll lead us further away instead. Shadow doesn't exactly look like a trustworthy rescue-dog if you ask me. He looks more like one of the Devil's own hellhounds." Tom argued, eyeing the dog suspiciously.

Shadow growled at him threateningly and padded back to loosely bite on Ashley's sleeve, tugging at him gently and trying to encourage him to follow.

"What other choice do we have? Neither of us brought a phone and we're lost in the middle of a giant forest. Go on, Shadow, take us home. *I* trust you, even if mean old Tom doesn't." Ashley pointed out, frowning nervously as he finally allowed the dog to pull him through the trees.

Sure enough, Shadow led them straight to the Morgan manor and gave Ashley's hand a farewell lick before bounding away back into the wild forest as a shrill whistle pierced through the air.

"Ha! Who's stupid now? See, he *did* know where we came from!" Ashley mocked victoriously, sticking his tongue out at Tom and padding over to type in the entry code for the gates.

Tom merely rolled his eyes and glanced back towards the trees, wondering how on earth the dog had known to bring them here.

They found their friends lazing about in the small living room between their bedrooms and Suzy gave a shriek of shock at seeing them both so filthy.

"Yes, I'm dirty. I know." Ashley growled, irritably. He was covered from head to toe in mud, with sticks in his hair and various leaves caught on his pyjamas and he felt absolutely gross.

"What the hell happened to you?" Luke exclaimed as Michael jumped up and grabbed a tight hold of Ashley's wrist. He roughly dragged his big brother out into the corridor before giving Ashley a firm shove into the bathroom and slamming the door in his face.

"I'm not letting you out 'til you're clean, Ash. You *stink!*" Michael shouted, reaching up to pinch his nose in disgust. "And you, Tom, go find some clean clothes too. You look like you went swimming in a mud-pool!" He added, turning to roughly push Tom in the direction of the boys' room.

"Yeah, well, I kind of did." Tom huffed, a little startled by Michael's sudden outburst since he was renowned for being the quiet one.

"Such a *sweet* boy." Ashley's voice grumbled from inside the bathroom as Luke calmly followed Tom into the boys' room and returned with a careful selection of Ashley's clothes. Heaven forbid someone should pick out the wrong outfit for him; they'd never hear the end of it.

Local History

Eventually, Tom and Ashley were both cleaned up to Michael's satisfaction and they all set off to explore the town again, with Ashley pulling his hood up to hide his offensive dark hair so they wouldn't be attacked by the townsfolk again. He didn't want anyone else to suffer a horrific nosebleed.

He couldn't help feeling slightly bitter about the fact that the locals only seemed to be abusive towards *him* while Rose was always left alone despite them both sharing the same rich black hair. He could only assume it was because it had been the Morgan men who became criminals whereas the women had never been much of a threat to the local community and therefore his gender automatically made him a target.

He was also the son of a murderer whereas Rose was the daughter of someone who'd done a lot to help improve the town, so he supposed that the reputations of their respective parents must have given people an opinion on what he and Rose were likely to become as they grew up. It was certainly a very peculiar experience to arrive in a new town and discover that everyone already knew your name and had firmly decided you weren't welcome.

Tom told their friends the story of their night-time adventure as they walked down the forest lane. But he forgot to mention the black dog Ashley had befriended since he was too busy wondering about the ghost train they had discovered.

Robbie didn't believe a word of Tom's tale while Ashley had fallen silent as he eagerly devoured the soggy toast Michael had saved for him. It definitely wasn't the most exciting meal he'd ever consumed but Ashley was too hungry to care.

At the edge of town, Tom, Michael and Rose split off to find the library, wanting to know more about the old mine and the story of the ghost train. Rose was amazed that she had never heard anything about the site before when she had lived in the manor the longest.

The others continued on towards the river, following a route that Rose had suggested to help pass some time. They had at least an hour before they were due to meet up with their friends again in the community gardens and thought it would be nice to see some more of the beautiful local scenery.

Robbie and Bryony rushed ahead eagerly, racing each other down the path towards a distant bench while Suzy and Jenna followed behind at a more dignified pace. Luke and Ashley hung back further still, occasionally glancing at each other and turning to look behind them at the three men who had followed them ever since they passed the old church, when a rogue gust of wind had blown Ashley's hood off.

Finally, Luke crouched down, pretending to re-tie his shoelace as he hoped the men would pass them and that he'd been getting jittery over nothing. Ashley waited with him while their friends gathered up ahead on a pebble beach, with Robbie and Bryony having a new competition to see who could skim stones the furthest across the river.

Unfortunately, Luke and Ashley were right to be unsettled, as the men stopped beside them, eyeing Ashley curiously. Luke gave his laces a final tug before he straightened up again, just in time to see Ashley scowl at the man in front of him.

"Stop looking at me like that." He snapped, automatically sinking into defensive mode from the way the newcomers were staring at him so intently.

"Can we help you?" Luke asked, his tone polite but firm.

The men ignored him, one even reaching out to push him aside slightly. Luke huffed. Meanwhile, the leader reached up to cup Ashley's face gently, turning his head from side to side and finally pulling his hood down to expose his distinctive black hair.

The men all glanced at each other in silent agreement and Ashley frowned uncomfortably as one guy snapped a photo of him.

"What do you want-?" He growled, tugging his hood back up yet again and smacking the leader's hand away from his face, scowling at him dangerously.

"You're Dean's boy." The man said, reaching out to roughly trace his fingers down Ashley's scar.

Ashley took a few steps back, retreating up against a tree and frowning at the way they had cornered him so easily.

"Don't touch me." He snapped, finally noting that the stranger had mentioned Dean a few moments later.

"You look a lot like him." The man commented, sounding a little surprised.

"Ugh, so everyone keeps telling me. Maybe I'll dye my hair blond and then you'll all leave me alone!" Ashley moaned, wrinkling his nose in disgust as the twins came to see what was going on.

"Hello!" Jenna smiled, warmly.

"Don't get friendly. We're leaving." Ashley told her, wrapping one arm around her shoulders and leading her back up the path.

"Bye!" Jenna called, turning to wave at the strangers while Luke rolled his eyes.

Bryony glared at the men a few moments longer before she turned to follow her friends. Unlike Jenna, she hadn't thought the men looked particularly nice and wondered what they had said to make Ashley so tense.

Tom, Michael and Rose had news too when they finally met up at the community gardens, choosing a spot that was quiet and private in a distant corner. They were very interested to hear that Ashley had been harassed by creepy strangers and it didn't take Luke long to work out the men's true intentions once he'd heard Tom's explanations.

Tom handed them all a photocopy, looking rather pleased with himself for finding it in the library.

"So, we managed to learn a bit more about the abandoned mine we discovered in the forest. We also found some information about the ghost train which I think is really interesting. Take a look. This is a local news report from 1895 and it talks about the site. Apparently, in addition to the small mine-carts up at the clearing, there was also a railway constructed to transport the goods down to the harbour in the next valley. They used one of the big old steam locomotives to haul the loaded wagons through the forest and into a tunnel that had been carved out to avoid building a massive length of track all the way around the moors. That would have been very time-consuming and expensive. The tunnel was still quite long but at the time it was praised as the more cost-effective solution. Here,

I copied a photograph from when the locomotive was commissioned. It shows the mining community all proudly standing to attention in front of the gleaming engine. What do you think, Ash?" Tom explained, passing another photocopy round.

Ashley gave a start when it came to him and studied the image intently.

"Yeah. I'm no expert, but it certainly looks familiar. I didn't take much notice of the ghost train last night since I was too shocked at it rattling past in front of my nose. I just remember that the funnel was quite unusual." He nodded, passing the photo to Suzy beside him. She eyed it curiously for a few moments before she raised it up in front of her face to squint at it suspiciously. Then she handed it over to Rose, peering down at her expectantly.

"Am I going crazy, or is that the Morgan crest displayed underneath the locomotive's name-plate? You've lived in the manor all your life so you'll be more familiar with the design. I only saw it for the first time a couple of days ago." She asked and Rose frowned, thinking that sounded very unlikely.

"What-? Why would that be on there?" She gasped, staring down at the image critically. Sure enough, the distinctive Morgan crest was fixed onto the side of the locomotive and her eyes widened in surprise. "Wow, I never noticed that back in the library!" She exclaimed, amazed that Suzy had spotted the crest immediately and deciding that she must have remarkable eyesight.

Intrigued, Tom crawled over to examine their new discovery before he peered round at the gloomy forest thoughtfully.

"That's interesting. I can only imagine that the Morgans perhaps sponsored the locomotive with the intention of using it later on to expand their stupid criminal empire. Why else would their family crest be displayed on the engine like that? It's basically an advert for their business! Maybe they were hoping that the honest and official purchase of the locomotive would make them seem more trustworthy to the local community when in actual fact they just wanted a way of secretly transporting their illegal goods around without arousing suspicion. So the crest is both an advertisement and a smokescreen." He exclaimed and Ashley frowned, not entirely convinced by Tom's theory and deciding to wait until he'd heard the rest of their news before he made up his mind.

"So, what happened to the train then? How did it end up becoming all ghostly?" He asked, causing Tom to glance back down at his notes.

"Well, everything was fine for a couple of years and the mine was quite prosperous. The train tunnel allowed goods to be shipped out quickly while another short track connected the mine to *this* little town nestled in the valley bottom and was used for bringing supplies and workers to the site. However, the tunnel was eventually closed due to a roof collapse, with the authorities labelling the place as dangerous and bricking it up for good. Therefore, the alternative railway had to be constructed around the moors at extra expense before being dismantled again when the mine was abandoned following a horrendous explosion. The site wasn't making much money anymore since it took so long to ship the goods out and the accident also wiped out a large chunk of the workforce. Therefore, the place was closed down." Tom began, pouting sadly as he looked down at the list of casualties.

"Jeez. What a horrible way to go." Ashley mumbled, feeling like he could relate to the men in some way since he had come quite close to death himself as a child.

"That sounds like pretty shoddy building work if the tunnel only lasted a couple of years before it collapsed." Luke muttered, raising one eyebrow in disapproval.

"However, one dark and cloudy night in 1898, the train went missing. Both the locomotive and wagons full of coal were lost and it was widely believed that the Morgan criminals had stolen them. The train simply vanished and it was a scandalous mystery at the time. The newspapers talked about it for weeks. Even now, the case remains unsolved." Tom continued, looking round as Robbie shook his head in disbelief.

"That's ridiculous. How the hell do you lose an entire train? I know I'm the worst for losing stuff but even I'm not *that* careless." He scoffed, thinking the whole thing sounded absolutely insane.

Ashley frowned as he considered everything he'd seen back at the ghostly mining camp and the way the spook train had just vanished into thin air.

"I think I'm starting to get the picture..." He muttered and Tom smiled to himself, pleased that Ashley had reached the same conclusion.

"The news report says that the gang leader, Aidan Morgan, was imprisoned along with his two sons, Kane and Ryan. Your ancestors." He said, glancing over at Ashley and Rose, the latter of whom was too excited to sit still. "Apparently, someone reported them to the police after seeing the way they kept gathering up at the old mine and looking as though they were planning something as they took a great interest in the transport infrastructure around the site. So, all three men were jailed and frequently questioned about the location of the stolen goods but they never told. Numerous searches of the area also failed to produce any results and eventually the hunt was called off. The police looked in all the local sidings, warehouses and engine sheds, etc. but were unable to find the goods. By then, the authorities couldn't afford to waste any more time and money in looking for the train, so they had to admit defeat. According to a later report, Ryan Morgan died in prison from a nasty disease, whereas Aidan and Kane were eventually released since the police had nothing to *prove* they were involved. But I remember Enid saying something when we arrived about how the Morgans had lost six of their men to world wars and that the family is now quite thin. Which means..." Tom added, looking round at them expectantly.

Luke grinned.

"...the train might still be hidden if they didn't have enough people to do anything with it." He finished, excitedly.

Tom nodded.

"Precisely. If you ask me, I don't think there ever was a roof collapse. I reckon that was a lie put out by Aidan and his sons so that they could capture the train tunnel for themselves and use it as a giant, underground warehouse for their stolen goods. But the authorities wouldn't just close the tunnel based on a rumour, so the gang probably had to stage something first in order to make the lie believable. I don't think it would have been too hard for them. After all, the Morgans have been criminals for centuries and Enid said the manor is full of secret passages so they must have acquired a vast knowledge of trickery over the years that they could use on the tunnel." He explained as Michael reached out to examine the faded photograph of the old locomotive curiously.

"Of course! The tunnel would have been the perfect place to hide things if people believed it was unsafe and no longer operational. I can see why they would want that and coal has always been a valuable commodity, so that's easy to explain. But I'm still a little confused about the engine itself. I can't see the criminals actually *paying* for it. That seems very unlike them from what I've heard. So I don't understand why the locomotive has the Morgan crest fixed to it." He muttered and Ashley nodded in agreement.

"Yes, I thought that was quite strange at first. I wasn't particularly convinced by Tom's idea that the criminals wanted to use the engine as a smokescreen for their illegal activities. As you said, Mitch, it seems weird for them to *spend* money on the locomotive when they usually just take whatever they want by force. So I've come up with a different theory instead." He began, frowning to himself as he considered everything he had learnt about the derelict old mine.

"Which is…?" Luke prompted as Ashley turned to glance round the empty park suspiciously, as though fearful that they were being watched.

"Well, I was very inspired to hear Enid talk about the way she had put her share of the Morgan wealth to *good* use by helping to restore the church tower and establishing this beautiful community garden. I'm sure there must have been other people like her over the centuries, who wanted to end the criminals' reign of terror. So I think it was probably one of them who paid for the locomotive in an attempt to return some of the stolen family wealth back where it belonged and improve relations with the local community. That's why the Morgan crest is displayed underneath the train's name. It shows who funded the engine. Maybe the buyer was hoping that the family crest would become a symbol of change and hope as the locomotive travelled around?" Ashley began and Bryony smiled.

"I bet their criminal relatives weren't too pleased. Assuming you're right of course." She muttered, easily able to picture his idea in her mind.

"No. I expect they would have seen it as a heinous betrayal. Therefore, since the locomotive was built from their money, I think they began plotting to reclaim it. Well, it wasn't *their* money since it was all stolen from other people, but you know what I mean. My theory is a case of 'why break-even when you could take more?' Instead of just settling for reclaiming the locomotive, the criminals decided to make the most of the opportunity to steal both the tunnel and numerous wagons full of valuable coal as well. I think that they were betrayed and turned it round to their advantage. But their schemes needed careful planning, which is why it took them so long to hijack the locomotive after it was purchased. They had to make sure everything would go smoothly." Ashley finished, staring round at them darkly.

Tom huffed.

"Okay, I'll admit, that makes a lot more sense than my idea." He grumbled, wondering if he should be at all concerned that Ashley seemed to have the same devious, criminal-brain as his evil ancestors. "I actually think we have a really good chance of trying to find the old tunnel now. Ashley, you said that the ghost train vanished by a decrepit signal box, right? What if that means the *real* train is still waiting somewhere nearby? Maybe that's the whole point of the ghost train, to help people find the lost one? After all, the tunnel would be really overgrown by now from decades of neglect if the Morgans weren't able to do much with it." He added, his imagination running wild with all sorts of exciting ideas.

Robbie scoffed.

"So how come no-one else has found it then? I'm assuming they haven't already if the whistles and the spook train still work. Otherwise, if someone had found the lost train, there'd be no reason for the ghostly one to hang around." He argued and Suzy smiled.

"Come on, Robbie! Who do you suppose has any cause to go wandering into that forest in the middle of the night? The townsfolk hate the place. They won't even go near the old manor, let alone venturing inside the dark forest. They seem to behave like this whole area is cursed and the forest certainly doesn't look very clean and well-managed. I don't know how far away the whistles can be heard but I don't think the townsfolk would go looking for them. I don't know why you've never heard them before, Rose, since you've lived at the manor all your life. Maybe your part of the building is better insulated? You and Enid have your own area, don't you? I'm guessing she must have modernised that part first since it was more important and left the rest of the house for later. Our room's not so bad, but the boys' one looks quite worn out and dated. I only saw it briefly the first day when Enid was showing us round but the windows looked quite thin. And your bed is right underneath them, isn't it, Tom? You're the one who first heard the whistles and your bed is closest to the forest too. You were perfectly positioned for hearing the ghost train." She explained and Luke nodded in awkward shame.

"Yeah, I was dead to the world last night anyway. I was so tired when I finally snuggled down that I would have slept through anything." He muttered.

Ashley rolled his eyes at the idea of Luke protectively watching over him again before he turned to offer Tom a faint glare of irritation.

"It was my first peaceful night in weeks too, so I might not have heard the whistles either if you hadn't gone and ruined my beauty sleep, Tom, you little swine." He huffed, obviously still quite resentful despite the exciting adventure they had shared.

Rose smiled to herself at the grumpy scowl on his face before she gestured round at the forest behind them.

"It may be true that the Morgans somehow started the rumour about the roof collapse but wouldn't it fall to the authorities to brick up the tunnel wall? So, assuming the train is still hidden inside the old tunnel, how would they manage to get it inside in the first place?" She asked, staring round at them thoughtfully.

Luke bit his lip as he considered the idea.

"I reckon the Morgan gang must have had some involvement with that too. Think about it. If they were able to fake the roof collapse, then they must have planned another illusion to help seal off the tunnel. Even if they *personally* didn't have any involvement with the construction of the tunnel wall, they must have had friends who could carry out the task for them instead. If there was some way the Morgans could have erected a fake wall, then it would be easy for them to steal the loaded train one night and switch the tracks to divert it off the main line and into the underground tunnel. I would imagine the tracks were kept on the old approach to the tunnel as that would have been a good storage spot for wagons or a passing place for any supply-trains coming the other way perhaps? That would at least explain why a signal box was needed there at all. Maybe the Morgan gang bribed the signalman, I don't know. They could've easily hidden the train in the tunnel and pieced the wall back together again, leaving it there until they had chance to come back with carts and collect the cargo. The tunnel would have been the perfect storage for stolen goods and what not and the old track-way at the other end would have allowed horse-drawn wagons and eventually motorised vans to come and retrieve the goods under cover of darkness. Only the Morgans would know the secret way to open the fake wall, so any outside observers would just think the tunnel had been sealed off by the authorities. It must have been quite an elaborate heist since everything had to be planned to perfection before they could risk stealing the train as Ash said. Timing would have been important." He finished, looking round at them curiously.

Robbie frowned.

"But why did the police never think to check the old tunnel? They must have been well-aware that the Morgan gang were cunning and clever if they had to deal with the remains of their criminal activities all the time. Surely, they would have learnt the identifying tricks and mistakes of the Morgans from cleaning up after their crimes. So why did the police never consider the possibility that the old tunnel worked fine and that it would be the perfect place to hide a train? The crime seems too easy." He asked, doubtfully.

Ashley smiled slightly.

"I don't think the Morgans make mistakes. After all, the locomotive has possibly remained hidden for decades while Dean managed to get away with the murders of Mum and Ethan too because the police never found him. He just disappeared into the night, so I'm guessing that he must have been taught how to evade the authorities as part of his criminal training." He sighed and Luke reached out to give him a sympathetic pat on the shoulder.

"If Aidan and his two sons never gave away the secret location of the stolen train then it makes sense for it to remain hidden. After all, yes, the three *leaders* were jailed, but there could have been *other* Morgans who still roamed free. We don't know how big the family was back then. Maybe these loose relatives committed other crimes that required police attention too and so eventually they would be forced to abandon the search for the train and it would be forgotten. Only the Morgans and their followers would know where it was hidden." He added, thoughtfully.

Bryony tugged the photo of the locomotive out of his hand and studied it for a moment.

"I suppose it's understandable that the police checked all the railway sheds and sidings first, because they would be logical places to hide a train when you believe the tunnel doesn't work and there would be a lot of them to check in those days. Think about it; the locomotive could be moved elsewhere and the coal itself could be removed from the wagons and stored in another hiding place or sold on. A single train consisting of a stolen locomotive and wagons full of coal would supposedly be easy to find because it's much bigger. But the police would have likely expected the criminals to break up the train into smaller sections to make it harder to find because they knew the Morgans were clever, as you say, Robbie. So then they would be looking for a locomotive by itself, possibly with a swapped name-plate and fake ID number and hidden amongst others of the same design, the wagons split up into smaller groups and hidden amongst others with covers over them, and perhaps the coal itself would likely have been removed and stored in numerous other hiding places too. When you consider how the stolen train could be broken up and spread across a wide area and that the police would surely have expected this, it makes sense that it was time-consuming and expensive to search everywhere. If they were distracted by other big crimes too then maybe they never had the time to realise that the tunnel was the hiding place? This isn't a very big community after all, so they wouldn't have had many people at their disposal to start with." She explained and they nodded in enlightened understanding.

Luke snatched the photo back from Bryony and examined it more intently as he imagined how the police would think it had been broken up.

"I believe we've hit the nail right on the head. Everything seems to fit perfectly. Good job, guys. I didn't know how much information there would be for you to find at the library. It seemed quite small when we passed it that first day on our way up to the manor." He smiled, gazing across at Tom, Michael and Rose proudly.

Bryony clapped her hands together.

"Well, what are we waiting for? Let's go find that tunnel! And hopefully the train too if it's still in there!" She chided, already halfway to her feet when Luke roughly pulled her back down again.

"Hang on. There's something I should probably tell you now before we go charging off into the forest." He added, looking round at Ashley cautiously. "Dean is here. He's been exploring the old manor behind Enid's back. I first caught him sneaking around when we retired early to bed after our long journey up from Cornwall. I was lying awake listening to Ashley's nightmares when Dean came in to search our room and he was very confused at finding the place occupied. He almost woke Robbie up at one point as he turfed everything out of the wardrobe. So, I had to go around and tidy up after him before I could get any sleep or you'd have known about our creepy intruder. Then, when we were walking down the lane into town, I turned back towards the manor and saw Dean watching us from a top-floor window before he moved back into the shadows. It must have been Dean who caused the breaking glass you heard, Tom, because I found a broken vase in the same room where I'd seen him watching us. Dean is here and he's looking for a secret passage in the manor. He knows there is one he needs, but he doesn't know where it is. Maybe there was a secret tunnel made to connect the manor with the big train tunnel under the moors, so that the Morgans could pass from one to the other with their stolen goods without being seen? Now I've heard about your adventure last night, I'm *sure* this is what Dean is looking for and it doesn't bode well that his minions recognised Ashley down by the river." Luke explained, darkly.

The scowl that passed over Ashley's face was truly terrifying as he considered the idea that his criminal father was sneaking around and Luke had cruelly decided to keep this important piece of information from him. He leaned over to give Luke's leg a hard kick as a punishment and glared at him coldly.

"Luke, you should have told me. I can't believe you kept that secret! How *dare* you? What if he'd come after me? I wouldn't have known to protect myself until it was too late. How am I supposed to watch my back if I don't know that it needs watching in the first place, you moron?" He growled, furiously.

"I know. I'm sorry. You know I hate keeping secrets from you. I only do it when I absolutely have to. I was worried that if I told you Dean was sneaking around, you might go looking for him and get hurt. I know your black temper, Ash. I know how unreasonable you can be when you're angry. So I kept Dean's presence secret from you to try and protect you a bit." Luke muttered, awkwardly reaching down to rub the spot on his leg where Ashley had kicked him.

Ashley paused, eyeing Luke critically as he considered his reasoning.

"I suppose that makes sense so I'll forgive you this time. But don't even think about keeping it secret from me in the future, do you understand? I *need* to know when Dad is nearby. He's the cause of my worst nightmares so I have to know if he's close by or I won't be able to defend myself properly if he comes looking for me." He muttered and Jenna let out a deep breath, relieved that Luke and Ashley weren't suddenly going to have a massive row in the middle of the park.

Tom turned to gesture round at the surrounding landscape.

"Come on. We need to find the train before Dean does. We've already wasted enough time as it is so let's go!" He said, straightening up and pulling Rose to her feet too.

Michael frowned, biting his thumb anxiously as he looked round at them.

"It's alright to say that the three Morgan ringleaders never revealed the location of the stolen train during their time in prison, but we don't know about the rest of the family or their followers. I would imagine that the locomotive and wagons will still be there since it's a bit difficult to secretly move something that big. Someone is bound to see you and wonder what the hell is going on. But we don't know if the stolen goods inside the wagons are still there. How do we know that they weren't rescued by other members of the Morgan family, either in the weeks and months following the theft or during later years? Even now, coal is still very valuable, so why would they leave that lying around in a dusty old tunnel? Maybe the ringleaders managed to slip secret coded notes to their friends with instructions to remove the goods somewhere else? Dean might be looking for a treasure that's been emptied already. We can only assume that the goods are still there but there's no real proof." He argued, reasonably.

Robbie gave a throaty growl of irritation.

"Thanks, Michael. Perfect way to ruin the excitement. Why do you always have to be so pessimistic?" He grumbled and Michael cringed.

"I'm just suggesting that there's no guarantee we'll find anything. We shouldn't get over-excited or it will be a worse disappointment when we find the tunnel empty." He protested, startled when Robbie suddenly reached over to cover his mouth with one hand.

"Shut up, you stupid little nerd. Of course the goods are still there. Don't be such an idiot. Why do you have to spoil everything?" He snapped, leaning in close to hiss in Michael's face before he stepped back to peer round at the others, recognising Ashley's scolding 'big brother' glare for picking on Michael and offering a defiant scowl of his own in reply.

Rose frowned as she considered Michael's warning for a few moments before she shook her head.

"No, I reckon the train and stuff is still safely hidden away. After all, Dean was brought up with the stories of our ancestors as he was trained to become a criminal himself. So he would probably know if the tunnel had been emptied and wouldn't bother wasting his time on it." She explained and Tom nodded in agreement.

"That sounds fair. I guess we'll only know for sure when we find the tunnel and see what's been left behind. Even if we only find the locomotive and the empty wagons, it'll still be an achievement. I reckon we should start by trying to find where Ashley said the train vanished before he knocked himself out on a tree. If the ghost train acts as a marker for the lost tunnel then that's where we should look." He suggested.

Luke promptly rounded on Ashley, his eyes concerned and soft.

"You knocked yourself out? Ash, look after yourself!" He scolded as they set off back through town towards the dark forest.

Ashley cringed, reaching up to examine the spot on his head where he'd hurt himself the night before and groaning when Luke immediately reached out to start pawing at him too.

"Thanks, Tom. You really didn't have to bring that up again. Now look what you've done. Get off me, Luke, you little pest! I'm fine! Stop fussing over me all the time; it's weird." Ashley grumbled, ducking away from Luke's anxious examination and hastily fleeing down the path to walk with Suzy instead.

A Wild Forest

Ashley quietly led the way through the forest, following the main paths for a while before he diverted off into the undergrowth. He couldn't remember much from after he'd knocked himself out so he was relying on his earlier memories instead and had a vague estimate of where the railway track-bed should be.

His friends exchanged quiet looks of confusion at Ashley's choice of route but followed in silence, eventually emerging from the bushes to find themselves staring at a derelict old signal box. It was easy to see where the railway had once sat, because the ground was still quite wide and level and the trees that grew there were much smaller. The iron rails may have long gone but the earthworks remained and Michael thought it was very interesting.

However, there was no sign of where the track split off towards the tunnel, so it was clear the route must have been out of use for a very long time and had been completely buried beneath the wild growth of the forest. Therefore, they split up in a long line down the track-way, hoping they would be able to find the train quicker if they spread out to examine the whole area at once.

Robbie eyed his section dubiously.

"Where the hell do you even start with such an overgrown forest?" He grumbled, stepping back a few paces to plan his attack.

Since the landscape remained so wild and hostile, he couldn't help wondering if this was *still* Morgan territory even now. Did they actually own this land? It certainly didn't look like the healthy, managed forests he was used to seeing. Maybe the locals just didn't care enough to take it on?

Beside him, Bryony had already begun her task, carefully clambering through the bushes to explore the area and trying to do minimal damage as she went.

On Robbie's other side, Ashley and Rose had decided to team-up together to tackle a particularly difficult section and were busy flattening the undergrowth to try and make a path through it. Rose had thought it a good opportunity to get to know her cousin better but was quite embarrassed that she only came up to his chest and wasn't entirely sure how to talk to him. She wanted the conversation to feel natural and friendly, but so far she just seemed to be asking silly questions about his favourite things. At sixteen, Ashley seemed to already be an adult and Rose found that quite threatening.

Nearby, Luke had chosen a different approach to looking for the lost tunnel. He had scaled a tree instead and was skilfully perched atop a wide branch as he surveyed the landscape from above, hoping that might reveal some clues about where the tunnel was hidden.

Back home, he had a big treehouse at one end of the garden that his parents had built when he was a kid as a consolation present for bringing a screaming baby into his life. So Luke was perfectly at home in the trees and always found it quite peaceful. It was nice having somewhere to think without people coming to pester you every minute of the day.

His siblings were eight, ten and thirteen years younger than him, and the large gaps could feel really awkward at times since Luke was a lot more grown-up than they were and wanted different things. He loved his siblings dearly, but it wasn't very fun having his bedroom door flung open all the time as they came to demand stories and cuddles and play-time. But his parents wouldn't let him put a lock on the door and so Luke had firmly declared his treehouse off-limits to anyone that wasn't Tom or Ashley, needing *somewhere* private to escape the madness. Frankie, Sara and Adam had complained bitterly about the rule, wanting to play in the exciting treehouse, but they obeyed it nonetheless, fearful of being shouted at when their big brother caught them invading his territory.

Unfortunately, Luke's grand plan of trying to survey the forest from above wasn't very successful and he sighed in frustration. The landscape below had grown too wild and tangled over the years and he couldn't make out the shape of the ground at all. He'd been hoping to spot a faint curve from the main track-way that would hint at where the train-tunnel was hidden, but he couldn't see anything. It was all too green and messy.

Meanwhile, his cousin, Tom, had disappeared from view altogether, having decided to lay down flat on his stomach and crawl under the bushes instead. It was going quite well for a while and he was making good progress, until he crawled straight into a thick patch of nettles.

Ashley smirked as a series of indignant swear-words floated back to him before Tom suddenly popped up out of the ferns, flapping hysterically as he tried not to scratch any of his burning stings.

"Wow." He muttered, staring at the blotchy state of Tom's face for a few moments before he playfully reached over to cover Rose's ears with both hands. "Tom, please! Watch your mouth! There are *children* present!" He called and Rose giggled. She'd been a bit scared of Ashley when he first arrived at the manor in a really bad mood, but now he'd confessed the story of his past, he seemed much more relaxed and she decided that he was actually quite fun.

"It's okay, don't worry. You're not the first person to swear in front of me. I'm eleven after all. I'm not a *child.*" She reminded them, understanding that she must seem really young and babyish compared to them since she hadn't yet reached her teen years.

They worked solidly for another hour or so, by which time Robbie had scratched his hand on a large thorn bush and dripped blood everywhere before Michael came over to help nurse him. Robbie had tried protesting that he didn't need anything, it was only a small scratch, but Michael had merely told him to shut up and bandaged his hand anyway.

Ashley and Rose had carved quite a long path through the undergrowth so far while Jenna and Suzy weren't far behind, climbing through the bushes carefully and doing their best not to get caught on the various prickly twigs that surrounded them. But they still hadn't found any sign of the lost tunnel and were starting to feel a little dejected.

It was only when Luke's branch suddenly snapped, pitching him down into the undergrowth with a scream of shock, that they finally located the old track-way. He'd made good progress so far, crawling through the trees a long way ahead of the others, before his luck finally ran out.

His friends all called out to him in alarm as he lay sprawled out on his front across the dead leaves, slightly dazed from the fall.

"Hey, buddy, are you okay? Did you break anything?" Ashley shouted, worriedly.

"Ouch." Luke groaned, cautiously pushing himself up onto his knees and scrabbling through the leaves to see what he'd fallen onto since it had been pushing uncomfortably into his chest.

Robbie reached him first, smirking at the sight of Luke frantically scraping at the dirt like a dog searching for a bone. Clearly, Luke was fine and unhurt despite dropping from a high branch. Robbie decided that Luke's bones must be made of rubber.

"Don't worry, he's fine." He called, turning to glance round at the others as they fought their way through the bushes, with Ashley giving Rose a piggy-back to make things quicker.

After a while, Luke's hand smacked into something hard and he yelped. Curious, he scraped the dirt away from it, proving himself a very careless and unmethodical archaeologist in his eagerness to see what he'd discovered.

"I'VE FOUND IT!" Luke yelled victoriously.

"Nope. I'd say that *it* found *you*, pulling you down out of that tree like a big magnet." Robbie argued as he peered down at Luke's messy excavation.

Michael promptly poked his head out from a nearby bush to see what was going on while Jenna tripped over a loose root and fell over with a scream.

Robbie quickly reached out to grab her, roughly hauling her back to her feet again as Luke pointed to the buried metal rail that had once formed part of the track.

Gradually, the others all climbed out from the bushes too and Luke proudly presented his find to them. Ashley playfully snapped a picture of his best friend, who was sitting on his discovery with a massive grin on his face, as though he'd just found something really important, like the true source of the River Nile or an alien spaceship, not just a rusty railway track.

Tom only gave it a brief look before he turned his attention back to the surrounding foliage.

"Well, if you just found an old rail that should help to narrow down the search. At least it shows *some* of the tracks are still there after all these years." He sighed, walking around them to study the area more intently.

Michael turned and fought his way back to the signal box with a sudden idea. Surely, its strategic position must give you a view of the track-way to the tunnel too? The route might not have been visible when they first arrived, but they'd flattened and broken quite a lot of the undergrowth during their search and he hoped they might now be able to spot the old tunnel in the distance.

He ran round the back of the tiny hut and up the rotten steps before carefully wriggling in through a broken window. Then, he pulled his sleeve down and firmly wiped away the grime and dust from a section of the front window before peering up and down the track-way.

"Anything-?" Bryony called, from where she'd followed him out of the undergrowth.

"Maybe. You can see things much clearer from up here now and I can just make out a faint curve in the landscape that must lead to the tunnel. It should be over there somewhere in the distance, where the ground rises upwards. After all, there had to be a reason why they'd put a signal box *here,* even if it's only a tiny one. Tom did mention something about there being a small supply-track down into town that linked up with the mainline, so they would have needed confirmation that the route was clear before they could proceed." Michael shouted back as he turned to point at various things in the landscape.

Following Michael's directions, they headed back into the bushes to search for the tunnel entrance, motivated by the news that the old track-way had begun to re-emerge from the undergrowth thanks to their hard work.

Jenna frowned, obediently following Luke and Bryony up the hill and reaching down to clutch at a painful stitch in her side.

"What do you think we're going to find up here? Shouldn't we be looking for the bricked-up wall first? I'd say that's where we'd be most likely to find a way in. There must be some kind of secret door into the tunnel, right? Why are we climbing up above it?" She asked and Tom shrugged.

"Don't look at me. Ash is leading the way." He muttered, gesturing up ahead to where Ashley was already standing on the level ground at the top of the banking and surveying the landscape quietly.

Suzy smiled to herself.

"We are such a flock of sheep, aren't we? As soon as one person wanders off, the rest of us just blindly follow them." She declared and Robbie huffed.

"Hey, don't call me a sheep! Do I look soft and fluffy to you?" He protested, indignantly.

"No, you're right. You're more likely to be a wolf in sheep's clothing. But Ashley is our resident wolf already from his criminal ancestry and I know you don't like to be associated with him." Suzy agreed and Tom sniffed, peering round at Robbie wearily.

"With that wicked cackle of his, I'd say Robbie is more like a hyena." He muttered and Robbie smiled to himself, obviously quite pleased with that description.

They finally caught up with Ashley at the top of the banking and he gestured round at the landscape in front of him.

"Mitch is right. From up here, the old track-way is a lot more obvious now. So, the tunnel must run somewhere beneath us. Let's just see what we can find up here first before we go to look for the bricked-up wall. We wouldn't want to miss anything important." He explained and Jenna nodded, understanding now why he had chosen to explore the banking instead of the track-way.

Once again, they spread out to investigate the area, wondering if they might find any other hidden archaeological treasures up here too, like the old rail Luke had discovered in the bushes.

Unfortunately, it didn't seem like there was much to find up here and Luke was about to suggest they go back to look for the tunnel wall when Ashley suddenly disappeared into the ground with a loud scream of shock.

Robbie frowned.

"What just happened? Where'd he go?" He asked, turning to stare across at where his brother had been standing and thinking it very odd how Ashley had just vanished.

"Ashley-?" Luke called, cautiously padding over to investigate the area with Tom and Suzy.

"Ow…" Ashley's voice groaned from somewhere beneath them.

"Where are you-? I can't see you." Luke asked, staring down at the surrounding foliage critically.

Nearby, Tom gave a sudden howl of panic and began waving his arms around madly as he struggled to catch his balance. Suzy quickly reached over to grab his arm and Tom gasped, clutching at her desperately as he took a hasty step back.

"Over here!" He called, shakily pointing down at his feet, where a deep hole lay buried beneath the foliage. He hadn't seen it at all when he was wandering around and Ashley's sudden disappearance showed that he'd not noticed the hazard either. "Thanks." He muttered, turning to offer Suzy a grateful smile before he crouched down to examine the strange hole.

On close inspection, he could see that the plants had been snapped where Ashley had fallen through them, but the hole was cruelly hidden from view by the shadow of a large bush that had taken root just beside it, making you believe the ground was perfectly solid. If he'd taken one more step forwards, he'd have disappeared down into the earth to join Ashley.

Difficult Discoveries

The others obediently walked over to see what they'd discovered and Luke knelt down to push the various plants out of the way before leaning forwards to peer into the darkness.

"Oh hey, there you are. The tunnel sort of *ate* me. I was just wandering around and then I fell into it." Ashley's voice explained from down the hole.

"Are you okay?" Jenna asked, worriedly.

"Yeah. I'm a little winded but I've no major injuries like broken bones or anything, which is a relief. I reckon I must have fallen a good fifteen feet at least before I hit the floor." Ashley answered, sounding a little smug.

Bryony frowned.

"Where are you? I can't see anything but darkness down there." She asked, raising one hand to her forehead in a feeble attempt to see better.

"I don't know. I can't really see anything either. My phone fell out of my pocket on the way down so I've no torch at the moment." Ashley replied and Luke sighed. It was all very well having a torch function on your phone, but if you needed a torch in order to find your phone in the first place then it wasn't very useful.

"Here. Use mine." He offered, reaching round to dig his own phone out of his pocket and switching the torch function on before calmly dropping it down the hole.

"Got it!" Ashley called, just about managing to snatch Luke's expensive phone out of the air and turning to study his surroundings curiously. He was shocked to find that he was knelt beside a loaded coal wagon and slowly turned to peer round behind him into the dark depths of the tunnel. "Oh my God..." He muttered as the powerful torch illuminated the hulking remains of the stolen locomotive.

"What can you see? Is there anything down there?" Jenna called and Ashley blinked, hardly able to believe what he was seeing.

"Wow…" He breathed, carefully picking himself up off the floor and padding deeper into the icy tunnel to gaze up at the enormous steam locomotive in silent awe. So it was true. The train had just been sitting here all this time. Ashley was amazed to find the wagons still firmly coupled together and loaded up with coal and thought it looked really spooky, as though the criminals had just left. It was only the rusting metal, thick cobwebs and damp smell that showed the place had been abandoned for years and Ashley thought it was really sad.

He stared up at the long train in blank shock for a few moments before he padded back down to update his friends on what he'd found.

"Hello-? Ashley-? Where've you gone?" Bryony called, having not heard from him in ages.

"You're not going to believe this." Ashley warned, turning Luke's phone round to illuminate his face instead while he was talking. "*I've found the lost train.* It's all still here. I can see the old locomotive up ahead, sitting quietly on the tracks with the wagons coupled up behind and loaded with coal. It's fantastic. I've found a place that no-one's visited in decades." He announced, proudly.

His friends all squealed in excitement, with Luke quickly pressing a hand over his mouth and glancing round nervously as he remembered that they might not be the only ones looking for this treasure. They didn't want to give away its location now by screaming about it.

"Are you serious?" He asked and Ashley nodded.

"Absolutely. Come on, Luke. You *always* know when I'm lying." He answered, pleased to have been the one to find the tunnel and secretly happy that he had some time to explore the place on his own for a while. "Alright. Either this weird place is my new home and you'll have to feed me and bring me bedding and entertainment, or you'll have to figure out how to rescue me. In the meantime, I'm going for a look around. If I find the secret passage Dean's after, I'll let you know." He added and Luke chuckled.

"Hey, you know we'd never leave you stuck down there!" He called and Ashley smiled to himself faintly before he turned to stalk off into the shadows. "So, any ideas?" Luke asked, turning back to the others.

Rose frowned.

"We need a rope." She said and Bryony turned to her expectantly.

"Do you have one?" She asked.

Rose considered for a minute before she nodded.

"I think so. There should be one in the garage somewhere. It's a separate building at one side of the manor, so I think it might once have been stables and was later converted to house automobiles instead. There are all kinds of things stashed away in there, including a vintage car that's up on bricks and covered with a sheet. It dates back to the twenties apparently, so I don't know why it's still stuck in there. I'd imagine someone would love to restore it for their collection." She explained and Suzy offered her a friendly smile.

"Okay, so Rose and I will go back to look for some rope. You guys should stay here to guard the tunnel from Dean's friends." She announced and they nodded in agreement, with Luke turning to consider the strange hole thoughtfully.

"I wonder what this was. It's got a brick shaft, so it obviously served a purpose. It's not a case where the ground just collapsed down into the tunnel." He wondered and Tom shrugged.

"I know some tunnels used to have shafts, or vents, like this to take away the smoke from the locomotives. So maybe it's one of those. It seems a bit strange to have one quite close to the tunnel entrance though. Perhaps this was how the Morgans entered the tunnel before their secret access passage from the manor was finished, or while they were busy modifying the bricked-up wall. I can't say." He suggested, as Robbie leaned forwards to peer curiously down into the darkness.

Luke and Bryony quickly reached out to grab a tight hold of him, nervous that he might suddenly fall down too and hurt himself.

"Wow, I can't see anything down there!" He muttered, sadly. He'd been really hoping to catch a glimpse of the lost train down below and was quite jealous that, once again, Ashley had been gifted the thrilling adventure instead of him. Little did he know that he was about to be granted his wish.

Underground, Ashley had carefully climbed up into the locomotive's cab to investigate how it worked and was currently peering round at the various dials and levers intently. He'd never been on the footplate of a locomotive before and he found it quite exciting. It was amazing to think how much power this old engine had once had, to be able to haul a load of heavy coal wagons through the hills day after day.

He cautiously reached out to tug on the whistle, alarmed when a shrill cry obediently blared down the tunnel. Almost immediately, there was a violent scream followed by a soft thump from somewhere behind him and Ashley spun round to see what had happened. He was surprised to find Robbie sprawled out on the tunnel floor beneath the old shaft and jumped down out of the cab to examine his brother.

"Are you okay? What happened?" He asked, crouching down beside Robbie and reaching out to check for any injuries.

"Ouch…" Robbie muttered, roughly smacking Ashley's hands away and picking himself up off the floor.

"Oh my God, Robbie, I'm so sorry! I didn't mean to drop you, I swear!" Luke's voice called from above.

"Yeah, thanks for that, *mate*." Robbie grumbled, glaring up at him coldly before he turned his icy gaze on Ashley instead. "Do you *have* to touch things? I was half-suspended down the hole when you pulled that bloody whistle and then Luke and Bryony let go of me in shock. It was alright for you, Ash; at least you fell in feet-first. What if I'd landed on my head? I could have freaking died because of you!" He snapped, reaching out to give Ashley a firm shove away from him.

"I'm sorry. I honestly wasn't expecting the whistle to still work. The train has been sat here for well over a hundred years already so the whistle *shouldn't* work. Seriously though, Rob, are you alright?" Ashley mumbled, awkwardly.

"Yes, I'm fine. Stop fussing will you? I don't need your help." Robbie snapped back and Ashley sighed.

Satisfied that his brother was unhurt, he padded back over to resume his examination of the old locomotive. He'd been really shocked to discover that the train whistle still worked after all this time and felt quite guilty that testing it had caused Robbie to fall down the hole as well. He could only assume that the spooky whistles of the ghost train must be powering the real one somehow down here in the tunnel as a supernatural plea to make it easier for people to find the lost train before it was gone forever. There was *no way* the whistle should work on its own after a hundred years of neglect. He quite liked the thought of the old locomotive crying out to him at the manor for help and firmly resolved that he would do everything he could to make sure the beautiful engine was returned to the locals to be properly displayed somewhere as a piece of their history.

Behind him, Robbie had turned his attention to examining the back of the tunnel where it had been bricked up. It was a huge structure that sealed off the tunnel entirely, causing the air inside to feel musty and stale. But, as they had seen from outside, it was now impossible to spot the tunnel wall due to the wild state of the forest, so it was no wonder the place had been forgotten. They'd only found it because Ashley accidentally fell into it.

Robbie had never seen anything like it in his whole life. Almost every surface was covered with thick cobwebs and the tunnel had an intense, suffocating darkness since the forest undergrowth had spread over the old steam vents and obliterated all the light. It was certainly very spooky.

However, Ashley and Robbie didn't get much time alone to explore the tunnel before Tom suddenly dropped down the vent to join them, raising one finger up to his lips as a silent gesture for Robbie to be quiet. A few moments later, Bryony arrived too and quickly stepped back into the shadows out of the way so that Jenna had space to land as well, a look of desperate fear on her face as she tried really hard not to scream.

Ashley peered round at them curiously, startled by this unexpected invasion of his exciting tunnel and wondering what they were doing. Why had his friends decided to jump into the hole now instead of waiting patiently for Suzy and Rose to return with a rope so that they could climb down safely?

Luke was the next one to drop down the hole and Ashley had barely parted his lips to ask what was going on when Luke rushed over to him and firmly slapped a hand over his mouth to stop him making a noise. Ashley stared back at him in alarm, his eyes wide at the rough, smothering touch. Luke raised one eyebrow in silent warning before jerking his head up towards the forest world above their head. Ashley nodded obediently, understanding that he had to be quiet for some reason, and Luke released him just as Michael dropped into the tunnel as well.

They waited in silence for a couple of minutes, staring round at each other anxiously, before voices were heard overhead.

"If he's that bloody fussed about finding this stolen train, why doesn't he come out here with us and look for it himself? Instead, he just sends us off to do all the dirty work while he lazes about doing nothing and reaping all the rewards." A man grumbled, bitterly.

"Come on now, don't be stupid. You know how this works. He's not *'lazing about doing nothing.'* He said he was going to search his old family home to try and find the secret passage that leads straight to the lost tunnel. He wouldn't take kindly to you calling him lazy. You'd better hope I don't tell him." Another man replied and Luke slowly turned to share a look of acknowledgment with Ashley as they recognized the voice of the guy who'd harassed Ashley earlier, down by the river.

"I don't think we should be talking about this. I mean, what if someone hears?" A third voice asked, nervously.

"Don't be daft. No-one comes into this forest anymore. People are scared of it. We can say whatever the hell we want out here. Look around. Do you see anyone? Relax, man!" The familiar stranger scoffed.

Jenna cautiously stepped back into the shadows as the men's footsteps paced overhead, getting closer to their hiding place with each second.

"Do you think we should tell him that we found his son?" Another man asked, also sounding rather anxious.

"No, that would only infuriate him all the more. Think about it. His long-lost son suddenly shows up just when he's finally put all that mess behind him? You're new, Chris. You don't know Dean Morgan when things don't go the way he wants them to. He's dangerous. I think it's better if we keep the kid's presence to ourselves, at least for now. What was his name again? I can't remember. It was A-something, wasn't it? Arthur?

Nah, that's too angelic. Alex? Nope, that's not it either. What about Anthony? Is that it? What goes well with Morgan?" The leader asked, pacing around as he tried to remember.

"Ashley." Someone muttered, helpfully.

"Yes, that's it! Well done. Ashley Morgan. Bit of a stupid name, don't you think? What made him pick that one? It's no wonder the kid went soft with a daft name like that. Isn't it usually a girls' name? Why would he choose it for a baby *boy?* I don't get it." The leader commented and Luke smiled to himself in amusement as Ashley shot a dirty scowl up at the vent.

The men paced around the area for a few minutes before their footsteps faded into the distance as they went to explore a different part of the forest.

Everyone breathed a sigh of relief and Ashley stepped back to perch on the footplate of the locomotive, doubling over slightly in stress.

"I swear my dad is a total pain in the ass. What are the odds that we *both* start hunting down the same treasure after all this time? Please, Dad, leave me alone! Why do you always have to make things so bloody difficult?" Ashley growled, frustrated.

Luke perched beside him quietly as the others went to examine the forlorn and sorry coal trucks.

"To be honest, I don't think it matters whether those men tell Dean about you or not, because I suspect that he already knows you're here. Tom certainly made your presence known by screaming your name for all to hear the other morning when we sent him up to find you. I reckon Dean was only two doors away from you at that point. If Dean really did choose your name then it would definitely be one that he'd remember, so it must have spooked him to hear Tom yelling it round the manor..." Luke began, peering round at his best friend with a hard look in his eye that Ashley had come to recognise over the years as meaning that Luke was trying to *read* him.

Tom smiled awkwardly as he padded over to join them, sensing that Ashley was feeling a little lost and wondering if there was anything he could do to help. It was clear from the stressed look on Ashley's face that the trip hadn't gone the way he'd been expecting at all and now he wasn't sure what to do with himself.

"Yeah, I'm sorry about that. I was just trying to locate you in the vast building and thought that shouting your name would make it easier. I never considered that it might put you in danger. At least you were wise enough to keep quiet." He apologised, cringing as Luke turned his steely gaze on him instead and gave him a dark scowl for interrupting his pep-talk.

"…Plus, I guarantee that Dean saw you as well that same morning when you were waiting out on the lane for us and sketching the forest. I caught him peering out the window, so I know he must have seen you, Robbie and Michael. People are always saying that you look a lot like your father, so he would have to be an idiot not to recognise his own son." Luke continued and Ashley frowned, trying to work out what he was getting at.

"So, what's your point?" He asked, wearily.

"*My point* is that I don't think you should hide yourself away. Dean already knows you're here, so it's up to you what sort of message you want to send him about the son he lost. You're not a helpless little boy anymore. You're all grown-up and confident and you can certainly take good care of yourself. You know exactly who you are and you don't let people try and put you down. You're strong, Ashley, really strong, and I think you should show Dean that. Show him that you're better than he is and that you're willing to stand against him. Show him that the days of the Morgan criminals are over. That you're strong enough to turn an entire family history on its head and return all the Morgan treasure hoards to their respective owners and fight for what's right and good in this world. I know that's what you want and it would be nice to think of Dean running scared after all he's done to you, don't you think?" Luke muttered and Ashley smiled faintly.

"You see? This is why I like having you around. Where I see ruin and disaster, you see opportunities and hope. You always believe in me." He muttered and Luke nodded.

"That's what best mates are for. I'm not supposed to *let* you wallow in your own misery and agree that your life is a complete mess and that you should just end it all. No, it's my job to step in whenever you get sad, haul you up off the hypothetical sofa of self-pity and kick your sorry ass out the door to start afresh. And that's what I'm gonna do right now. I won't let you sit here all day thinking about Dean and feeling sorry for yourself. We're gonna find out everything we can about this tunnel and see this adventure through to the end, alright?" Luke told him and Ashley sniffed.

"Yeah. It's just hard, you know? I never got on very well with my father; you all saw that from my baby photos in the attic back at the manor. So now it feels like the last twelve years have just been deleted. Don't you see? Nothing has changed. We might not have seen each other for over a decade but we're still fighting. We're still enemies. How long do I have to wait before it's finally *over?* I knew it was a mistake to come back here." He sighed and Luke reached out to lay a firm but encouraging hand on his arm.

"Hey, no-one ever said this was going to be easy. You can't say that it was a *mistake* to come back. I saw your face in the old bedroom as you explained about Heidi and Ethan's deaths. I don't think I've ever seen you look so peaceful. I'd say that coming back here was something you *needed* to do. I think that visiting the room helped to give you a sense of closure. Dean may have haunted your dreams the past twelve years but you don't have to fight him on your own anymore. You know we'll always be around to help you out. It doesn't matter whether it's back home in Cornwall or here in Wales; if you need help, all you have to do is ask. Come on, Ash. What do you say? Are you ready to dive into this adventure?" He coaxed and Ashley nodded, a look of grim determination on his face.

"Yeah, let's do this." He declared as Rose and Suzy finally returned with the rope, surprised to find no-one waiting by the vent.

Bryony advised them on the best place to anchor the rope at the top before coming over to join Tom, Luke and Ashley by the old locomotive.

"Well, Dean's minions didn't find the vent so our secret is safe down here for the time being. I don't know how they missed the obvious tunnel track-way since we destroyed a load of the undergrowth. Maybe they just haven't been properly motivated so they're not really *looking.*" She smiled brightly.

"Mmm, but I still won't sleep easy, if at all, knowing that my evil father is lurking about the house somewhere. It's okay telling me to be strong and that I can take care of myself just fine, but I can't exactly watch out for him in my sleep, can I?" Ashley sighed, hugging himself anxiously.

Luke draped one arm over Ashley's shoulder gently.

"He's not gonna get anywhere near you. Promise." Luke insisted and Tom nodded in agreement.

"Yeah! Don't forget, there are four of us in that bedroom who can help protect you if the worst happens and Dean does manage to sneak up on you. Plus there's the three girls down the hall. Do you really think Dean would stand a chance being outnumbered like that? Trust me, we've got your back. Not to mention you're harder to reach anyway up in that top bunk. But, quite frankly, I don't think you'd need our help. I've seen the way you handle yourself against your school bullies, so I have every faith you'd be able to send Dean packing all on your own. I wouldn't advise it though." He pointed out which made Ashley relax a little as he thought about the chaos Dean would cause.

"Hey guys? Come over here a sec, this is odd." Michael called, from where he and Robbie were busy examining the brick wall at the end of the tunnel.

Ashley stayed perched up on the locomotive footplate as he considered Luke and Tom's words, gazing around thoughtfully while the others all went to see what Michael had found.

Jenna couldn't see anything obvious, but then she didn't have the same eye for detail that he did, unless shopping was involved and then she could spot a bargain a mile away.

"What's up?" She asked, reaching out to lay an encouraging hand on Michael's shoulder.

"This. At first glance, the wall looks normal, but Luke was right about it being fake." He told them, gesturing to the wall and smiling.

"What can I say? I'm a genius." Luke boasted, grinning round at them all smugly.

Michael merely rolled his eyes.

"Yeah, if you look closely, the bricks seem to be different. This block *here* looks different to that group of bricks over *there*. You can trace your finger around each different group, so I think we were right and the wall was erected and dismantled in sections. Maybe they built the fake wall up somewhere else to check it all worked properly and then brought it over here when it was ready. I'm not sure. Perhaps they let the authorities build the official wall and then came over one night to destroy it and replace it with their own fake wall instead. I don't know what it looks like on the other side in the forest, but on this side it looks a lot like a giant door. Maybe they used to drive vans into the tunnel or something, I can't be certain. But they've parked the train quite far away up there in order to leave enough space behind this last coal wagon that would allow the wall-door thingy to swing open and let carts or vans inside." Michael explained.

"Looks all the same to me." Robbie shrugged, turning to the others with a weary sigh.

Tom raised his arm up slightly to shine his own torchlight onto the brickwork curiously.

"Wow, look at that! Well spotted, Mitch!" He exclaimed and Michael shrugged, scowling slightly as Robbie patted him on the head.

"Michael is all about solving mysteries. Back home, he has a huge collection of detective stories and he loves trying to figure things out, like where Ashley sneaks off to every other night or locating my lost possessions. It's quite cute really. You should see his determined little pout." He explained as Ashley finally padded over to join them again and fixed Michael with a disapproving look.

"You really shouldn't tail me like that, Mitch. I hate it. You might think you're being careful and quiet, but I always know when you're behind me." He scolded and Michael frowned in obvious confusion.

"I don't get why you're so mad. It's not like you go somewhere really bad. You just sneak off to explore that creepy, abandoned theatre on the promenade. It's gross. I really don't know what you see in that place. It looks like it could fall down at any minute." He protested and Ashley sighed.

"I guess it's just one of the few places where I feel like I can be myself. At home, there's always someone shouting at me for making too much noise or complaining that my art materials are taking over. At the theatre, I can do as much singing and sketching as I want without getting yelled at. The place has amazing acoustics and the Victorian decorations are absolutely stunning, so I find that it's a really good place to chill out and gather my thoughts. It's my sanctuary, which is why I really don't like you following me there." He replied and Robbie pulled a face.

"You're bloody weird, do you know that?" He muttered, eyeing Ashley critically for a few moments before he turned to gesture round at the dirty old locomotive. "I bet you're both really excited by this adventure, aren't you? For once, Mitch, you've got a proper crime to investigate, while you, Ashley, have found another strange, abandoned place with great acoustics. You must be absolutely delighted." He mocked and Ashley shrugged, obediently stepping back out of the way as Bryony moved over to examine a nearby coal wagon.

"How did they even manage to steal the locomotive in the first place? I highly doubt any of your ancestors were train drivers, Ashley. They wouldn't have had the time or the patience for learning that. So does that mean they blackmailed the real train driver into helping them out or something? What happened to him?" She asked, peering round at them expectantly.

"Wow, I never even thought of that." Tom muttered, reaching down to dig his research out of his pocket and flicking through it urgently. "Ah! Here we are. I must have missed this section earlier." He exclaimed, holding out an old news report for them to read.

Luke accepted it quietly and Suzy moved closer to help illuminate the paper with her phone.

"It's only a small paragraph at the bottom, but it says that the driver went missing along with the stolen train, which makes sense. The criminals would have needed him if they wanted their plan to work. Let me have a look at some of the later reports, Tom." Luke began, holding one hand out expectantly. Tom handed a few more papers over and Luke squinted down at them intently. "Yes, it's just as I suspected. The report says that the man was never found. That also makes a lot of sense to me, because the Morgans wouldn't want him running off to the authorities after all their hard work. It would be nice to know what actually happened to him though. Was he forced to leave the area, or did the criminals deal with him another way? It feels very ominous to have no closure on the matter. It's like the town just gave up on him." He added, pointing down at a section of a different news report. Ashley leaned closer for a quick nosy before he turned to gesture round at the gloomy tunnel worriedly.

"You know, this is all very interesting, but has anyone found my bloody phone yet? I can't afford to lose it. Will someone please help me look?" He begged, frowning to himself anxiously as he shone Luke's phone-light down on the ground.

"I'll help you look, hun; don't worry!" Jenna smiled, obediently padding over to search the area beneath the vent with him while the others spread out to examine more of the tunnel.

"Oh God, where is it?" Ashley moaned, dropping down onto his knees to peer under a nearby workbench.

Unfortunately, they'd still not found the device ten minutes later and Ashley was starting to get very irritable. He couldn't understand why his phone had totally vanished from underneath the vent. It wasn't like he'd purposefully thrown it deeper into the tunnel. The stupid thing had just slipped out of his pocket when he fell in, so logic stated that it should be fairly close.

Further up the tunnel, Bryony gave a sudden howl of shock and jumped to one side slightly, obviously horrified by her new discovery and turning to beckon at them urgently.

"Hey, guys! Come quick! Look what I found!" She called, sounding a little shaken-up.

Ashley and Jenna turned to each other curiously before they wandered over to join their distressed bandmate, finding Bryony to be doubled over a short distance in front of the old locomotive.

"Oh my gosh; that's disgusting!" Jenna gasped as her torchlight revealed a human skeleton half-buried in the dirt at the side of the tunnel. She stared at the bones in dismay for a few seconds before she turned to bury her face in Ashley's shoulder, suddenly feeling rather nauseous.

"Please tell me that's not a real person..." Suzy frowned as Robbie carefully knelt down beside the shallow grave.

"I think it is." He answered, staring round at them grimly.

"Gross." Ashley muttered, wrinkling his nose as he pulled Jenna into a comforting hug.

"It's the missing train driver." Luke announced, having crouched down to examine a wonky wooden cross that was lying in the dirt next to the dead man. "Well, at least now we know why he was never found." He added, shaking his head slightly in disapproval.

"What's that in his hand?" Bryony asked, having finally managed to compose herself. She had definitely not been expecting to find human remains when she agreed to this holiday and felt absolutely terrible.

Robbie obediently leaned forwards to examine the skeleton before he turned to stare up at his big brother in amazement.

"Ash, he's got your phone." He muttered and Ashley blinked.

"What-? How's that possible?" He demanded, raising his eyebrow slightly as he wondered whether Robbie was playing another trick on him.

Recognising the dubious look on Ashley's face, Luke leaned forwards to examine the bones himself.

"He's right! That's definitely your phone." He confirmed and Robbie huffed.

"Told you." He muttered as Ashley gently separated himself from Jenna and crouched down beside them.

"How the *hell* did that get here?" Ashley gasped, shocked to find his missing phone trapped underneath the dead man's fingers. He'd been expecting to find it somewhere near the last coal wagon since that was where he had fallen down the vent, but instead his phone had ended up near the front of the train with a corpse. Ashley couldn't understand it at all.

Suzy shuddered.

"I've heard that some spirits, known as poltergeists, are able to move things around. But the items don't usually travel very far. This is really quite impressive to find your phone all the way down here, Ashley! Look, you can see a faint trail in the dirt from where it was pulled along. We must be dealing with a very powerful ghost if he's capable of doing that." She explained and Ashley frowned.

"I thought I heard a weird rushing sound while I was busy wandering around the locomotive. I just dismissed it as the wind, but now I think that must have been my phone zapping across the floor behind me. How odd." He muttered, staring down at the bones thoughtfully for a while before he reached out with one hand to try and rescue his lost possession. But he changed his mind at the last second and Robbie smirked.

"Hey, I'll get it for you if you're scared." He mocked and Ashley rolled his eyes in obvious irritation.

"I'm not *scared,* you moron. It's just…well…they always say not to touch the body, right? I don't want to get in trouble with the police for messing up a crime scene. Besides, do you think the train driver would even let me reclaim my phone now that he can see I'm a Morgan? Maybe he wants revenge on the people who killed him, so he's decided to take my phone hostage and make things difficult." He explained, hovering uncertainly over the dead man as he debated what he should do.

Fortunately, he didn't have to think about the situation for very long before his phone suddenly slid out from its bony prison and spun round to face him. Shocked, Ashley stared down at it in disbelief, understanding that there was *no way* his phone could have moved like that on its own and so obviously it must have had supernatural help.

"There you go. Problem solved. He must have heard you complaining." Robbie announced as Rose stepped forwards to peer down over his shoulder at their grisly find.

"Maybe the poor guy just wanted someone to find his body? He's been lying there for over a hundred years now, so I reckon he only nicked your phone, Ashley, because he knew you would come looking for it and then you'd discover his remains too. I think he just wants a proper burial and someone to tell his descendants what happened to him." She suggested and Suzy smiled faintly.

"Well, we can certainly do that. Once we climb out of the tunnel, a few people should go straight down to the police station and report everything we've discovered the past few days. Don't worry, sir; we'll have you back with your family in no time. I'm sorry you've had to wait so long." She promised and they all nodded in agreement.

"Absolutely." Ashley vowed, awkwardly reaching down to snatch his phone up off the floor and shoving it in his back pocket with a grimace.

"Ew, I can't believe you actually picked it up!" Jenna moaned, pressing one hand over her mouth in disgust.

Michael wrinkled his nose slightly before he stepped forwards to roughly haul his older brothers away from the grave.

"Come on, stop crowding him already. We shouldn't be disrespectful to his spirit. How would you feel about having a bunch of strangers gazing down at your bones? Honestly, some days it feels like I'm the only person in this family who has any sense." He scolded, firmly pushing Ashley and Robbie back down the tunnel towards the locomotive and causing them to peer round at each other critically.

"What-? We might not have found the missing train driver at all if his ghost hadn't gone and hijacked Ashley's phone. I'd say the man was *expecting* to be stared at." Robbie protested, indignantly.

"Not by so many people!" Michael argued, glaring up at Robbie darkly as the others obediently traipsed after him as well, glancing round at each other guiltily.

Tom paused to snap a few photographs of the stolen locomotive before he turned to offer Suzy a calm smile through the gloom.

"I'll come down to the police station with you. I'm the one with all the evidence anyway and I'm the oldest, so it's kind of my duty to set a good example. Besides, we need to show the hostile town that Ashley can be trusted, so it's *especially* important to report this discovery straight away seeing as we know there are other people looking for it. Otherwise, it will look as though Ashley is associated with the criminals and we don't want that. We're trying to clean up his dirty reputation, not make it worse." He announced and she nodded at him gratefully.

"And me! I want to make sure everything is done properly so we don't get into trouble." Michael insisted, finally releasing Ashley and Robbie as they arrived back at the steam vent.

Robbie promptly set about clambering up the knotted rope while Ashley turned to survey the fascinating old train one last time.

"Count me in. As Tom said, I need to improve my relations with the town residents, so I can hardly sit back and let you report the stolen goods for me. That would just be wrong." He frowned, wondering how the police would react to *him* turning up at their door. Would they be suspicious of him too, just like the rest of the town?

Luke considered the idea for a while before he reached up to gesture at the arched tunnel ceiling.

"Well, if that's the case, I'd really like to go out tonight and look for the ghost train myself. This might be our last chance to see it before the police start investigating the old tunnel. Then the lost locomotive and missing train driver will have been discovered so there'd be no need for the phantom ones to stick around. Does anyone want to come out with me? I know Tom and Ashley have already seen it, so they don't have to come if they want to catch up on sleep, but it would be nice to have some company. Guys, you should've woken me up! I'm really jealous of your adventure last night! Wake me up next time so that I can come too; do you hear me?" Luke complained, turning to glare at Ashley and Tom, the latter of whom returned his dark scowl with one of his own.

"Hey, I *tried* to wake you up, Luke, but you were fast asleep and wouldn't budge. You were nearest to me so of course you were my first pick but you ignored me. That's why I chose Ashley instead. It's your own fault you missed out, you lazy git." He grumbled, hotly.

"Well, shake me a bit more next time. You can't have tried very hard. Slap me, shake me, pour water on my face, scream in my ear, anything! I don't like being left behind when adventure is in the air!" Luke huffed, idly tapping his foot on the ground as he waited for Suzy to climb off the rope above them.

Ashley wrapped his arm around Luke's shoulders, smiling at the look of sulky resentment that had taken over his face at being left behind.

"Easy, boy. I'll come with you. After all, you need someone to show you where the mine is. Only Tom and I know that at the moment." He offered and Luke nodded.

"I'd have just followed the railway track up through the forest until I found the mine, but I suppose it might be quicker if you lead the way. So, does anyone else want to come or will it just be me and Ash?" He asked, peering round at his friends expectantly.

"Yes, please! I'm coming! I'm interested to know if the driver's spirit actually materialises with the ghost train or whether he just remains imprisoned inside the tunnel with his corpse. It would make sense that the spook train and driver would join together since they both remain hidden down here, but I want to see if I'm right. I mean, a train doesn't exactly have a soul, does it, so how would it become supernatural without some kind of human help?" Bryony replied, enthusiastically.

Michael also nodded, eager to see the ghost train for himself.

"Me too. I'd like to know how it all works. It's not very often you get an opportunity like this, is it? I want to make the most of it." He declared.

Rose cautiously looked round at them, wanting to join their adventure as well but worried they'd think her too babyish if she admitted that the dark forest scared her during the night.

"Can I come?" She asked, stepping back out of the way as Ashley began his ascent up through the steam vent.

Luke smiled at her cheerfully.

"Sure you can." He agreed and she beamed. "So, that's Ashley, Bryony, Michael and Rose coming out with me tonight to look for the ghost train, right? Anyone else want to go?" He continued, looking round in amusement as Tom gave a large yawn.

"Nah. This has been a pretty hectic day already and I'm still really tired from looking after Ashley last night too. So, if you don't mind, once I've gone to report the stolen train to the police, I'd rather stay at the manor and get some rest." He muttered, seeming completely exhausted.

But, despite Tom's best intentions, the trip down to the police station proved a total waste of time and he, Suzy, Michael and Ashley arrived back at the manor looking dejected and indignant.

"So, how'd it go?" Luke asked, from where he was now lounging across the window-seat of their private living-room and sharing a blanket with Rose.

"Awful." Michael replied, pouting slightly.

Tom nodded in agreement.

"Yeah. Bloody awful. They just laughed at me and told me to grow up and stop inventing fairy-stories and that if I came in again with nonsense tales like that I'd be charged with wasting police time. I'm *seventeen* for Christ's sake. I'm almost an adult too. But they wouldn't listen and treated me like a small child. I have never been so insulted in my entire life. I can't imagine how you must be feeling, Ash, after they asked if you'd had any contact with your father." He huffed, flopping down into the nearest spare seat and glancing round awkwardly as Ashley mumbled something under his breath and stomped over to claim the empty spot beside Robbie, who visibly tensed.

Suzy carefully perched on the chair-arm beside Tom and reached down to gently pat him on the shoulder.

"At least we tried. You did your best, they just wouldn't listen. Clearly, they haven't read up on the history of this area to know about the missing train." She murmured, eyeing him sympathetically before looking round at the others instead. "He tried to show them the newspaper reports and the photos he took back in the tunnel, but the sergeants just dismissed us without even looking at them. I'm guessing they must get a lot of time-wasters around here, so they didn't think we were very important. I couldn't believe it when they asked Ashley about Dean's whereabouts. That was very insensitive. I reckon they were just hoping for a quick arrest, but they made it sound like Ashley was a villain too. Honestly, you should have seen the look on his face! I don't think I've ever seen him so cross. I would be too. It was so inappropriate." She added, wearily.

Luke frowned, peering across at his best friend thoughtfully for a few moments as he attempted to read him a little deeper. Ashley had wasted no time in digging out his precious journal and was currently sketching the old fireplace in an attempt to distract himself from the insulting trip down to the police station. But since his pencil-strokes were quite sharp and jagged and bold, Luke concluded that Ashley must be *deeply* offended and was just trying his best not to let his friends see it.

"Wow. It's not very encouraging if they won't even believe Tom, the eldest and most mature member of our group. Suzy and Michael are both honest, sensible and respectful too and we all know that Ashley has a good heart, so we certainly sent down our best team for dealing with the authorities. I guess the adult world still views us all as mere children. Sorry, Tom; I know you meant well." He said, sympathetically.

Robbie shrugged.

"Well, I guess we'll just have to stop Dean ourselves then." He declared, looking quite pleased with this outcome.

Luke nodded.

"It certainly looks that way." He muttered, glancing round as Bryony pushed herself up out of her chair and gestured out the window at the dark forest.

"Come on; let's not worry about going up against Dean just yet. We've already agreed to go out tonight and look for the ghost train, so let's focus on that instead. We should try to learn all we can about the old tunnel before we make a plan for tackling Dean and his gang. It would be foolish to confront them without proper preparations. We've still got some time until Dean discovers the secret passage, so we should make good use of it. What do you say?" She said, clapping her hands together to try and motivate her friends.

Ashley scowled as the tip of his pencil suddenly snapped off from the silent rage of his drawing before he turned to offer Bryony a solemn nod.

"Absolutely. I won't let my father get away with this. Let's show the police what a bunch of *kids* can really do. They'll be sorry they ever mocked you, Tom, when we reclaim that tunnel for them." He vowed, sourly dumping his sketchbook on the sofa and padding over to stand beside Bryony to show his support.

"Well, I wouldn't put it quite like *that*, but yes." Bryony corrected as Robbie quickly snatched up Ashley's journal to snoop at his latest drawing.

"Oh-kay, that's clearly the fireplace from hell. I thought you were meant to be good at this, Ash? I guess you can count me in for your dangerous adventure. You're no fun to prank when you're like this. You look like you might rip my head off..." He muttered, turning the journal round to show everyone Ashley's nightmare-ish fireplace sketch.

"Give it back, you nosy little brat. That's private!" Ashley snapped, reaching out to try and rescue his precious journal and rolling his eyes when Robbie promptly leaned back to hold it out of his reach. They struggled against each other for a few moments until Ashley eventually managed to reclaim his book and shoved it safely back in his bag. "Do you *have* to stir up trouble all the time, Rob, you menace? This is exactly why Dean might win. His gang is organised and obedient whereas we just spend half our time bickering and fighting over stupid little things. We need to be united if we stand a chance of successfully completing this adventure. Could you at least try and work with me for once?" He grumbled and Bryony nodded.

"Yes, I'm sure you guys would make a really awesome team if you tried. After all, you both have a reason to hate Dean, so maybe this adventure is just what you need. Finally, you have some common ground." She suggested, glancing between them pleadingly.

Awkward Family Reunion

It was Michael who waited up that night, fearful that the others might forget to wake him up and leave him behind. Rose had been so scared of being forgotten too that she had refused to go away to her own room and was instead asleep on Michael's bed while he had settled himself in the grand old armchair by the dusty fireplace.

He passed the time reading a book by candlelight, wanting to save the torches they had for their night-time adventure and not waste them before they'd even set off.

Eventually, the grandfather clock in the banquet hall struck midnight, its ghostly chimes sweeping through the dark corridors and catching Michael's attention. He glanced down at his watch briefly to double-check the time before blowing out his candle and padding over to Luke and Ashley's bunk. He chose to wake Luke first and leaned over him quietly, eyeing the sleeping boy critically as he tried to work out how to rouse him.

"Come on, Luke, it's time to get up." He whispered, not wanting to wake Tom and Robbie since they had opted to stay behind instead.

"Huh, don't hurt me!" Luke moaned, automatically curling up into a defensive ball in his sleep.

Michael scowled, carefully sitting beside Luke and studying him intently. Maybe he should have climbed up to wake Ashley first instead. Hearing Ashley make strange little howls of protest as Michael tried to wake him would have roused Luke in no time, so that would have killed two birds with one stone. That was just how Luke worked. Ashley was his entire world, so if his sleepy brain thought his friend was under attack, he would of course wake up to try and protect him.

Michael frowned, reaching out to grab a cushion from the end of Luke's bed before he gave the older boy a firm whack around the head with it. Luke gave a muffled grunt of surprise before he blearily opened his eyes and peered up at Michael expectantly.

"Is it time?" He yawned and Michael nodded.

"Yes. So you go and rouse Ashley while I wake up Rose. Then someone will have to fetch Bryony too from down the hall. She'd be really mad if we accidentally left her behind just because she's in a different room." He whispered, cringing when Tom gave a faint huff of irritation nearby as they disturbed his rest.

Luke glanced round at his cousin before he obediently twisted round to climb up the ladder to Ashley's bunk instead. His best friend was still fast asleep on his front with one foot hooked over the edge of the rail and the duvet cuddled up to his face. Luke smiled to himself faintly, pleased to see that Ashley had managed to get some stress-free sleep for once and feeling a little guilty about having to disturb him.

"Wake up, Ashley! It's midnight! We're going out looking for the ghost train, remember?" He murmured, kneeling over Ashley and shaking him gently.

Ashley groaned.

"Aww, I was having such a good dream for once. I had cake! I never get to have any cake! You always steal it before I have chance, you thieving rogue." He grumbled, pouting slightly as the nice images from his dream slowly began to fade away in his mind.

Yawning, Ashley clambered down the ladder and grabbed his phone and trusty bag, determined that he would not be spending *another* night cold and lost in the forest. No, tonight he would be wiser and take his phone out with him so they could call for help if they needed to.

He pulled on his comfy black coat and his boots and loosely wrapped a scarf around his neck before going to rouse Bryony down the hall while Luke, Michael and Rose gathered up their torches.

Soon, they were all gathered outside the gates and Ashley led the way into the forest, following the path he and Tom had taken the night before.

Rose scuttled after him, shyly reaching out to hold his hand for some comfort amongst the spooky trees. She'd only known her cousin a few days but already loved him a lot. Once you learned to look past his dark exterior, you discovered that he was actually really nice and Rose was a little sad that they had never met before.

Ashley looked round at her, eyeing her hand in his for a few moments as he debated whether to allow it. Eventually, he loosely closed his fingers around hers and turned his attention back to the forest lane, his sudden stiff posture making it obvious that he wasn't completely happy with the contact but was willing to endure it for the time being to help earn Rose's friendship.

Luke, Bryony and Michael hung back slightly, with Michael swinging his torch round to stare into the trees suspiciously every time a twig snapped from the movement of nocturnal animals.

Ashley was the only one at ease since he'd slept on the forest floor the night before and grown used to the different sounds. He found it very inspiring to watch the crescent moon peering down at him through the trees and gaze round at the twinkling stars while bats flapped about overhead. He'd always loved the darkness of the night. It was like entering a secret world that no-one else ever saw and the rich, lapis-lazuli sky felt both ancient and mysterious. It was no wonder people talked about stars being the spirits of their ancestors, watching over them from above.

"Good thing we all have torches!" Luke called, trying to sound cheerful and bold, but a sudden owl hoot made his voice increase in pitch halfway through so he sounded like he'd inhaled a helium balloon.

Ashley turned to smirk at him and Luke scowled in embarrassment.

"Oh, so you'd have come out here all alone if no-one else was interested, would you?" Ashley teased.

Luke merely gave a sniff of contempt and turned to shine the beam of his torch into the bushes as a low growl echoed through the night.

"Okay, what the hell was that-? There aren't, like, bears or anything in this wood, right?" Luke demanded and Michael gave a loud snort of derision.

"Bears. You think we still have wild bears in *Wales*, do you? Come on, Luke. I thought you were supposed to be smart?

Bears, I ask you. What an idiot." He scoffed, turning to fix the older boy with a look of disgust, so outraged by Luke's ridiculous comment that he'd forgotten the reason why Luke had made it in the first place.

"Hey, I panicked, alright? But still, whatever made that noise sounds quite big to me. And I'm pretty sure that deer don't make that kind of growling noise. Not unless they're like some really weird, alien species of deer that no-one's heard of. Like giant, monster deer or something." Luke replied, hotly.

Ashley merely grinned, understanding exactly where the strange noise had come from and wondering how the enormous beast had managed to find him again.

"Shadow..." He breathed, grimacing slightly as Rose tightened her grip on his hand in silent fear.

After a while, Ashley turned off the main track, beginning the climb up a steep banking and awkwardly pulling Rose up behind him. Luke followed them quietly, smiling to himself as Michael grabbed a fistful of his hoodie, hoping Luke would pull him up the banking too and save him from having to search for a decent path in the dark.

Luke stopped dead when he reached the top, gazing round in wonder at the ghostly camp and causing Michael to accidentally walk into him from his sudden halt.

Ashley calmly reached over to help steady his little brother and fixed Luke with a look of hard warning.

"Yeah, I wouldn't stand there. You'll be in the train's path. Mind, I don't suppose it'd matter. The ghost train would probably just go straight through you. But I wouldn't risk it." He called out, and Luke obediently moved over to stand at the side of the track-way instead.

"This is incredible." He muttered, as the others stopped to catch their breath, with much panting from Rose and Michael.

"Wow...I never knew...this was...here." Rose gasped, staring round in amazement.

Bryony pointed down into the clearing.

"Hey, Ash-? There's a guy down there who looks a lot like you." She whispered, leaning closer to him.

"No-one looks like me, don't you ever say that again. And why are you whispering? It's not like he can hear you! He's dead, remember?" Ashley frowned, having always loved his distinctive appearance.

"Sorry, but it's true. Look at him!" Bryony protested, pushing Ashley down the other side of the banking and tripping over in her haste.

They tumbled down the bank together, falling over each other until Ashley finally came to rest at the feet of a ghostly man sitting on a wooden box and smoking a pipe. Ashley stared at the man, finally sitting up amongst the leaves to study him properly as Bryony wandered off to explore the mine a bit more.

"Oh, it's Kane Morgan. I recognise him from the news report Tom showed us in the park." Ashley called, reaching out to slowly wave his hand in front of the man's face but with no response. "Well, hello ancestor. I can see you, but you'll never know of me. Never mind. Your loss. I wonder how many generations ago he was? Four? Five? It must be something like that." He muttered, peering up at the man curiously. Bryony was right. They did look quite similar so Ashley decided he must be Kane's great-great-whatever grandson.

"HEY." Michael called from where he was still standing atop the old railway banking.

They all turned to him expectantly and Luke felt a cold shiver run down his spine as a ghost walked right through him. He automatically twitched and shifted over into a clear spot, glaring furiously at the man who had invaded his space.

"What-?" Ashley asked, standing up in front of his ghostly ancestor as he wondered what Michael had discovered.

"No whistles." Michael told them, gesturing round at the silence of the night.

Ashley frowned, staring round at the landscape thoughtfully.

"That's odd." He muttered, as ghostly whistles from the night before obediently echoed round his head.

Luke looked round, bitterly disappointed by this news but still desperately hoping to glimpse the train approaching in the distance.

"Maybe it only runs at certain times? Like, it only runs the same ill-fated route on the anniversary of when it was stolen all those years ago? So it's a once-a-year kind of thing?" He suggested, but Ashley shook his head.

"No, the date's wrong. According to the news report, the train was stolen in March. But it's August now, not that you'd believe it since it's so bloody cold. If your theory worked, then there wouldn't have been any ghostly whistles for Tom to hear last night, so we wouldn't know anything about the train." Ashley pointed out as Bryony wandered back over to join them.

"What time was it when you came out here last night?" She asked.

"I don't know. We only came out to investigate something in the dead of night, so neither of us had a watch. I didn't even have my phone, 'cause I didn't know I'd get lost and end up spending the night out here since Tom has no sense of direction whatsoever. We'd only been intending to spend maybe half an hour out here, just to find out what the noise was, before heading back to the manor. All I know for sure is that it was some time after midnight." Ashley shrugged, a little defensively.

Luke peered round at the abandoned buildings curiously.

"Did you get to explore much of the mine last time? Where do you suggest we start? Is there anything particularly fascinating you'd like to show us?" He asked and Ashley shook his head.

"Honestly, we didn't even get a chance to properly explore the place. The ghost train showed up just after we arrived and then we got lost trying to chase it through the forest. So I don't know anything about these old buildings." He admitted as Michael slithered down the banking and gazed round at the brick structures in wonder.

"Wow, this is really cool! Normally, the only way you get to see the past is through re-enactment events but this place has its own ghostly workers wandering about everywhere you look! I love it." He exclaimed, stepping aside to let a transparent gentleman stomp past, who was carrying a sheaf of papers in one hand and looked more official and administrative compared to the dirty, run-down labourers.

Bryony turned to watch the ghost for a few moments before she gestured onwards.

"Shall we have a look around then while we're waiting for the ghost train to show up? It won't take us long to run back if we do hear it whistling through the trees in the distance. We might as well explore a little since we're here." She asked and they all nodded in agreement, with Michael happily leading the way around the exciting old structures and pointing out things he recognised from his studies.

They were busy staring up at the overgrown remains of a great stone chimney when a scruffy, middle-aged man suddenly emerged from a nearby building and jumped slightly on finding other people exploring the area.

"Hey! What are you doing? Go away! You shouldn't be here!" He shouted, angrily striding towards them and reaching out with one hand to indicate that they should leave.

"What-? Who said that?" Bryony gasped, turning to locate the unfamiliar voice. She had thought they were the only ones wandering around the forest in the middle of the night and was quite alarmed to learn otherwise.

"Oh, great. That's just what I need." Ashley sighed, eyeing the newcomer with a cold scowl and shoving his hands deep in his jacket pockets.

As the man drew closer, he paused, staring across at Ashley in disbelief for a few long moments before he finally marched over to join them.

"What the hell are *you* doing here?" The stranger demanded, raising a threatening finger up to Ashley's face and narrowing his eyes suspiciously.

"Hey Dad." Ashley muttered, straightening up a little taller and glaring back at Dean sourly.

"So, where have you been hiding all these years then, my boy?" Dean asked and Ashley's scowl darkened a little further.

"I'm not telling you that. You don't need to know anything about me." He replied, feeling quite uncomfortable as Dean slowly circled around him to examine him from all angles.

"You look like your mother." Dean muttered, sounding quite curious. This was the first time he had seen his son properly in over a decade and he was very interested to see how Ashley had grown-up. The boy was taller than he had expected and Dean was alarmed to discover they were already the same height.

Ashley also had an air of bold confidence that Dean found a little unsettling. He'd thought the kid would be a whimpering mess after that night so he was quite surprised to learn that Ashley was brave enough to look him in the eye.

Ashley flinched. Most of the time, he quite liked being compared against Heidi as it made him feel like she wasn't completely gone from his life. His guardian certainly liked to highlight all the ways Ashley and his mother were similar whenever she got the chance. But hearing Dean acknowledge their resemblance just felt offensive and cruel.

"How dare you? My mother is *dead* because of you. Families don't do that to each other. We're supposed to be loving and respectful and devoted, but you were never that. You almost *killed* me that night! Seriously, what kind of parent tries to murder their own kid? I've been through hell and back thanks to you." Ashley snapped, taking a bold step forwards to angrily shout in Dean's face and causing his friends to glance round at each other uneasily.

Ashley didn't lose his temper this badly very often so they weren't entirely sure how to react. Luke didn't know whether to pull Ashley away before he made things worse or leave the two hot-headed Morgans alone to argue. After all, Ashley hadn't seen his wicked father since the bloody attack twelve years ago, so his furious black rage was perfectly understandable. But would it *help* for Ashley to give Dean a piece of his mind or would he just come away from the fight feeling even more frustrated and upset? That was the last thing Luke wanted for him.

Dean's eyes narrowed slightly, clearly insulted by something Ashley had said.

"Families also don't *betray* each other either, but that's exactly what your mother did to me. She deserved all she got, the stupid witch. I hope she burns in hell. That'll teach her not to put a dirty curse on my kid and then run off with another man. I was so excited to have a baby son at last but then she went and poisoned you against me right from the start. After that, you were just one big disappointment and I wished you'd never been born. You never showed me any respect and preferred spending time with that girlfriend-stealing ape, Ethan

Slater, instead. So you deserved to be punished as well that night for your sins. Now, seeing how you've turned out, I'm ashamed to have produced a weak little boy like you, *Ashley*. Why couldn't you just be normal and crave adventure like all the other kids in our family? You're nothing but a miserable waste of precious Morgan blood." Dean shouted back, reaching out to give Ashley a violent prod to the chest.

"Yeah? Well, maybe I wished for a father who wasn't a bloody psychopath! My friends have always felt more like a family to me than you ever did. At least *they* love me and support my dreams. You only cared about teaching me to become a master criminal. What is it with you people and this stupid obsession with crime anyway? I don't get it. Why did I have to be born into such a dark and wicked family? Believe me, I wish I didn't bear the Morgan name either. It has caused me nothing but pain and embarrassment. Maybe I'll do us both a favour and ditch my poisoned surname altogether and then you can finally pretend we're not related. Anything to be free from *your* dirty curse." Ashley complained before giving a furious howl of pain when Dean suddenly lashed out to smack him hard across the face.

"Absolutely not. I *forbid* you. Do you hear me, Ashley? I won't have any kid of mine commit such an atrocious act. You were born a Morgan and that's how you're damn well staying, alright? If you want to change something, go ahead and switch up your *ridiculous* middle names. But you *can't* change your blood. You're a Morgan whether you like it or not and one of these days you'd better start acting like one." Dean scolded as he reached out to grab hold of Ashley's jacket collar and roughly pulled him closer so they were practically nose to nose.

Luke and Bryony promptly jumped forwards to try and pull Ashley back but he threw his arms out to block their path, forcefully holding them behind him where they were safe. Luke eyed him curiously for a moment, alarmed at Ashley's fierce strength. Then he considered that he would probably do the exact same thing if he was in Ashley's shoes and gave a faint chuckle of amusement at their similarity.

"I don't think you get any say now in what Ashley chooses to name himself. If he wants to use something else instead then that's his decision and there's nothing you can do about it. You've no right to suddenly barge in like this and start bossing him around. After everything you've done, I'm not surprised Ashley doesn't listen to you." He declared, reaching out to lay a supportive hand on Ashley's back instead since he wasn't allowed to step any closer to Dean.

Bryony nodded in agreement.

"Yes, exactly! What planet are you living on? Do you honestly expect Ashley to still respect you after all this time? You're just an overgrown child who doesn't like being told 'no' and throws a nasty little temper tantrum if he doesn't get what he wants. I'd say Ashley's mother was right to leave you. At least she cared about her son. I'm just sad that Heidi had to put up with you for so long." She said and Dean's gaze hardened slightly as he turned to consider them.

"Who are you? Get out of here; this is none of your business. It's private *family* stuff between me and my son." He snapped, frowning when he spotted Michael amongst Ashley's crowd of loyal friends. He was about to take another step forwards to examine him more closely when Ashley calmly slid over to plant himself in-between them.

"Back off. I swear, if you lay so much as a god-damn finger on him, I'm going to send you straight to hell." He snarled, absolutely determined to protect Michael from Dean's rage. He'd already failed once with Robbie and couldn't bear to think of young Michael getting hurt too.

Dean eyed him curiously for a moment before he swivelled his gaze round to peer at Michael over Ashley's shoulder.

"Ah, yes. It's *Michael,* isn't it? How could I forget the snivelling infant?" Dean muttered, sneering at Michael in disgust as Ashley reached out to firmly push his father back a few paces. "How does it feel, being the least-favourite son? Your mother didn't even *try* to shield you the night she died." He remarked and Ashley's furious scowl darkened a little further. Michael, however, remained unfazed.

"You can mock me all you like. I know that my parents loved me very much. And I know that my brothers will always take care of me. So your words mean nothing." He muttered, trying to sound a lot braver than he felt. Dean's insults may not bother him but the man was still pretty terrifying.

"Come on, let's go. I'm not wasting my time with this selfish jerk any longer." Ashley declared, offering his father a final menacing glare before he turned to pull Michael and Rose up the path. He didn't want to leave them in danger any longer than was necessary.

Luke sighed, gazing after Ashley sadly for a few moments before he turned to face the angry criminal.

"He deserves so much better than you." He declared and Bryony nodded in agreement. She merely gave Dean a dirty look and a loud sniff of contempt before she turned to follow Luke back through the abandoned mine buildings.

"Watch your backs. I don't know what you're doing out here in the middle of the night but if anything goes wrong with my plans then you will be the *first* ones to be punished. Mark my words. I will make you suffer." Dean called after them and Ashley turned to fix him with a look of dark loathing.

Michael and Rose glanced at each other nervously as Ashley pulled them onwards past the various ruins and spectral workers. They didn't like seeing Ashley in such a horrible mood and felt quite angry at Dean for spoiling their adventure.

"He has some bloody nerve..." Ashley growled as he roughly dragged them over to a row of rusty old mine carts at the edge of the site. It didn't take long for Luke and Bryony to catch up and Ashley turned to his friends awkwardly as he jumped up to sit on the edge of a nearby wagon. "I'm sorry." He muttered and Luke blinked.

"For what?" He asked, confused by Ashley's apology. He'd been really proud of the way Ashley dealt with his difficult father and couldn't understand why he looked so guilty. Ashley may have lost his temper and yelled at Dean a lot but he hadn't physically assaulted him. Luke thought that Ashley had shown a lot of restraint and maturity.

"I'm sorry for dragging you into this mess. And I'm sorry that Dean threatened you all just now. I can't believe he did that and it makes me feel like a really terrible friend." Ashley explained, peering round at them mournfully.

Luke pouted, hating to see his friend so conflicted and reaching out to lay a supportive hand on Ashley's arm.

"You're *not*. Believe me, you are a fantastic friend. None of this is your fault at all. How were we supposed to know that Dean was snooping around the forest too? I thought he was still searching the manor for his elusive secret passage. Don't beat yourself up about it." He insisted and the others nodded in agreement.

Bryony laid a soft hand on Ashley's knee and stared up at him with a look of serious concern.

"Absolutely. I'm sorry you have such an awful father, Ashley. I know it must have been really hard to meet him again so unexpectedly. And I can't believe he's still so offended by your middle names after all this time. The man certainly knows how to hold a grudge! So what if your mother chose something else at the registry office? Dean got to pick your first name, didn't he? It's not like he was excluded. What's his bloody problem?" She exclaimed, frowning to herself darkly as she reached up to gently examine the angry red skin on Ashley's cheek where Dean had hit him. "What would you like to do now then, Ash? Do you still want to look for the ghost train or should we just head back to the manor and get some rest? How can we make you feel better?" She added and he cringed.

"Honestly, I think I need to be alone for a while." He muttered, eyeing them nervously. He didn't want to be rude by suddenly ditching them in the middle of the dark forest, but he still felt really angry about his row with Dean and he didn't want his friends to see him like that.

Luke frowned. He wanted to give Ashley some good advice but he didn't think he had much to offer at the moment and hated feeling so useless when his friend was hurting.

"Don't listen to Dean. Don't let him affect you like this, saying stupid things like your mother deserved to die and you're an embarrassment. He's just trying to twist his way into your head. Come on, Ash; you can't let Dean spoil your mood. What does he matter? He may be your family by blood but we're the ones who really care about you." He pleaded and Ashley nodded solemnly.

"I know. I just need some time to process everything. A lot has happened the past few days and I've not really had chance to sit down and think about how I feel. Now, after meeting my father again, I think it's important for me to go and reflect on stuff and get my brain in order. So, if you don't mind, I'm going to head back." He mumbled, hopping down off the old mine cart again and turning to stalk off into the forest, wisely choosing the opposite direction to Dean.

"Be careful." Luke called and Ashley turned back to offer him a faint smile before he pulled his hood up for some privacy and set off into the night.

Rose stared after him blankly, surprised that he'd just left.

"Where's he going?" She asked and Luke shrugged, staring after his friend anxiously.

"Thinking time. It's nothing new. Ash always wanders off whenever he's upset about something. He thinks we'll judge him and call him weak for having feelings. Of course he's emotional about coming face-to-face with Dean again, that's understandable. But, knowing Ash, I reckon he's just as angry about the way Dean threatened us. He's always been protective of his friends, so he'll blame himself for that and think he's a failure. I wish he wouldn't. It was *my* idea to come out looking for the ghost train so if anyone is to blame it should be me. But Ash won't see it that way. He'll think this mess is *his* fault because he was the one who invited us on holiday to begin with." He explained, biting his lip anxiously.

Rose frowned as she considered the way Luke had just let Ashley wander off unsupervised when they knew Dean was still lurking somewhere nearby.

"Are you sure it's okay to let him go out there all by himself? What if Dean manages to sneak up on him? Should we follow him, just in case he gets into trouble?" She worried, turning to stare off into the darkness after her frustrated cousin while Michael gave a soft chuckle.

"Nah. I reckon Ash will be alright. He's quite clever and he can normally defend himself from school bullies really well, so I'm sure he'd be fine if Dean came back for him. But I doubt he would. The man seemed a bit preoccupied if you ask me. Honestly, don't worry about Ashley. I know my brother. He'll bounce back soon enough. He always does. Have you forgotten the way he's started taking the bullies' insults as compliments and playfully turning up the next day rocking whatever look they'd described him as? Trust me, no-one handles trouble better than Ash. He just turns it into a big game." He promised, startled when Luke merely shook his head and let out a miserable little whine.

"No, he won't! This is very different to anything we've handled before. It's not the same as dealing with Robbie's snide comments or a bunch of mean bullies at school. This is Ashley's *father* we're talking about! The man who gave him that ugly scar! You heard Ashley yesterday; Dean has haunted his dreams for years and caused him immense grief, so this is much more personal and I don't know how he'll react to it. I'm telling you, one day Ash will snap and I won't be there to save him from his dark thoughts. What then? Will you be saying 'everything's gonna be okay' when you're standing at his grave? At *our* grave? How would I go on without him? He's always been there as long as I can remember. It's like he's a part of me." He protested, wildly.

Bryony stared at him in shock for a few seconds before she reached over to pull Luke into a tight hug. She'd never seen her bandmate this vulnerable before and she was quite concerned after hearing him accidentally spill one of his darkest fears. She had always known that Luke and Ashley were really close, anyone could see that, but she'd never realised just how scared Luke was of losing Ashley and what that might mean for him.

Luke was the one who kept everyone in check and offered motivational pep-talks whenever they were needed, so it was quite alarming to see him break down like this. He had always been really strong and optimistic and his friends weren't sure what to say now that would help to cheer him up. Bryony had to remind herself that Luke was only human; of course he had feelings too, just like the rest of them, and sometimes those emotions must get complicated and overwhelming. Everyone lost their way sometimes, it was okay. She supposed he was only feeling broken because, for once, he didn't know how to help Ashley and that terrified him.

"Come on, Luke! Don't say that! You know Ashley better than anyone. Do you really think he would take his own life? He's tougher than all of us put together. No matter how bad things get, he always finds a way to keep going and I know he'd never dream of making you sad. He'd think that was the worst thing he could do. It might seem scary now, to let him wander off into the darkness, but I guarantee that Ashley will be back by morning. It's not like he's gone chasing *after* Dean. He's not that stupid. He went the other way, remember? Ash is trying to *avoid* Dean, which means he's got a head-start on the criminal." She smiled, hugging Luke tenderly and gesturing for Michael and Rose to join in too.

Luke sniffed.

"You sound like me." He muttered, clutching at his friends tightly.

Michael patted him on the back a few times before he pointed towards the way they had come.

"Let's go back to the manor. I think we've had enough adventures for one night." He muttered, eyeing the older boy anxiously.

Rose nodded, unsettled by their encounter with Dean and hating the spooky dark forest.

"I agree. I don't really want to be out here anymore" She mumbled as she quietly slipped her arm through Michael's, feeling suddenly very young and small beside them and hoping he would offer her some comfort since he was the closest to her age.

Bryony glanced round at the old track-way curiously as she considered everything that had happened.

"You probably don't want to hear this right now, Luke, but I have an idea about why there was no ghost train tonight." She began, pausing as her friends turned to her expectantly. "Well, do you remember when we found the body of the train driver in the tunnel? I said then that I thought the skeleton and the lost train must be connected. I'm sure the guy wants someone to find his body so that he can be properly buried and his descendants can find out the truth about what happened to him. So, he uses the ghost train to try and help people find them. But he doesn't want the stolen goods to fall back into the hands of the Morgan criminals, which explains why there was no ghost train tonight, because Dean was sneaking around. I think the lack of a ghost train shows that we're dealing with an intelligent spirit. After all, the driver would have controlled the train in life, so I'm sure he must also have some control over the phantom one too in death and he can dictate when it will run. I'm not sure why the ghostly mine still showed up though. Maybe that is always visible. The real mine is pretty obvious anyway, so there'd be no point trying to conceal those ghosts." Bryony explained, looking round at them proudly.

Michael nodded.

"Sure. That makes sense. Still would have been nice to actually see the damn train though." He sighed while Rose frowned in confusion.

"But if the train driver doesn't want the locomotive to fall back into the hands of the Morgans, how come Ashley managed to see the ghost train last night?" She argued and Bryony shrugged.

"Well, technically the ghost train didn't call out to *Ashley*. It was Tom who was startled awake by the whistles and he was the one who then woke Ashley. Otherwise, Ash would have slept through the night. Besides, I've heard that people are supposed to have different coloured 'auras' depending on their personality, so maybe the train driver saw that Ashley didn't have the same kind of angry glow as his criminal relatives and decided to take a chance on him." She reasoned, calmly.

The walk back to the manor seemed to last a lifetime as they reflected on everything that had happened, so they were all very relieved when they finally reached the old gates again.

Time to Grieve

Unfortunately, there was still no sign of Ashley the next morning.

Luke hadn't slept a wink since they got in, sitting up in bed and biting his thumb as he hoped Ashley was alright, wherever he was.

Luke had tried texting Ashley to check on him, but Ashley hadn't replied, not even answering when Luke rang him a couple of times. He had once quietly padded through the dark old house to see if Ashley was hiding in the murder scene on the top floor, but he wasn't there either. Luke couldn't think where Ashley would be, unless he was still lost in the spooky forest, and he hated not knowing what had happened to his best friend.

His brain had unhelpfully conjured up an image of Ashley's lifeless body dumped across the forest floor, covered in blood after Dean had caught up with him again, and now Luke couldn't get the sickening thought out of his head.

The conversation over breakfast was awkward to say the least, with Michael calmly telling Enid that Ashley wasn't feeling very well and had decided to stay in bed a little longer.

They had agreed not to tell Enid the truth of their adventures or that they had encountered Dean again. Tom had argued that maybe they *should* tell Enid what had happened and that perhaps she would be able to help since she was part of the Morgan family too. But he had been outvoted, with the others all insisting that if they did tell Enid the truth, she would likely just pack them off back to Cornwall, out of harm's way. Then, without anyone to defend the stolen train, Dean's gang would easily be able to take it back. No, for the time being at least, it was much better to keep Enid in the dark about what they had discovered.

Thankfully, it didn't take them long to find Ashley after breakfast and Luke was very relieved to have him back safe and sound. As it turned out, Ashley hadn't been very far away and it was Michael who eventually found him.

Ashley had discovered a beautiful, private graveyard behind the manor, reserved for the fallen members of the Morgan family and with a spectacular view down over the long lake in the valley below. He was fast asleep when Michael found him, stretched out across the wall above a particularly attractive gravestone that had an old oak tree blowing gently in the wind beside it. This grave was located just outside the main cemetery, making it clear that while the occupants may not be Morgan blood themselves, they were still an important part of the family history.

Ashley was resting his head on one arm while the other hung down beside the wall, his journal gripped loosely in his hand and the pages blowing back and forth slightly in the breeze. He also had a pen in the hand beneath his face and a little ink had smeared across his cheek. He had wrapped himself up in a fleecy blanket for warmth and his bag was still fastened around his shoulder, dangling down from the wall and looking quite dirty.

Michael texted the others to say that he'd found Ashley before quietly going over to examine the gravestone beneath his brother. Just as he suspected, it marked the graves of both Heidi and Ethan, and was decorated with a beautiful poem and a prayer of love and good luck to Ashley, Robbie and Michael inscribed at the bottom.

Michael sat down on the grass, studying his parents' gravestone curiously and occasionally flicking his gaze up to monitor Ashley's sleepy expression of peaceful innocence.

Soon, the others had all found them too, with Rose, Tom, Suzy and the twins all hanging back awkwardly, perching on an old stone bench a few metres away.

Robbie dropped to his knees beside Michael, reaching out to trace his fingers across their parents' shared gravestone in obvious grief.

Michael frowned, gently laying one hand on Robbie's shoulder in silent comfort. He'd never known their parents for long enough to be particularly affected by their loss or to even remember them. To him, they were just names. He didn't have the same emotional connection that his brothers held dear.

He suspected that Robbie didn't really remember their parents that well either; he just knew the stories that people had told them and had memories of photographs rather than real events.

Growing up, Robbie had been absolutely fascinated by the fact Ethan had been a pilot and had respectfully decorated his bedroom with clouds and model planes. He had a strong desire to follow in Ethan's footsteps and make his father proud by spending his own life above the clouds as well. But Robbie wanted to get there *himself* rather than relying on machines and so he dreamt of becoming a skilled mountaineer instead. His aim was to scale the highest and toughest peaks in the world and he had been an enthusiastic member of a local rock climbing club since he was eight, even taking part in a few trips abroad when they could afford it.

Michael had always been very interested in Robbie's ideas and loved to hear about the logistics of how everything worked. But Ashley wasn't quite as encouraging, which only created more friction between him and Robbie. Ashley thought that Robbie was too reckless and impatient for his chosen career and he couldn't bear the thought of losing any more family members to a catastrophic young death. It terrified him. But he also knew how it felt to have people scorn your dreams with his own musical profession and so he had generously donated some of his earnings towards Robbie's last trip to the Alps, wanting his younger brother to be both happy and, more importantly, *safe*.

Michael wasn't sure yet what he wanted to do in life. He had always loved to read and learn new things and excelled at school with consistently high report cards, but he hadn't found anything to obsess over, like Ashley had with his music, or Robbie and his mountaineering. He didn't want to grow up in their shadows and found himself wondering, as he sat on Heidi and Ethan's graves, what advice they would give him about looking for his purpose in life. What would they tell him to focus on?

While Robbie and Michael were busy grieving for their murdered parents, Luke quietly wandered over to perch on the wall beside sleepy Ashley before reaching down to carefully tease the journal out of his hand. He studied the last few additions curiously, eyeing Ashley's colourful depictions of the moonlit forest and Morgan graveyard before turning the page to find a small sketch of Heidi that he'd copied from an image on his phone. The rest of the page around Heidi's portrait was filled with scribbled memories, descriptions and associated words as well as a little sketch of her gravestone. Clearly, Ashley had spent his alone-time quietly reflecting on his early childhood and so Luke's panicking had all been for nothing.

Luke smiled to himself and looked down at exhausted Ashley beside him, still fast asleep despite the chatter of his friends. Thankfully, the red slap-mark on his cheek had disappeared but now Ashley's skin looked rather blue instead from the cold air and he was shivering a bit. Hoping to make things a little better, Luke carefully reached down to pull Ashley's blanket further up around his face and patted him on the shoulder briefly before he crouched down in front of him to pick up the various things that had fallen out of Ashley's bag while he was asleep.

Thankfully, they didn't have to wait much longer before Ashley finally stirred, blinking round at them all vacantly for a few seconds as he tried to work out where he was.

"Morning." He yawned, sitting up and stretching beneath his blanket while Luke eyed him in soft concern.

"Did you lie there all night? You must be frozen!" He asked, worriedly. He reached out to lay one hand on Ashley's forehead for a moment before he firmly tugged off his own thick coat and wrapped it around his icy friend. "You really must stop sleeping outside, you know. That's the second night in a row already! It's not good for you. Why didn't you come back inside the manor and sleep on the sofa or something if you wanted to be alone? At least that way you'd be safe and not in danger of catching hypothermia." He scolded, shaking his head at Ashley sternly.

Ashley shrugged, holding his hand out for his precious journal and hugging himself for warmth.

"Yeah, I'm quite cold and stiff but I'm alright. I was quite surprised to stumble across Mum's grave last night during my aimless wanderings and I decided to stay with her for a bit. It's almost like she was calling to me and wanted to help. No-one ever told me where she and Ethan had been laid to rest, but I definitely wasn't expecting to find them so close to the manor. I thought they would be in a churchyard somewhere. I just wanted to feel close to Mum while I considered the issue of what to do about my criminal father. People have always told me stories about how Heidi was a good person and I decided I should focus more on that, rather than let myself become so bitter and angry about everything that Dean has done. Unlike him, Mum only ever wanted the best for me and I need to remember that. She wanted me to have the safety and freedom to be myself, so she ran away from Dean to give me that, which I've always thought was really brave." He replied, gesturing down at the weathered inscription while Luke eyed him critically.

"Hey, you've got a little bit of ink on your face. Right there." He muttered, helpfully reaching across to point it out.

Ashley frowned in awkward embarrassment and reached up to scrub his face clean, feeling quite ashamed that his friends had found him sleeping on a stone wall. He must have been a lot more tired than he realised. He hadn't planned to spend another night sleeping outside after all. He'd only intended to stay with his mother for an hour or so while he thought about things before heading back inside to bed. But obviously his body had decided otherwise and he'd just crashed.

Below him, Robbie self-consciously rubbed his eyes, hoping that no-one had seen his tears and feeling a little stupid that he'd broken down at his parents' grave. He'd always thought himself to be tougher than that.

Michael smiled to himself.

"Rob, it's okay. No-one is going to tease you for crying at your parents' grave. Who cares about your strong reputation or the silly 'boys don't cry' rule of society? *Everyone* cries and this is an emotional situation for you. It's understandable that you're upset so please don't feel ashamed. We're your friends; we'd never make fun of you like that." He murmured, hugging Robbie tightly and trying to offer him some comfort. Robbie sniffed.

Ashley considered them for a while before he crouched down beside his brothers and wrapped his fleecy blanket around all three of them, pulling Michael close with one arm and Robbie with the other. Robbie automatically struggled in protest for a few moments before he went limp, reluctantly allowing Ashley and Michael to comfort him and hoping someone would invent some kind of mind-eraser to prevent the moment from being preserved in anyone's memory.

They stayed like this for a few minutes until Ashley stepped back and peered up at the manor darkly.

"I want revenge. Dean has hurt us a lot over the years and I think it's about time we fought back. After last night, I don't want him to think he has any power over us. And I'm definitely not going to let him get away with threatening my friends. Believe me; he's really going to pay for *that*." He declared and Suzy frowned to herself dubiously.

"What exactly do you mean by 'revenge'? I hope you're not implying we do anything violent. That doesn't seem like a very mature solution." She asked, wanting to hear more about Ashley's ideas first before she decided whether or not she was on board with them.

"Well, I've been thinking about something Luke said to me yesterday in the train tunnel. His little speech about being defiant and reversing the Morgan legacy by returning their stolen goods really inspired me. As you've already seen, I don't like to be associated with my father so responding to his violence with my own aggression wouldn't solve anything, no matter how satisfying it may feel in the moment. It would just end up putting me on the same level as him and make people even more suspicious of me if they think their fears are coming true. So, I want to have fun messing up all of Dean's plans instead and absolutely infuriate him. That would be a much more satisfying revenge, I think. And right now, the first way to make his life unpleasant is to stop him getting the goods in that tunnel! Come on, who's with me?" Ashley explained, gazing round at his friends expectantly.

Luke grinned, feeling quite proud of himself. He was delighted that he had inspired Ashley so much and given him something to work towards. It really made him feel valued and respected.

Beside him, Tom merely groaned, eyeing his young cousin wearily and thinking it was going to be a very long day.

"Oh great, now he's gonna be strutting around all day like a flamboyant peacock with an ego the size of Africa…" He grumbled, having shared that many camping trips with Luke during their childhood that he knew exactly what his cousin was like when he either did something right and got praised for it or managed to get away with doing something bad.

"Aww, you're just jealous because I have such great ideas." Luke beamed, sidling over to stand beside Tom and giving him a brief pat on the back. In that moment, Tom swore he could see a glistening halo above Luke's head and rolled his eyes slightly in exasperation.

Bryony clapped her hands together eagerly.

"Okay, Ash, so what's the plan? I like your idea of getting back at Dean by messing up all of his evil schemes, but how do you propose we do that?" She asked and the others turned to him curiously.

"Last night you suggested we do more research before tackling Dean and I have to agree. I think that's a great idea. He caught us completely by surprise up at the old mine and we can't afford to let that happen again. That's why I think it's important to find out all we can first and then decide how to act upon it later. Maybe the police will believe us if we bring in more evidence? So, I want to explore the rest of that tunnel to see where it goes and what other treasures it guards. I think a few people should stay here at the manor too and try to look for the secret link-up tunnel that Dean wants so badly. If we find it first, then we can protect it and stop him getting into the train tunnel that way." Ashley suggested and Suzy nodded.

"I'll stay here to look for the secret passage." She offered, deciding that she didn't much fancy spending the day exploring a cold, damp and gloomy train tunnel.

Tom moved over to stand beside her.

"I'll look with you. We know what Dean's like so we should always stay at least in pairs now for safety." He said and she gave him a grateful smile.

Michael considered them for a few moments before shaking his head.

"Yesterday, at the library, we found an old map of the tunnel route and I want to see if we can follow it from above over the moors using modern maps for comparison. The old map was little more than a sketch, but I'd still like to give it a try." He suggested, looking round at them hopefully.

Rose and Jenna both moved over to join him, leaving Ashley, Luke, Bryony and Robbie to walk through the tunnel.

Michael nodded in satisfaction and turned to head off into the forest with Rose and Jenna while Tom and Suzy departed together to walk around the manor and investigate it properly from the outside, starting with a curious nosy through the old graveyard.

Ashley yawned, leading the others back inside since he had to get changed again after spending another night outside. He left them in the banquet hall and disappeared off down the narrow corridor that led to their wing of the manor, understanding that he'd have to be quick and trying to mentally organise his clothes as he went.

Robbie and Bryony turned their attention to the old tapestry on the wall, taking the chance to examine it more closely than the passing glance they'd given it on their arrival.

It was an exquisite piece of art that showed the Morgan lands with the manor in the centre, surrounded by the misty forest and the occasional glistening stream and waterfall. The hostile town featured in the bottom right corner and the beautiful long lake was proudly displayed too, where it lay in the valley below the manor. The lonely moors had also been carefully presented in the tapestry, complete with moorland wildlife and a cloaked figure walking across the landscape, guided by a small lantern and accompanied by a black dog. On the opposite side of the tapestry to the hostile town, a wild and stormy sea had been depicted, with rocky cliffs, an old galleon ship riding the waves and a cluster of buildings packed into a secret little cove. Another port featured at the top right of the tapestry too, except this place was clearly a busy town with docks and warehouses. Then, there was a lighthouse and some other buildings stitched onto a large island at the top left that was just off-shore from the main harbour-town.

It was a magnificent, detailed tapestry and Bryony felt she could have admired it for hours. She couldn't imagine where you got the patience to complete a difficult project like that and felt a huge respect for the people who had made it.

Luke, meanwhile, had gone over to examine the grand piano at one end of the banquet hall. It was a beautiful instrument and Enid clearly took great care of it, for the wood was perfect and gleamed slightly beneath the antler chandeliers.

Luke perched on the piano stool and gently ran his fingers across the polished wood, pulling his hand back automatically when he encountered a different texture. Curious, he leaned forwards, eyeing the wood intently for a few moments and finally spying the initials 'H.C.' neatly engraved onto the instrument in an elegant font.

He paused. The only person he knew within the Morgan family who had those initials was the mother of Ashley, Robbie and Michael. Ashley had always said that his mother used to sing him to sleep and his guardian had often said too that Ashley had inherited his mother's musical talent.

But why was Heidi's old piano *here*, at the Morgan manor, rather than back home with the guardian of her three children? Maybe Pamela simply hadn't had the space for it? Her house had become crowded enough with the arrival of Heidi's children without adding to that chaos with her piano always getting in the way too. Maybe Pamela had asked Enid to keep the piano safe here at the Morgan manor since she had neither the space nor the maintenance money for it. After all, the care of Heidi's children was much more important than that of a piano.

Luke smiled to himself, hovering his fingers over the keys for a few moments before settling himself properly and beginning to play Heidi's favourite song. Ashley had always known this motivational composition and had once explained that it was one of the precious few memories he had of his mother. Whenever she sang that song to him as a child, it made him feel a lot better and still worked miracles even now. It didn't matter that Ashley was singing the lyrics to himself; it felt like Heidi was there with him and that made everything right again. So, a few years ago, Luke had decided he should probably learn this magical song too, as a cheering-up tool for when Ashley was feeling low, like he surely was now, deep inside, after they'd found him fast asleep beside Heidi's grave.

The piano was well-maintained and Luke was a skilled musician so the tune sounded exactly as it should and the high ceiling of the banquet hall gave the place excellent acoustics.

Luke played the tune calmly, but he chose not to sing the accompanying lyrics, instead voicing them in his mind. He was not the usual singer of these lyrics; that was Ashley's job. Ashley's voice was strong and powerful and perfectly suited to the song, so he could easily hold the long, loud notes that it required. It wasn't that Luke was a bad singer; quite the opposite in fact thanks to years of practice, but this was a very personal song for Ashley, so he had asked his bandmates never to sing it. He feared that if his friends sang the lyrics too, he would begin to associate the song with them instead and it would lose its special meaning. It was one of those rare pieces that could be performed really loud and bold or quiet and gentle and Ashley could never decide which version he liked best.

Outside the room, Ashley paused as he returned from the boys' room, recognizing the tune instantly and feeling immediately soothed. Luke really was the most amazing best friend. He always knew what Ashley needed and how to make him feel better, it was spooky. It was like Luke was his own personal spirit-guide.

Ashley cautiously padded back out into the banquet hall and walked over to perch beside Luke on the narrow piano stool, smiling to himself at the amusing sight of Robbie and Bryony dancing round the room together. Robbie *never* danced, always insisting it was below him, so it was obvious that Bryony had dragged him into it and he looked a little embarrassed as a result, but also a lot brighter and happier.

Of course, Robbie and Michael both knew about Heidi's favourite song as well, but they associated it more with Ashley since they'd both been too young to have many memories of Heidi. Ashley had also sung them to sleep with it countless times over the years when their guardian was unavailable, or to comfort them when they were ill. Therefore, in their opinion, it was more *Ashley's* song than their mother's, but it still held a special place in their heart even so.

Ashley smiled slightly and opened his mouth, loudly singing the concluding verses of the song and watching Robbie and Bryony's goofy little dance. It was a beautiful, magical moment and he couldn't help wishing that Michael had shared it too, instead of Bryony. He'd always considered Luke to be part of his family, like an adopted brother, but Bryony didn't really fit into the family category and he wished Michael had taken her place for this moment.

Luke nudged him gently as he played the final few notes and jerked his head towards the engraved initials. Ashley studied them quietly and his eyes seemed to sparkle a little as he reached out to trace his fingers across the beautiful letters. Once Luke had finished, Ashley offered him a silent nod to show that he was grateful for the tune and Luke smiled back at him brightly, happy to have cheered everyone up.

A Guiding Beacon

Ashley trudged along behind his friends as they navigated their way through the forest back to the old signal box. He wasn't sure what to think any more; it was all so complicated and emotional.

Finding his mother's old piano and hearing her favourite song played through it had been really special and he'd felt so peaceful sitting beside Heidi's grave. But he couldn't escape the fact that he was also related to Dean and found that thinking of both his parents at once just gave him a headache since they were so wildly different.

Thinking about Heidi made him sad and thoughtful while Dean just made him angry and hot instead. Ashley wasn't entirely sure how he felt and didn't know how he'd go about explaining it to his friends, so he felt a bit lonely and lost since he couldn't discuss his thoughts with anyone. How could they ever understand his pain?

As far as he was concerned, Dean was *his* problem and no-one else's. Dean may have issues with Robbie and Michael too, but Ashley stood in the way, so Dean would have to deal with him first anyway before he could even get close to them. As for Luke, he had only become a target because he'd foolishly decided to defend Ashley and challenge the criminal. Dean wouldn't have given him a second thought otherwise.

Ashley sighed. He'd never expected to actually meet his father again when he agreed to this trip. If he'd known that was going to happen, he might never have come. And he certainly wouldn't have invited his friends along too. He was already quite embarrassed that they had had to deal with his dark side a lot recently as he worried about the trip and felt very ashamed that he had just stormed off after meeting his father and left his friends to fend for themselves in the spooky forest. That wasn't very nice. He wasn't usually in a permanent bad mood, but this place just made his skin crawl and he was having quite a hard time dealing with his emotions.

Part of him was wishing he'd not invited his friends up here at all. He hated to think of them getting caught up in a fight with Dean and decided it might be best to try and distance himself from his friends a little more for the time being. He didn't want Dean's calculating, predatory gaze to slide over onto anyone else. No, it was far better to face Dean by himself. At least that way there'd be fewer casualties.

Eventually, they reached the old signal box, where Michael, Jenna and Rose had split off on their own task, heading deeper into the forest to follow the tunnel from above. Their route would take them up out of the trees and onto the wild and lonely old moors before they dropped down towards the busy harbour town in the distance. The tunnel wasn't shown on their modern map at all, so they would have a difficult task trying to match up the old map to the current landscape but were quite looking forward to the challenge.

Robbie silently dropped the rope down the steam vent, checking it was securely anchored before quickly slithering down into the darkness with a head-torch pulled on over his hair. He'd been unusually subdued ever since the discovery of his parents' beautiful gravestone and his lifelong bitterness towards Ashley was slowly beginning to fade.

Luke was next into the hole, sliding down with ease and clearly loving the thrilling adventure. He eyed Robbie quietly, thinking the younger boy looked a little lost, sore and lonely, but, like Ashley, Robbie was too proud to let any emotional weakness show through much.

A few moments later, Ashley dropped down beside them and studied his little brother with the same quiet concern as Luke.

Robbie folded his arms and scowled at them self-consciously.

"What are you both staring at? Do I look like a zoo animal?" He grumbled, hating it when people tried to force their way inside his head.

Ashley smiled to himself, reaching down into his front pocket and carefully taking out an old identity-tag for the air-force. He spread it out across his palm and held it out towards Robbie, the beam of his head-torch glinting down on the metal and illuminating it brightly in the tunnel.

"Take it. This belonged to Ethan and I think now is a good time to pass it on to you after we found his grave. You know that he was a military pilot for a while before he met Heidi and I've seen how you've always been immensely proud of that fact. So I thought you might like his old identity tag now to help you remember him better." Ashley murmured, an affectionate little glint in his eyes as he waited for Robbie's reaction.

Robbie hesitated, staring down at the heirloom in silent awe and shock for a while before he reached out to take it, trying not to let his fingers graze against Ashley's hand too much in the process. They might be getting along better at the moment but that didn't mean Robbie was willing to let his guard down altogether. Ashley was still his arch-enemy.

"How long have you had this?" He asked, raising the tag up to his eyes and momentarily blinding himself in his own torchlight as he attempted to read the words engraved on the tag.

Ashley smiled faintly in amusement.

"I've had it for years. Pamela inherited most of Heidi and Ethan's stuff when they died. Well, to tell you the truth, *we* inherited it, but we were too young to appreciate it back then, so Pam just hid it away in the attic. She had the painful task of sorting through our old house and I don't know how she managed as Heidi's best friend. I know if it was me trying to clean up after Luke's death, I wouldn't even be able to set foot in his house, let alone being calm enough to decide what to keep and what to give away. Anyway, years later, I rescued stuff down into my room when I found Mum's old diaries up there. Now, I can see that coming here has brought back your faded memories of Ethan and your bond with him. So I want you to have this. There are more of Ethan's old things I could give to you, like his military badges and his uniform, but I think this is good enough for now." Ashley replied, as Bryony finally joined them down the hole as well.

Robbie looked up at him briefly before hanging the tag around his neck and tucking it underneath his top so that it sat next to his heart.

"Why didn't you tell me the stories before or that you had these things?" He asked, a little moodily.

"I didn't want to hurt you and Michael by giving you these family treasures before you were ready and reminding you of the parents and childhood family adventures we lost. My innocent childhood was brutally ripped apart by the memories of Heidi and Ethan's murders and I didn't want you and Michael to lose your purity as well. I was just trying to protect you." Ashley told him, gently.

Robbie nodded at Ashley briefly in silent thanks before setting off into the shadows of the tunnel with Bryony to begin their adventure of following it the whole way through.

Luke slowly turned his gaze on Ashley beside him, pursing his lips slightly and frowning.

"Ruined childhood, eh? Liar." He said, a soft hint of mischief hidden within his voice. "What about me? What about all the exciting adventures we shared during our time together? Don't be forgetting all the happy times of your life in favour of one giant storm-cloud in your past. I've already stitched together your old teddy this holiday; don't tell me I need to heal your broken memories too?" He scolded, raising his eyebrow in disapproval.

"No one could ever be miserable for long with you around, Luke. You're too much fun. I don't know how you do it. You're always so happy and your good mood is infectious." Ashley explained as Luke walked up the tunnel alongside the stolen train, finally pausing beside the cab of the old locomotive and turning to beckon at Ashley.

"Get up there, you menace. I'll show you that your childhood was far from ruined. You just need a change of perspective." Luke smiled, climbing up into the locomotive cab and settling himself on the footplate.

Ashley followed him silently, clambering up into the dark cab and leaning out the opposite side to gaze down the length of the locomotive and round at the wagons coupled up behind.

"What are you doing?" He asked, turning to peer round at his friend nervously as he tried to read Luke's behaviour.

Luke merely offered him a secret little smile as he dug his phone out of his pocket and Ashley frowned to himself uncomfortably. Luke spent a few moments flicking through the device before he gently placed it on the driver's seat.

"This is a song I wrote for you months ago and the twins helped me to record it back home in my garage studio. It's mostly about *our* friendship in particular and I think it's time you finally heard it. I wrote it when you got Enid's invitation to stay here and it put you in a really low mood. I thought someday you might need a little reminder about the people who truly care about you, from your family members to all your closest friends. Sometimes, I think music is the only thing you really listen to, so that's how I'm going to lecture you from now on." Luke muttered, as the song's catchy guitar intro echoed around the locomotive cab.

Ashley's eyes widened in surprise and he turned to study Luke properly, who had tugged off his head-torch and set it up on top of the coal tender behind the locomotive, the beam illuminating the shadows of their bodies on the wall of the tunnel.

Luke confidently danced around the cab, his shadowy-self copying the moves on the tunnel wall and looking good despite having never taken any real dance lessons. There wasn't much of a pre-planned routine to his movements, he was mostly just making it up on the spot, but it didn't look at all awkward.

Both the song's inspiring lyrics and Luke's smooth, strong voice were absolutely captivating and Ashley found himself gazing round in a trance. As he looked across at their figures outlined on the wall, they seemed to shift and change in his mind, until Ashley was staring across at themselves as children.

He watched in amazement, seeing the scenes of their childhood together presented in a rich play of light and shadows on the wall as Luke described them. Only Luke had ever held the power to capture Ashley's imagination this way and he knew it.

Ashley gazed round in wonder, hearing ghostly snippets of children's laughter echo down the tunnel and feeling his heart ache as he wished he could go back and live it all again.

In his mind, the great old locomotive slowly seemed to come to life, as though wakening from a hundred years of sleep, with all the dials flicking on inside the cab and the firebox giving off an expectant crackle. He staggered slightly as the train slowly moved forwards in his vision, adding smoke to the captivating images on the wall and moving them forwards through the years in time with Luke's lively, fun song.

Ashley smiled to himself, watching the shadowy scenes on the wall and admiring the gleaming train in his mind, with smoke billowing from the funnel and the great strong wheels spinning round in a wonderfully hypnotizing manner.

It was true. Luke had always been there for him and Ashley valued his friendship above all else in this world. They had been almost inseparable since they were four years old and had become a strong partnership over the years. Nothing would ever come between them. No matter what happened in their lives, no matter who came and went; Ashley knew that they at least would never part.

Eventually, Luke's song faded away and he quickly snatched up his phone again before another tune could play and spoil the mood. Then, he stowed it back in his pocket, giving Ashley a few moments of precious silence as he pulled his head-torch back on.

Ashley slowly turned to face him, leaning back against the cab and studying Luke thoughtfully.

"That's my new favourite song, right there." He murmured and Luke smiled to himself proudly.

He had spent a long time before the holiday furiously scribbling lyrics and tunes in his room back home, trying to write the best song for Ashley that would convey all the right messages and stories he wanted to tell. His room had become a mess of inspiring old photographs and scrunched-up paper that he'd tossed over his shoulder, the failed attempts of his song-writing. Of course, he'd also been harassed by his three nosy young siblings too, who had come to see what he was working on as they always did when he was busy and wouldn't play with them.

Finally, he'd dreamt up the perfect song, knowing it to be good from the way it had given him chills up his spine when he heard the finished version on his laptop. He thought the song was a great representation of their friendship, with the deep bass chords in the background symbolising dark, moody Ashley while the hopeful, uplifting tune on top seemed to match quite well against Luke's own optimistic personality.

No matter how many times Luke stressed that he would always be there for Ashley, the message had never seemed to penetrate Ashley's strong, defensive shield before and Luke had wanted this new song to remind Ashley of those truths.

Ashley's favourite songs tended to focus on themes of freedom and survival and his own compositions seemed to feature similar ideas of personal identity and the desire to pursue your own dreams and stay true to yourself, so Luke had worked hard to include some of these powerful messages in the song he'd written for Ashley. He'd wanted it to be one that would stick in Ashley's head so that he would appreciate the point that Luke was trying to make, that Ashley was never alone and that he shouldn't dwell on the past so much. Luke had spent ages trying to craft the right lyrics that would be personal and meaningful to Ashley but would also be quite generic and motivational to anyone else who heard the song.

Ashley had always loved music and Luke thought it was the perfect thing for him, since it allowed Ashley to balance the light and shadows of his own life and the world around him and helped to give him focus and direction. He had the most amazing, powerful voice and Luke had once said that it would be a great shame not to share his talents with the world and inspire people with the beautiful music that he wrote.

Ashley's music and stage persona were so magical and strong that his bullies would temporarily become his fans as they watched him perform and Ashley always found that really satisfying. He just wished they'd treat him with the same respect when the tune ended.

But, as much as he enjoyed being all flirty, mischievous and expressive on-stage, Ashley wasn't particularly motivated by the idea of getting filthy rich and the whole 'celebrity' lifestyle that came with it. What really drove him was the desire to help people.

Music had guided him through some pretty difficult times and Ashley knew there were lots of people around the world suffering from things like mental health issues and domestic abuse. Ashley felt that if he could make those people a little bit happier for a few minutes, then that would be the greatest achievement. He wanted to show that he could relate to people and that he had actually lived through his lyrics. That was very important to him. Of course, not all of his songs were intimate and serious. He was also quite good at writing exciting party songs when he was in the right mind-set, but his deeper compositions were the ones he was the most proud of.

It was certainly true that Ashley's darkness gave him strength, but Luke feared having to see Ashley swallowed entirely by moody, black shadows as he fought against the troubled memories of his past and the offensive criminal family that he was descended from. Therefore, Luke saw himself as the candlelight to guide Ashley through the gloom, a bright beacon of hope and safety. He would always be there to help point the way, regardless of whatever challenges were thrown at them.

If Ashley described himself as a stricken ship sailing through stormy waters and fearful of being run aground on treacherous rocks, Luke would reply that he would be the old lighthouse to guide Ashley safely through the danger, withstanding countless storms but standing strong through the years and refusing to be swayed or brought down.

But if Luke's guiding beacon wasn't lit in time and Ashley saw himself as the ship already dashed on the rocks, his cargo robbed and thinking himself beyond all hope, then Luke's answer would instead be that he was the brave lifeboat rowing out time and time again to rescue Ashley, patch him back together again and set him safely off on the right course.

It sounded a little soppy but that was Luke through and through. He'd always been the noble romantic and a complete gentleman and his friends were forever teasing him about it, saying he was the perfect knight in shining armour and it was no wonder everyone liked him. Robbie always took great delight in mocking him with "Yes, Sir. Sorry, Sir." or "Right away, your Lordship." whenever Luke was trying to boss him around. It never failed to produce an exasperated moan and Robbie would immediately leave him alone again.

Looking at Ashley now, in the private peace of the locomotive cab, Luke could see that his message of friendship, loyalty and guidance had finally pierced through Ashley's shield and would never be forgotten.

"Don't lock yourself away. It only makes the problems hurt more." He murmured, glancing round as Robbie padded back down the tunnel towards them.

Ashley smiled faintly.

"I know I get lost sometimes. I lose myself in the darkness of my mind and can't find a way out. It's like I'm stuck in a permanent nightmare and can't wake up. No fun at all. But you always know exactly what to say or do to help cheer me up. You're amazing, Luke. You make people feel like things will get better. You make them feel special and appreciated and you can't stand to see anyone upset, whether it's comforting Jenna over a lost boyfriend, tending to your siblings when they hurt themselves or helping me work out my identity amidst the chaos of my past and issues with school bullies. You make people feel like they matter, regardless of their background, or race, or anything, and that they should never give up. You believed in me right from the beginning when I was just a scared little boy being dropped off by Pamela at playgroup. None of the other kids wanted to play with me because my gruesome scar was still quite fresh and it really frightened them. But you didn't care about that. You were the first person to approach me, and I remember you just told me your name and then gave me one of your toy dinosaurs and asked if I wanted to play. You befriended me when no-one else did and it made me feel really safe and happy. You were there for me when I needed a friend the most. Even as a four-year-old, you cared a lot about people. I wish I had your optimism and your happiness; I really do. You inspire people." He muttered, sincerely.

Luke merely grinned proudly, turning to clamber down out of the old cab as Robbie finally joined them, studying them with suspicious eyes.

"Hey, lovebirds. You do realise we're trying to keep this tunnel a secret, don't you? What do you think you're doing, making all that noise? Do you *want* to attract the criminals?" Robbie scolded, raising his eyebrow at them in exasperation.

Ashley rolled his eyes, jumping down off the locomotive and stalking past Robbie into the shadows of the tunnel, fixing him with a dirty scowl on the way.

Luke frowned, irritably.

"Don't talk to me like that. I wasn't that loud. Come on, I'm not daft; I know we're trying to keep the tunnel hidden. Besides, I think *you're* the noisy one around here, Robbie. I could hear you rummaging through that crate of glass bottles from all the way back here. You're the one who doesn't know how to be quiet, so don't start lecturing me about it, you snarky little brat." He snapped and Robbie bit his lip.

"What were you doing up there with Ashley anyway, besides having a spontaneous concert? You're always sneaking off together back home too or sharing secret smiles and inside jokes, it's weird. You two really freak me out sometimes." He grumbled, offering Luke a hostile glare that was sharply reciprocated.

"How would you understand the truth? You were always so independent, never needing anyone's help and insisting that you would do everything by yourself. You don't understand that sometimes it's good to talk about things. You just see that as a sign of weakness and that you'll be fine and tough on your own. Seriously, Rob, would you *please* stop poking fun at me and Ashley? You should see our bond as a sign of strength. Okay, we need help sometimes and it's nice to have someone to talk to, but that doesn't make us weak. We're a team and that makes us stronger. No hero ever succeeded on their own and you're just making yourself look afraid by refusing to let anyone too close. Grow up, Robbie." Luke growled, threateningly.

Robbie stared at Luke in shock, alarmed at his shrewd judgements. Luke rarely misread someone and he could be a little scary sometimes when he revealed what he'd discovered. Luke fixed him with a final hard stare before following Ashley up the tunnel, thinking they should really make some progress or they'd still be down here at midnight.

Robbie shoved his hands deep in his pockets and sighed. It wouldn't be easy, but he had to change and prove to them all that he really did want to help with things and be their friend. But he'd dug a hole so deep that it would take a lot of hard work and patching up before people would trust him again. Sometimes, he got the impression that his friends only let him tag along with their adventures because they couldn't fob him off to anyone else and that made him feel quite bad.

Clearly, since he'd always hated and bullied Ashley throughout his life, making him suffer more than he deserved, Robbie knew that he would have to work especially hard at convincing Ashley of his refreshed view on life. All their adventures and family stories during the past few days had made him think and he'd begun to realize just what a sour and sulky little brat he'd been. It was no wonder Ashley always referred to him as a changeling. Robbie had lost his innocent childhood cuteness long ago, becoming so full of dark, bitter hatred for Ashley that it had turned him into a rude bully and a mean prankster and his face now displayed a permanent scowl.

But Ashley wasn't so bad and Robbie could see now that his older brother had suffered a lot over the years to protect him and Michael from the same hurt that he'd endured. Regardless of how much Robbie tortured him, Ashley had always defended him at school and helped Pamela to nurse him and Michael back to health whenever they were sick. Looking back, his childhood jealousy of Ashley's first-born power seemed petty and ridiculous.

Robbie sighed. If only his younger self had seen what was clear to him now; things would've been so much easier. But his hatred for Ashley had grown deep and it would take time to change his behaviour. He had always blamed Ashley for the deaths of his parents, never really knowing why but needing to direct his anger and grief at *someone* and Ashley was the perfect victim since he didn't really fit in properly with his different surname and profoundly different looks.

Robbie hung back, watching the others quietly as he considered the situation. As far as Ashley was concerned, if Robbie could help out with these adventures and the whole Dean situation, maybe his big brother would forgive him. As for the others, it wasn't quite so clear what he should do, but Robbie had to make them see he was a changed man.

Hunted

Up above, the map-team of Michael, Jenna and Rose hadn't made much progress either. The old and modern maps didn't match up very well at all and they had walked round in a circle twice already. The older map of the tunnel route was basically just a simple sketch and had faded somewhat during the last hundred years so it wasn't very easy to pick out on their photograph.

Michael had always heard Luke, Ashley and Suzy moaning about the twins' awful habit for getting lost and their absolute inability to map-read. Tom could easily get lost too, which was why he and Ashley had ended up sleeping on the forest floor one night, so it was probably a good thing they'd left him safely behind at the manor. And Rose was equally unreliable since she was from the sat-nav generation and had never had much experience of map-reading as she said they always programmed a walk or a drive into a gadget, so this was a new experience for her as well.

Therefore, Michael had firmly put himself on map-duty after Jenna had led them astray a few times. They had made good progress in the last half hour but were still nowhere near as far forward as they should be, judging by the length of the tunnel.

They had tracked the tunnel through the forest for a while, taking care to test the ground before they stepped on it properly to make sure no-one else fell down a steam vent by accident. Ashley and Robbie had both been very lucky to fall down the last one without injuring themselves anywhere.

Now, as they followed an old cart-track up onto the moors, the tunnel became harder to trace, burrowing through the hills somewhere below them. They hadn't found another steam vent in ages and Michael couldn't decide if this was just because they were really overgrown and impossible to find after a century of neglect, or whether there weren't as many vents up here to begin with. They'd already climbed up a long way so the tunnel must be very deep now and it would be quite costly and impractical to try and dig down to it. Besides, the route wasn't as important as a busy main-line one that would handle passenger and freight trains from both directions, so it might not have needed as many ventilation shafts anyway if the tunnel would only receive a single goods train once in a while.

There was also the possibility that the Morgans themselves had destroyed some of the old vents to make it harder for people to find the tunnel and the stolen goods that were hidden within it and Michael thought that this was perhaps the most logical explanation for why the vents were so hard to find. If the Morgans had gone to a great deal of trouble in somehow staging a roof collapse and erecting a fake tunnel wall, they wouldn't want to risk someone simply hooking a ladder onto an old vent and climbing in that way. Michael felt sure the criminals would have made absolutely certain their precious tunnel was safely protected by bricking up some of the vents, so this definitely helped to explain why they hadn't found one in ages.

The three of them walked on in silence for a while, keeping a wary eye on the moorland fog to make sure they didn't get lost in it. At the moment it was still creeping down the other side of the valley and so they could follow the track without much worry for now.

Presently, they found themselves out on the moors properly, standing amongst the bleak and lonely view of bracken and heather. Here they were exposed to the harsh cold wind and Michael was the only one who didn't have to endure his hair blowing across his face because it was cut quite short. But Jenna and Rose were both struggling desperately, with Jenna holding her hair back in one hand while Rose's was blowing around so badly that she could hardly see.

After a while, Michael stopped, gazing round at the view in awe.

Hugging themselves within their jackets, Jenna and Rose stopped beside him, wondering at the delay.

"It's kind of beautiful, don't you think-?" Michael asked, hugging himself too but staring out across the valley with a slight smile at the corner of his mouth.

Rose nodded, visibly trembling against the cold winds and pulling a hat on to try and contain her fly-away hair.

Michael opened his arms to her and pulled her close, half-wrapping his coat around her to share warmth.

Jenna smiled brightly, gazing round with a thoughtful look in her eye.

"It's an incredible view. This landscape has so much history. People have lived here for thousands of years." She remarked, gesturing around at the purple heather and occasional shafts of sunlight piercing through the clouds to cast certain areas in bright light while other areas remained in darkness.

Michael nodded eagerly.

"Imagine what it must have been like in the past. This is just the kind of place where you can picture a lonely traveller crossing the moors with only a single lantern to guide his way, caught in a storm and soaked to the skin, but he staggers on through the dark. I've heard these moors are riddled with bogs and that many an unfortunate soul has fallen in and drowned. This is a fascinating place, both beautiful and deadly at once. It conjures up all sorts of romantic images in your head. Modern towns and cities just don't do that. They don't have the same exciting magic as the old settlements." He added, thoughtfully.

Jenna and Rose both turned to scowl at him, already feeling quite cold and exposed without wanting thoughts of lost skeletons in the ground beneath their feet. They'd suffered one too many skeletons already with the discovery of the murdered train driver in the tunnel.

But Jenna's eyes widened as she turned to glare at Michael, instead staring across at something over his shoulder.

Rose turned to follow her gaze and gave a yelp of fright, automatically jumping back to hide behind Michael in terror.

He eyed them curiously for a moment before turning to see what they were both staring at with such fear.

Rose gave a soft moan, cautiously peering out from behind him.

"The Black Dog." She moaned, clutching at Michael's arm tightly.

"What? Oh, come on. It's just a stray dog. Why are you both so scared of it? Poor thing; someone must miss it dearly. What's it doing all the way out here?" Michael scoffed, gazing across at the furry black dog crouched down amongst the bracken.

Rose whimpered.

"Mum told me the legend of a bloodthirsty great black hellhound that roamed these parts, but I always thought it was just an old story. I never thought it was true!" She moaned, still gripping Michael firmly as the dog slowly moved through the landscape, coming closer with each step.

As though sensing his scorn, the beast slowly raised itself up from where it had been crouching amongst the bushes. It was still some distance away, but they all stared across at it in shock.

Michael gulped.

"Alright, I take your point. That's definitely no ordinary dog. I thought satanic creatures like that only existed in folklore, not in real life!" He muttered, staring across at the enormous black dog in horror as it gave a low growl, exposing a set of razor-sharp teeth beneath sinister dark eyes.

The dog padded a little nearer, sniffing their scent curiously and giving a few threatening barks to make them leave.

Michael glanced round behind him as they retreated back a few paces, checking to see he wasn't being herded to his death in a bog too, just like the unfortunate souls he'd mentioned.

The beast cocked its head to one side, eyeing Michael intently as he turned back to face it. There was a brief pause as the beast considered them and Jenna gulped. Then, with a decisive snarl, it bounded towards them, coming closer with each second.

Rose squeaked, promptly turning on her heel and fleeing across the moor away from the terrifying creature.

Michael and Jenna glanced at each other quickly before they turned and fled too, fearful for their lives.

Of course, the dog could have easily outrun them, having evolved with higher speed and stamina than its human prey, but it chose instead to just chase them since its duty was only to guard the Morgan lands, not to maim and injure, unless it was specifically instructed to do so.

But these thoughts didn't occur to Michael, Jenna and Rose, who were all too scared and desperate, simply running for cover and trying not to get hurt in the process.

Rose suddenly screamed as she tripped over a hidden rock and came crashing down amongst the bracken.

Michael immediately skidded to a halt, having to use a tree to stop himself as he looked back at her in horror, wondering what the beast would do now.

Behind him, Jenna awkwardly leapt over the small bush that was in her way before she ground to a halt as well, turning to look back as the dog stopped to pad around Rose, who curled up amongst the bracken, crying and whimpering in fear.

"What do we do?" Michael asked, staring across at the gigantic dog anxiously.

"I don't know!" Jenna moaned, turning to look round the area desperately to see if she could spot anything that might help them. Eventually, she settled for simply hurling a few sticks at the beast to try and draw it's attention away from the younger girl.

The menacing dog slowly circled around Rose a couple of times, sniffing her intently and bending over to examine her in more detail. After a few intense seconds that seemed to stretch on forever, the beast slowly turned its satanic black eyes on Michael and Jenna.

Throwing back its head to let off a blood-chilling howl, the dog bounded towards them, leaving Rose unharmed and trembling in the dirt.

Jenna gave an automatic scream of terror, once again turning to flee down the track towards the hopeful safety of the forest.

"SORRY!" Michael yelled, forced to turn and run away too as the dog headed straight for him.

Rose bit her thumb, watching them both flee down the track as fast as they could. Now she was left out here on her own, covered in scratches and wondering why the beast had left her and gone after the others instead. Surely she was easier prey?

"Jenna, split up!" Michael called, dodging round the trees a few metres behind her.

She obediently veered off in a different direction and Michael continued the way he was going. Naturally, since he was behind, the beast chased after him instead of Jenna.

Michael scowled, glancing over his shoulder at the beast to monitor its location. In this brief moment, he glimpsed Rose in the distance, standing on the moor top and looking like a warrior queen with her long hair blowing in the wind and this great dog bounding away from her.

With this image emblazoned across his mind, Michael misjudged the jump over a log and so tripped over it instead, crashing to the floor with a scream of shock.

He was sent rolling head over heels down the hill, getting covered in twigs and sticky plants as he went. He could feel the branches of the undergrowth snapping across his face and knew that he was covered in blood, which would only make it easier for the beast to find him.

Finally, he came to rest amongst a deep patch of nettles and groaned. Things really couldn't be worse for him right now and he half hoped that he would wake up and find that it had all just been a really bad dream.

But no, as he lay there, covered in dirt and bloody cuts, with nettle stings raging across his face, ripped clothes and twigs in his hair, the beast only padded closer, sensing Michael was weak and exhausted.

Michael sighed, firmly picking himself up out of the nettle patch and studying the creature. The hellish thing certainly didn't seem to have any weak spots that he could see from this distance.

The dog let out another threatening low growl and Michael promptly turned and fled, going deeper into the forest with each step and desperately trying to out-run the beast. It was a foolish idea and he knew it, but it was all he had.

He wasn't the fitness enthusiast of the family; that was Robbie's area of expertise with his love of mountain climbing. Michael had never had much interest in physical exercise, seeing it as a complete waste of his precious time and preferring instead to work on mental exercise by curling up on the sofa with an exciting pile of books to explore. Even sport-hating Ashley got more exercise than he did since he was always dancing around the house with his headphones on, or running off for various midnight adventures around the town with his mates. They were a pretty dysfunctional family really and didn't seem to overlap much in terms of their interests and abilities.

Even so, Michael was wishing they'd interacted with each other a lot more during their childhood as the dog drew ever closer, seeming to have infinite stamina. If only they had been more accepting and interested in each other's hobbies, then Michael wouldn't be feeling quite so unfit right now and convinced that he would die from exhaustion and become dog-food. Instead, they had spent all their time making fun of each other and now he had to face the consequences of that decision.

Michael crashed through the undergrowth, periodically glancing back over his shoulder to check on the beast. The forest was so dense and overgrown that he could barely see where he was going amongst this gloomy mass of trees.

He was ploughing through the bushes in desperation when the ground suddenly vanished from beneath his feet and he was pitched down into a dark hole. He flailed round for a moment, screaming in panic until his hand caught hold of a thick root.

Overhead, the dog paced around the area, confused by Michael's bizarre disappearance and tracking his scent to the old steam vent.

The structures had once been protected by a small stone wall built around the top and a grating to stop people falling into them like this or gaining unauthorised access to the tunnel. But over the years, the walls had begun to collapse, with the stones and protective grating tumbling down into the dark tunnel below.

The wild growth of the forest now meant that it was almost impossible to find the tunnel vents as they lay buried beneath the various bushes and plants, so they had become quite dangerous since their hidden locations meant it was quite easy to fall into one, as Ashley and Michael had both demonstrated.

The landscape had also changed a lot over the past century, with new saplings taking root in the open space around the vents where there was more light, so that didn't help much either. The clearings that had once existed by the vents had long gone, but even if they had still remained, Michael probably wouldn't have recognised their significance, his brain being too panicked at the devilish creature that was hunting him down.

He hardly dared to breathe as the dog stopped right above the vent shaft he'd fallen into, blocking out any remaining light and leaving him almost in complete darkness.

He could feel the forest bugs crawling all over him, having decided to make him their new home since he'd destroyed their last one by falling through it. He shuddered in disgust, keeping a firm grip on the root as he didn't know how far down this hole went. All he could see below was a black abyss that was bitterly cold and silent.

He didn't know which was worse, being chased by a savage and half-starved hell-hound or being covered in bugs with a drop to certain death below.

Tunnel Invader

Down below in the tunnel, Bryony flinched as a loud howl echoed through the forest overhead.

"Did you hear that-?" She gasped, grabbing Robbie's arm and gazing up at the tunnel roof anxiously.

Ashley shrugged.

"It's probably just the wind." He assured her, as the four of them gathered in the tunnel to listen.

Luke nodded in silent agreement.

"Mmm, it does sound kind of ghostly sometimes when it blows through the trees." He agreed, shoving his hands deep in his pockets and tilting his head slightly as he listened. There was nothing but silence for a few moments until a distant scream was heard and Bryony stiffened.

"That was my sister. I'd know that scream anywhere." She moaned, an expression of confusion and worry carved across her face like stone.

Then, a second scream was heard and this time both Ashley and Robbie tensed up, with Robbie's face displaying a rare expression of anxiety.

"Mitch." Robbie frowned, while Ashley's hands clenched up into fists.

Luke gently wrapped his arms around both of their shoulders.

"Okay. I'll grant you that. I heard that scream too and it was definitely not the wind." He agreed, rather reluctantly.

"What's happening up there? Why are they screaming?" Ashley asked, worriedly.

"I don't know; I can't see through stone and soil, can I?" Luke grumbled, indignantly.

Ashley scowled at him, blinking as the ground overhead trembled, showering him in dirt and dust. He firmly pulled his hood up to protect himself a little better and peered round at the tunnel critically.

Bryony edged closer to Robbie nervously, feeling a bit left-out and seeking some comfort and reassurance as she worried about her twin-sister up above.

"I hope they're alright, I haven't heard anything from Rose. Do you think she might be hurt?" Bryony worried as Robbie awkwardly patted her on the arm and turned to examine the tunnel around them.

"I hope the tunnel doesn't cave in either. It was a stupid idea really, to start exploring without checking first to see if it was safe. This place could fall down at any minute and we just set off on our reckless exploration. I don't wanna die down here in this God-forsaken place. Only our friends know where we are, no-one else. What would Enid think if we all just disappeared like that? And what about Pam, our guardian? She'd be heartbroken." Robbie added, looking quite guilty.

Luke frowned as Bryony cautiously moved further up the tunnel to examine the wall there.

"Hey, this tunnel has been here well over a hundred years. I hardly think it will cave in now, just because *we're* exploring it. Don't you think-?" He replied, following her up the tunnel and firmly pulling Ashley along behind him by the wrist, wanting to know he was safe if the tunnel did start to collapse.

"Don't jinx it." Ashley scolded, obediently padding after Luke and glancing round at the tunnel nervously as he considered the way he'd been showered in dirt a few moments ago. "As soon as you say something like that, you can be damn sure it's going to happen. You know how it works. I may have the luck of the devil, but that doesn't mean you can put it to the test." He frowned, peering round in silent curiosity as Luke dragged him onwards past the gloomy opening of a smaller access-tunnel at one side and wondering what other mysterious secrets lay buried underneath the vast forest.

They continued up the tunnel in silence for a while, each of them lost in their own worried thoughts about Michael, Jenna and Rose and trying to work out what might have happened. Had Dean found them?

Eventually, a menacing low growl from above made them all look up in silent horror. Both the growling and the earth tremors moved further up the tunnel towards Bryony, who promptly clenched her hands into nervous fists.

Ashley cautiously walked up the tunnel towards her, reaching out with one hand to try and calm her as he wondered what was going on above their heads.

Bryony suddenly let out a loud scream, stopping Ashley in his tracks and sending a cold shiver down his spine.

"Ooh, there's a load of bugs raining down on me! Get them off, Ashley, get them OFF!" Bryony moaned, doing a strange little dance around the tunnel as she tried to shake off all the insects that were now crawling over her.

An eerie snapping of twigs from above made them look up again and Ashley gave an automatic cry of shock and pressed his hand over his mouth at the writhing figure outlined by their head-torches.

"What's that-?" Luke hissed, the fear obvious in his voice.

"What's going on?" Robbie called from further down the tunnel, where he was busy examining it to see just how stable it really was.

Before the others had chance to reply, the mysterious thing above gave a desperate howl and crashed down upon the three of them, showering them in even more twigs and bugs. They all screamed in terror, though Ashley's was abruptly cut off as the thing landed on top of him, knocking the breath out of him and leaving him spread-eagled out on the ground with both the thing and Luke sprawled over him.

Bryony quickly snatched up a metal pole that was lying on the ground and gave the dark figure a few sharp prods.

"Cut that OUT." Michael's voice snapped and she dropped the pole in surprise, though judging by Luke's cry of pain, she must have dropped it on him by accident.

"Oh, thank goodness; it's only you. For heaven's sake, don't do that! You scared the life out of me!" She gasped, reaching up to press one hand over her heart in relief.

"What's wrong, what happened-?" Robbie called, having turned to run up the tunnel towards them when they all screamed in terror.

"No, Rob-!" Ashley gasped, quickly snapping his mouth shut before a large spider could enter it.

Robbie howled as he tripped over Luke in the dark and was brought crashing down on top of them, causing Ashley to give a violent yell of pain at the sudden impact.

"Ow." Robbie grumbled, peering round at them critically and looking a bit dazed.

"Would whoever is crushing my lungs please get the hell off? I can't breathe…" Luke gasped, eyeing the muddy trainer by his face and trying to remember who it belonged to. "Mitch, is that you? Why are you so damn heavy?" He asked as Bryony cautiously stepped forwards to help untangle them.

"Oh boy…." Ashley groaned, still flattened face down on the ground with his two brothers and best friend sprawled out on top of him in a rather painful, chaotic mess.

Robbie frowned as he considered what Luke had just asked.

"Huh-? Why would Michael be down here? I thought he was still up on the moors with Jenna and Rose. What are you talking about? Did you hit your head on something when you fell down, Luke?" He asked, reaching up to accept Bryony's hand and allowing her to pull him back to his feet.

"Hey, Robbie." Michael's voice muttered from where he was still tangled up on the ground somewhere with Ashley and Luke.

"What the hell are you doing down here?" Robbie asked, crouching down to help free his little brother from the mayhem and habitually giving Ashley's foot a hard kick, as though Michael's misfortune was somehow his fault.

"He fell down the vent, dummy." Luke growled, pulling flattened Ashley back to his feet and dusting him off while Robbie devotedly set about picking all the leaves and sticks from Michael's hair.

"Well then what was he doing in the vent?" Robbie demanded while Michael merely stood there staring up at the vent and visibly trembling.

Eventually, he pulled Robbie into a tight hug and refused to let go. Robbie gave a disgruntled squawk of protest and squirmed slightly, trying to free himself from the unwanted hug.

"Robbie, I've never been happier to see you in my life! I thought I was dog-food!" Michael gasped and Robbie frowned.

"Dog-food? What the hell is that supposed to mean?" He asked as Michael reached out and firmly pulled Ashley into the hug too. "No! Get off me, Ashley, you freak!" Robbie protested as Michael forcefully pinned them together.

"I love you. Both of you. Do you hear me? I need to know that I said it and that you understood." Michael declared, causing Ashley and Robbie to peer round at each other awkwardly as they wondered where this sudden proclamation of brotherly love was coming from.

"Uh, sure. You too, I guess, baby bro." Robbie muttered, reaching out to give Michael a fond pat on the arm.

"You know I do." Ashley agreed and Bryony rolled her eyes at the way they both refused to say it back to Michael properly. Was it really that hard?

Michael frowned, standing in traumatised silence for a few minutes as he replayed the chase in his mind, his body still shaking as he clung to his brothers desperately, having thought he'd never see them again.

"So, what happened to you? I don't think I've ever seen you so scared. And you've definitely never said, well, *that* to me before. What inspired that? Normally, you're shouting that you hate me." Robbie asked, peering down at Michael curiously.

"The b-black d-dog." Michael stammered, staring up at the vent and refusing to let go of Robbie no matter how hard he wriggled and moaned.

"Oh." Ashley muttered, biting his lip as he considered the furry new friend he'd made in the forest the other night.

Robbie chuckled.

"Hey, it was probably just a weird shadow that you saw, that's all. Nothing to worry about." He said, tousling Michael's hair fondly.

"I know what I saw, okay? That thing just tried to kill me and would've succeeded, had I not fallen down the vent." Michael snapped, hating how they never believed him and always treated him like a baby.

Taken aback, Ashley and Robbie turned to each other, slightly subdued after his sudden outburst.

"Okay, calm down. You're safe now and that's what matters. No need to bite my head off…" Robbie murmured. Clearly, his brother had suffered quite an ordeal as Robbie had never seen him so scared and he'd dealt with Michael's childhood fears a lot over the years: fears of the dark, monsters under the bed, Ashley's scar, being left behind, strangers, yucky food, everything.

"It was huge, with shaggy black fur and cruel dark eyes. If I hadn't fallen down that vent, I'd have collapsed from exhaustion and would probably now be half-eaten." Michael moaned as Ashley rocked him gently and Robbie finally prised himself free with a grunt of embarrassment.

A little impatient, Bryony padded over to join the three brothers and fixed Michael with a hard stare.

"What about my sister?" She demanded, firmly interrupting their family-time with her own concerns for her twin.

"Jenna had to run off too, but we split up to try and improve our chances. Unfortunately, the beast chose to harass me. I don't know where she is now, but I'm sure she's fine. The dog chased me for ages, so Jenna should be far out of its way by now." Michael replied, looking up at her.

"And Rose?" Ashley asked, anxiously.

Michael bit his lip and frowned, the last image of Rose still clearly stamped across his mind.

Luke looked down at Michael quietly, marvelling as always at how similar Michael was to his own baby brother, Adam. They had the same angelic innocence and desire to please since they were both the youngest child in their family.

"Mitch?" Luke asked, cautiously. "What happened to her?" He demanded, moving round to add his own hard stare to Ashley's so that Michael felt as though he was looking at two sets of bright lasers, one a vivid blue and the other a shocking green.

"Well, it kind of looked like the dog would....*obey*....her. She fell over and the dog stopped to investigate her but left her alone and chased after us instead." He muttered, looking up at Ashley nervously.

"Obey her, eh? That's interesting." Ashley muttered, thinking of his own encounter with a giant black dog and wondering if there were more Morgan secrets they had yet to learn.

"You weren't there; it certainly looked as though she's hiding something." Michael protested, smacking Robbie's hands away from his hair where he was still hunting for twigs and standing there with his arms folded and a sulky little frown.

Ashley sighed, taking a few moments to consider Michael's behaviour before raising his gaze up to the roof of the tunnel instead.

"The black dog. Is that you, Shadow, I wonder? Or do you have friends?" He smiled, talking mostly to himself and missing the suspicious look that Luke shot him.

Robbie stubbornly picked the final few twigs out of Michael's hair and studied him quietly.

"Things aren't always how they seem. You should know that by now. Remember the time you thought there was a monster living under your bed? You even got Ashley to lie down and try to reason with it and he found the noises you'd been hearing were coming from a stray cat. This is just the same. It wasn't a terrifying creature out to maul you, it was just somebody's over-excited dog that wanted to play. To say you spend all your free time studying, you don't have much logic. Trust me, there's always a rational way to explain things." Robbie murmured, turning Michael's face towards him and smiling.

"You know, you and Ashley are just the same. You both think you're so strong and powerful and that I'm just a helpless little child who always needs protecting. Stop treating me like a child, the pair of you. Would you have had the same reaction if it were Tom who had fallen down the vent instead of me? No, of course you wouldn't. Tom's the sensible, grown-up one; you'd believe anything *he* tells you and you wouldn't start petting him like a kitten, the way you are with me. Why can't you treat me like that too? Just because I'm the second-youngest and the second-smallest of the group, you seem to think that I'm stupid or something and dismiss everything I say. You're only a few years older than me, but you seem to think that you're so wise and clever. You should show me more respect. I didn't *have* to come with you on this holiday, I *chose* to, so you should try being nicer to me." Michael growled, roughly pushing them both away and stomping up the tunnel in a huff.

"Well, forgive me for trying to help. You weren't so feisty a moment ago, clutching at me and sobbing about dog-food." Robbie shouted after him, his short temper flaring up as usual.

He boldly tried to set off after his angry little brother to try and make amends but found himself firmly held back by his big brother instead. Ashley calmly pulled Robbie across the old railway tracks to the other side of the tunnel and fixed him with a look that was almost parental.

"Leave him. He's obviously had quite a shock so the last thing he needs is you shouting at him. Don't worry, Michael will be fine, I promise you. Just give him some space and let me talk to him instead." Ashley murmured as Bryony and Luke followed him into the darkness too, with Luke's face displaying a particularly critical frown as he studied Ashley curiously.

"Okay, I saw your face, Ash. You know something about that dog, don't you? Admit it. That's another secret you've kept from me this holiday, you bad boy. I don't like your new independence, so stop it. You know I hate being shut out." Luke muttered, sternly.

Ashley shrugged.

"I think, in this case, you would *all* need my help where that dog is concerned. I met it too the other night, when Tom and I got lost in the forest. The same thing happened then as with Michael, Jenna and Rose today. The dog was perfectly friendly towards me, but when Tom tried to introduce himself as well, it turned hostile and savage. I'm wondering if the dog is another Morgan secret we need to learn about. Think about it. I'm a Morgan and so is Rose. The dog wouldn't harm either of us, yet turned hostile towards Michael, Tom and Jenna, the non-Morgan blood." Ashley told them, raising his eyebrow slightly.

Luke nodded in agreement.

"Yeah, I don't think Michael is lying. I've never seen him look so scared. You three brothers all have a give-away tell when you're lying and Michael's didn't appear when he told us about the beast. His eyes were steadfast and he flicks them around more when he's lying. Right now, I imagine that he's more embarrassed about the way you treated him like a child than his desperate hugging of you when he first arrived down here. That behaviour was understandable; he was still in shock and trying to calm down from the intense adrenaline, so he was just happy to see you and realise that he was safe at last. But he's right; you do tend to baby him a bit. Even my sisters hate that and they're a lot younger than he is." Luke murmured and Robbie twitched slightly in alarm.

"Wait, we have a give-away tell? So that's how you always know when Ash is lying! What's mine then? What do I do?" He demanded, hating that Luke and Ashley were so much taller than he was and couldn't be bullied into submission. Robbie had always prided himself on being tall for his age and used this as a weapon of intimidation whenever he wanted his classmates and Michael to do what he said. Unfortunately, that trick had never worked on Luke and Ashley, so Robbie had found other sneaky ways of getting what he wanted.

Luke smiled to himself and shook his head.

"No. I'm not going to tell you what you do when you're lying because you'll stop doing it. Then how will I know that you're up to no good? Knowing when people are lying is one of my secret tricks for working out what's going on in their head." Luke replied, calmly.

Robbie pouted, tugging at Luke's sleeve pleadingly.

Bryony frowned, irritated by this idle chatter and worried for her sister and Rose, who were still missing out in the wild somewhere with Michael's evil dog patrolling the forest. Ashley and Robbie may have their own brother safe and sound down here with them, but she had nothing to prove that Jenna was okay.

The Outcast

Meanwhile, Jenna had run through the forest until she could take it no longer. She'd seen the dog chase after Michael but that had been ages ago and the dog could well be after its next victim by now. She couldn't bring herself to think about what might have happened to Michael and really hoped he was safe and that Rose had managed to look after herself too after they'd just abandoned her out on the moors.

Jenna just wanted to collapse amongst the undergrowth, but she feared the beast too much to simply give in now. She fled through the wild forest a bit longer before she burst into a spacious clearing and found a small but well-maintained stone cabin. It was located close to the old track-way that led away from the tunnel, so Jenna presumed the building must once have had something to do with the lonely railway.

She was so glad to find some kind of shelter away from the vicious dog that the cabin's maintained appearance and smoke rising from the chimney didn't register in her brain and she simply burst through the door. She just saw the building as somewhere she could finally rest without worry of being torn to pieces. Slamming the cabin door closed behind her, she collapsed back against it and closed her eyes in relief, thankful to be safe at last.

"Excuse-me-?" A male voice protested, indignantly.

Startled, Jenna's eyes flew open and she stared across the room to find a middle-aged man with scruffy black hair scowling over at her.

"I'm sorry, I didn't realise this place was still in use!" She gasped, feeling completely rude and invasive.

"What's that supposed to mean?" The man demanded, getting up out of his chair and crossing the room. "Get out. Go on, shoo! Who do you think you are, bursting into people's houses like you own them?" He grumbled, shaking his fist in Jenna's face and making her feel very uncomfortable.

"D-Dean? Are you Dean Morgan?" She asked, cautiously. She could only assume this was who the man was, judging by the black hair, piercing eyes and furious scowl. If she was right, then she had just made a very dangerous mistake.

The man stopped, pointing one finger in her face as his eyes narrowed with cold suspicion.

"How do you know that name? Your accent doesn't sound local." He demanded, moving closer until he was almost nose to nose with Jenna.

"My friend. Dean's son. Ashley Morgan." She stammered, feeling very intimidated and unnerved by this severe invasion of personal space.

The man gestured over to a stool by the open fireplace.

"I think you and I need to have a little chat." He growled, his eyes still narrow and guarded.

Jenna perched herself awkwardly on the small stool while the stranger settled himself back into his rocking chair and gazed into the fire.

"I'm sorry…" She blurted out, looking up at the man nervously and really not liking the hard look in his eyes.

"I haven't heard my brother's name mentioned in a very long time." The stranger muttered and Jenna frowned.

"Your *brother?*" She asked, only now remembering that Enid was the youngest of three children.

"Yes, my brother. Dean is older than me by five years. I'm Glen Morgan." The man explained, finally turning his gaze back onto Jenna, who bit her lip in confusion.

"But I'm staying at the old manor with Enid and she never mentioned you. It was her daughter, Rose, who told us that you'd been banished." Jenna replied, curiously. She thought it was really sad that Glen had been thrown out of the family and wondered what he had done to deserve such a cruel punishment.

"Well, why would Enid tell you my life-story? Our family history is none of your business." Glen growled, staring across at Jenna intently.

"No, but I think it's Ashley's business. He's a Morgan too since he's your nephew, so I think he has a right to know all about your family history and why you were disgraced. At the moment, he only seems to know your name and nothing else." She protested, surprised when the man merely shook his head.

"That boy has suffered enough, don't you think? He doesn't need an exiled uncle adding to the pain. And if you truly are his *friend*, then I would strongly advise you to put him straight on a train back home. This place isn't safe. Once you've picked your side, you have to stick with it and face the consequences. Not all of our ancestors have fully passed on, so it's important to bear that in mind when you're choosing what kind of life you wish to pursue. In this family, our dead have a habit of sticking around to make sure the rest of us are behaving properly and following the criminal traditions. So it's not just the living relatives you have to worry about. There are at least seven ghost-Morgans who haunt this landscape and only one of them is good. That's why I say Ashley should leave and never return. If he's anything like his mother, then he's likely already in danger. And I really don't want to see him get mixed up in all of this. Look what happened to me. I tried to fight against the Morgan traditions and ended up being kicked out." Glen scowled, gesturing around at the cabin where he had lived for over twenty years.

"What happened, if you don't mind me asking? Why were you exiled?" Jenna asked, feeling a little rude but unable to hide her curiosity.

Glen sighed, staring across at Jenna coldly. She may be Ashley's friend, but that didn't mean she could start poking her nose into their private family affairs. So far, with forcefully bursting into his home and asking invasive questions, the girl hadn't made the best first impression and Glen found himself wondering what kind of people his nephew hung out with. Had Ashley fallen in with a bad crowd?

"I was cast out of the family when I was nineteen. I was too angelic and righteous for the traditional Morgan values, so both my father and my brother *hated* me. But I did something that really offended them, so they cast me out and I've lived here ever since. I'm a forester and prefer to live a simple life as you can see by this cabin. It brings peace to my troubled mind and I enjoy the tranquillity of nature. These mountains and forests are truly beautiful across the seasons and I like the solitude. I have no use for all these fancy modern gadgets; they destroy the soul. Instead, I get my entertainment the old-fashioned way from books that my sister lends me from the manor library. Books are wonderful for firing up your imagination and learning new things. Outside, I grow most of my own food in the garden and then I buy everything else I need from the local market. What more could you want?" Glen explained, peering round the little cabin quietly.

Jenna studied him thoughtfully, trying to consolidate everything she had learnt about Dean in her mind. She'd never encountered someone who had such a violent stranglehold over their family and found it very sad to consider all the different situations.

First, there was the tragic tale of Heidi and Ethan, who had been brutally murdered at Dean's hand after they decided to become a couple. Then, Dean had tried to murder his own son, leaving Ashley scarred for life both physically and mentally since he still suffered from post-traumatic stress over a decade later and had been viciously bullied for most of his life over his gruesome appearance. Robbie had also gained an ugly scar from Dean's rage that night too before he, Ashley and Michael were shipped off to live with Heidi's best friend instead, something that had caused a great deal of distress at having to adapt to a lot of complicated changes at once. Even Enid and Rose couldn't escape Dean's cruelty since they had been left to guard the old manor and didn't seem to have much opportunity for chasing their own dreams. Now, Jenna was upset to discover Glen's lonely existence out here in the middle of the forest and couldn't believe he had been discarded like a broken toy. It was horrible!

She might not have met the infamous Dean Morgan herself so she didn't yet know what he was really like, but she imagined him as some kind of master puppeteer, juggling the lives of those around him and holding the cards of life and death over their heads. No-one was safe from his violent temper and Jenna was sorry for all the pain he had caused his victims over the years. She couldn't believe this was Ashley's ancestry and felt very relieved that he seemed to be more like his mother than his father. It was strange to think how differently things could have been otherwise.

Glen watched her quietly, trying to work out what kind of person she really was in the hope it might tell him something about his beloved nephew. He'd thought Jenna quite bold and unpleasant when she first burst into his cabin, but now he wasn't so sure.

"So, how is my nephew? I haven't seen him since the night he was attacked twelve years ago. Does he still have that long scar across his face? I'd be surprised if he didn't; it looked quite deep." He asked, cautiously.

Jenna nodded.

"Yes, he still has that scar. I'd always wondered where it came from, but he only just told us the story the other day so I'm still trying to process everything." She told him, biting her lip as she considered her friend's threatening appearance.

Glen frowned slightly, reaching out to prod the fire with an old metal poker.

"I think about that day a lot. I never thought my brother could be such a ruthless killer. He was always more of a petty criminal in his youth so I couldn't believe he'd actually murdered people. I'd only gone to the manor that evening to return a few books and I was shocked to find a load of police cars and ambulances swarming round the place. I didn't know what was going on. I remember seeing the paramedics bring little Ashley out of the house with his face covered in blood before he was lifted into an ambulance and driven away. Enid was frantic. She wanted to go with Ashley and Robbie and make sure that they were okay but she had baby Michael to look after too and the police wanted to ask her a bunch of questions. So she sent me to go with the two injured boys instead while she remained at the manor. I stayed with Ashley and Robbie all night in hospital while I waited for their new guardian to turn up. I don't think I'll ever forget that day as long as I live. It was horrific." Glen sighed, closing his eyes for a few moments as the firelight flickered across his face, revealing it to be thin and gaunt and exposing years of stress. He may have presented his lifestyle as a perfect existence, but his face suggested otherwise and Jenna wondered if Glen was still bullied by his criminal brother despite being outcast all those years ago.

His black hair was already going grey before it's time and this, along with Glen's worn and haggard face, made him look much older than he really was. Yet he still had the typical Morgan inner strength and determination that reminded Jenna of feisty Ashley. She smiled to herself as she recalled that Glen's eyes had the same piercing, soul-searching nature as Ashley's too. Sure, their eyes were different colours, but it was obvious that the Morgan traits ran deep.

She nervously reached out to lay a hand on Glen's arm, wanting to reassure him that Ashley was okay. She suspected, from the tone of his voice, that Glen blamed himself a lot for what had happened to Heidi, Ethan, Ashley, Robbie and Michael. Obviously, the man had spent the years wondering what might have happened if he had arrived at the manor a bit earlier that day and felt guilty that he hadn't been able to prevent the awful tragedies from happening.

"Don't worry! Ashley is well! He's one of my best friends. We're actually in a band together. Ashley says the memories of that night still haunt him too and probably always will, but otherwise he is healthy and strong. I think you'd like him; you seem quite similar." She mumbled, a little flustered under Glen's intense gaze.

The man considered her thoughtfully for a few moments before he gave a faint smile, obviously very pleased by her words and suddenly seeming a lot friendlier.

"Yes, he always did like music. Here, look at this. I only visited him once as a baby but he was *very* noisy even then so he must really like being part of a band. Ashley spent the whole duration of my visit making funny little sounds with his voice. I thought it was quite cute, but Dean hated it." Glen murmured, standing up to pluck an old photograph off the mantelpiece and handing it to Jenna.

She looked down at it curiously, smiling when she found it was another image from Ashley's infancy and thinking that he looked absolutely adorable with his tufty black hair sticking up all over the place. The photograph showed Dean seated on a tatty long sofa with baby Ashley cradled in his left arm, happily shaking a rattle and kicking his feet about. The look on Dean's face was one of weary disgust as he stared down at his tiny son, one eyebrow raised in disapproval at Ashley's noisy toy and trying to offer him a plushie little wolf to play with instead.

Glen was seated on Dean's right, leaning forwards slightly to coo at Ashley and loosely holding a picture-book in one hand. Then there was Enid seated on Dean's left, staring down at Ashley with a look of nervous anxiety on her face as she firmly reached over to adjust Dean's arm to make sure that he was holding Ashley properly and wasn't going to hurt him.

Finally, there was another black-haired man seated beside Enid at the end of the sofa, except he was much older than the other adults so Jenna presumed this must be Ashley's paternal grandfather. The man was watching baby Ashley with an intense, predatory sort of look as though he was busy planning out Ashley's life in his head and Jenna thought he was really creepy. He had a very dark aura and clearly didn't get on well with Glen since they were sat at opposite ends of the sofa.

Jenna thought it was very interesting to see the Morgan family all seated together like this and the way they interacted with each other. Judging by the landscape visible through a window in the background, the photograph had been taken at Dean and Heidi's flat in London and a note scribbled on the back stated that Ashley was about four months old.

Glen gestured at it sadly.

"That's the only photo I've got. I've another one of young Rose of course, but that's the only one I have of Ashley. I've often wondered what became of him. I was really excited when Ashley was born as I'd never had a nephew or a niece before so I wanted to help out and be involved. I may have been kicked out of the family but Enid still wrote to me with regular updates so I knew what was going on. But Dean would never let me come and visit, saying that he didn't want me corrupting his impressionable young son. As you can see, Ashley never had much interest in the toys that Dean chose for him anyway, but I still wasn't allowed to visit. It was only because Heidi insisted on getting us all together for a family photograph that I finally got to meet little Ashley. Even then, Dean wouldn't have me in the house for more than an hour. But Heidi had never had much family of her own, so it was very important to her that Ashley be allowed to meet *all* of his Morgan relatives. From what I've heard, Heidi grew up with only her father for company, but he died a few years before Ashley was born. I've always suspected that Heidi was still grief-stricken when she met my brother and that he took advantage of her need for companionship. Anyway, Dean only agreed to the photograph to stop her nagging at him and he was very careful not to let me touch Ashley even once. Heidi said that she'd never seen him so devoted and parental and she was absolutely amazed. Dean kept hold of Ashley the entire time I was there as a clear message that Ashley was *his* kid and he didn't want me hanging around and interfering with things." Glen explained and Jenna nodded, studying the photo a little closer and frowning when she realised that Dean was not only offering out a more suitable, Morgan-themed toy for Ashley to play with, but he was also blocking Glen's access to Ashley by raising his arm up in front of Glen's chest like a barrier. Glen may be leaning forwards slightly to coo at baby Ashley, but Dean was still quite protective about how close Glen was allowed.

"I'm sorry." Jenna muttered, gently handing the photo back and staring round at the tiny, old-fashioned cabin in wonder. She couldn't believe that Glen had ended up living in such a strange place. How on earth did he manage?

Entering the cabin was like stepping back into a different era and she was quite shocked by the simplicity of everything. One end of the cabin housed a crackling open fire and Glen's rocking chair, along with a small bookshelf and a few ornaments scattered across the window-ledges. The floor below was bare stone apart from the occasional rag-rug that had been spread out for extra warmth and there was a basic wooden bed pushed up against the wall behind Jenna. A separate door led off to a narrow, primitive-looking bathroom while a nearby window offered a view out across Glen's garden of various herbs, fruits and vegetables. An old cooking range had been squeezed in by the main door along with a small wooden table and a single chair, so it was obvious that Glen didn't get many visitors.

Overall, the cabin had a cosy feeling of days gone by and Jenna thought that the open fireplace would be quite romantic in winter. Glen clearly found it comfortable enough, but she couldn't imagine swapping her own materialistic lifestyle for the simple, old-fashioned one that he had chosen. It was really quite remarkable.

Painful Revelations

Underground, the tunnel-team had become quite dispirited and grumpy, having lost interest in their task of following the route of the tunnel long ago since the place was so dark and everything looked the same. Most of the stolen goods had been removed years ago before the place was abandoned, so only the empty crates remained now.

Ashley sighed, reaching down to dig his phone out of his pocket to check the time.

"For God's sake, it's almost two o'clock! How much longer is this bloody tunnel? I didn't think the moor was that big!" He moaned, scowling to himself irritably as he stared round at the dirty brickwork. His head-torch hadn't revealed anything interesting for a while now and he was getting very bored.

"Two o'clock? Oh no! How long is it going to take us to walk all the way back? I hope we're not late for dinner! I'm already starting to get hungry! Should we turn round?" Luke complained from somewhere behind and Ashley rolled his eyes.

"You're always hungry." He muttered, idly thinking about the amount of food Luke had nicked off his plate over the years during various sleepovers and school trips.

Robbie snickered.

"Nah, let's keep going. We should be nearly there by now, right? It would be a shame to just give up." He decided and Michael gave a miserable little whine from where he was wearily hanging onto the back of Robbie's shirt and letting himself be pulled along like a baby elephant.

"I can't walk much further. I'm exhausted." He protested, giving a large yawn and stumbling slightly against the uneven ground. His terrifying ordeal with the black dog had completely drained him of energy and he just wanted to curl up somewhere and go to sleep.

Ashley turned to eye him quietly, seeing that Michael could hardly keep his eyes open and wondering what they would do if he actually passed out. He didn't think Michael would appreciate being carried since he was thirteen but he looked absolutely shattered.

"Come on, little brother. I think I see a light up ahead!" He chided, padding over to stand behind Michael before he set about firmly pushing his two siblings up the gloomy tunnel.

"What light? I don't see any light!" Robbie protested from the front of the little group, tripping over himself slightly from the speed of Ashley's encouragement.

Ashley glanced round briefly to offer Bryony a scheming wink through the darkness and she nodded, reaching up to point into the distance with a loud shout of joy.

"He's right, I see it too! We must be nearly there!" She lied, understanding that Ashley was trying to give Michael a bit of friendly motivation to keep going. In truth, she had no idea when the tunnel would end since everything was still in complete darkness, but the idea of emerging into daylight again was very inspiring and she found herself eagerly skipping forwards with renewed excitement.

Robbie shook his head in disapproval.

"Hey, don't get too excited. We might end up having to walk all the way back through the tunnel anyway if there's no way out at this end." He warned, thinking it very unlikely the Morgan criminals would have created multiple access points to their secret warehouse.

They walked in silence for another fifteen minutes or so before Luke gave a sudden howl of pain as he walked into something in the dark. Almost immediately, a loud rumbling sound echoed down the tunnel, along with the desperate screeching of an old mechanism that hadn't been used in decades.

Startled, the others turned to see what had happened, finding Luke to be hopping about in distress next to a rusty iron lever that was sticking up out of the ground.

"What did you do?" Ashley demanded, eyeing the lever suspiciously before he glanced around to see what might have caused the loud screeching sound.

"I was so busy watching you three idiots charge up the tunnel all linked together like a human train that I forgot to look where I was going." Luke grumbled as Bryony padded over to investigate the strange lever he had found.

"What's this doing here? Bit of a strange place for a lever, don't you think, right in the middle of the path?" She wondered, crouching down to squint at it before she cautiously reached out to pull it towards her.

Once again, a loud rumbling sound echoed down the tunnel and Ashley flinched, automatically pulling Michael close against him in case the lever unleashed anything dangerous.

"I don't think you should touch that." He called, looking round the tunnel nervously.

"I want to know what it does!" Bryony protested, this time pushing the lever away from her to see if that did anything.

"Don't worry, I'm fine…" Luke huffed, a little offended that no-one had asked.

Bryony stared round the tunnel expectantly for a few moments before giving a loud shout of victory as a sliver of daylight appeared at the side of the tunnel.

"Look! It's a door! We can get out!" She shouted, rushing to examine their latest discovery in giddy excitement.

Robbie frowned, padding over to join her and eyeing the iron door critically. From what he could see, the forest outside must be *very* wild and overgrown, because the door had only shifted an inch or two before it got stuck on the foliage.

"Well it's not very useful if it won't even open. How are we supposed to fit through that tiny little gap?" He muttered, dubiously.

Bryony frowned, padding back over to investigate the old lever again while Ashley stepped forwards to take her place by the door, wanting his own delicious nosy at the outside world.

"Mmmm, I can smell fresh air! It's soooo good!" He called, taking a deep breath to savour it and then grunting in protest as Robbie roughly hauled him out of the way.

"Hey, stop hogging all the fresh air and let me have a turn! Why do you get to go first every time?" Robbie whined, pushing Ashley back into the stale darkness of the tunnel.

"Because I'm older than you and I'm bigger than you." Ashley retorted and Bryony sighed, shaking her head at them briefly before she turned her attention back to the fascinating lever.

"Maybe the gap will get wider if we try the lever again? After all, nothing happened the first time when Luke accidentally tripped over it. Then, when I pushed it open again, we got daylight. Each time we push the lever, the door opens a bit more." She suggested and Luke nodded.

"I agree. I am more than ready to get out of this stupid place. I'm worried that if I spend any longer down here, my eyes will start glowing or I'll end up looking like some hideous cave monster." He complained and Michael shrugged, staring across at the exposed greenery anxiously.

"I'd rather walk back through the tunnel than go out there. What if the beast is lying in wait for us? At least we know it's safe in here. It can't get into the tunnel." He said, waking up slightly at the horrifying thought of meeting the great black dog a second time.

Bryony considered their arguments thoughtfully before she directed her torch over to highlight Ashley and Robbie by the door, deciding that it was only fair to let everyone have their say.

"Boys? What do you think? Should we try and force our way out through the door or head back through the tunnel?" She asked, eyeing them expectantly.

Ashley raised one hand up to point at the door.

"I think we should see what's out there. We still don't know what happened to Jenna and Rose so I reckon we should go and look for them." He answered while Robbie turned to stare back into the tunnel.

"We also need someone to go and retrieve the rope from the other end. We just left it hanging there when we set off and we don't want to make it easy for Dean and his gang. But it might take longer to retrieve it if we go out into the forest because we don't know how to find the tunnel from this direction. If we go back through the way we came, we could just climb out again and then bury the rope in the bushes." He suggested and Bryony smiled.

"That's true. Unfortunately, it looks like you've been outvoted. Only you and Michael would rather go back through the tunnel, whereas Luke and Ash want to go outside with me."

She said, reaching out to play with the lever again in the hope it might reveal some more of the wild forest.

She thought it was quite strange to have a door-opening switch located somewhere on the floor rather than on the wall, but then again it was probably quite a smart idea by the Morgan criminals. After all, if you were laden up with various stolen crates and sacks to carry outside and load up into a waiting cart or lorry, you wouldn't want to waste time carefully putting them down again in order to open the door.

Having a switch in the floor meant you could just kick it on your way out and let the door open itself. Saving time was obviously very important if you wanted to avoid being caught by the police so this floor-switch was quite a useful idea.

You couldn't assume that the Morgan gang had always had a lot of people at their disposal to afford the luxury of posting someone on door-duty. Sometimes there may only have been a few people running the operation while others were locked up in prison and therefore anything that would help save time would be of the utmost value.

Sadly, it seemed that the door wouldn't open any further no matter how many times she pulled the lever back and forth and she sighed, padding over to join Ashley and Robbie as she wondered if they could push it open instead. It took a while since the door was so old and heavy, but eventually their combined strength allowed them to force it halfway open and they stepped out to admire the view.

Bryony frowned, staring round at the wild forest critically for a few moments before she dropped down onto her knees and began crawling through the bushes. It had taken them ages to hack the undergrowth into submission the first time when they were looking for the lost tunnel, so she hoped that crawling through it would be easier since they had a much smaller area to clear.

Luke crouched down behind her, smiling to himself as he considered all the different challenges they had encountered during their adventure so far. He eyed Bryony's little green tunnel for a moment before he obediently crawled in after her, wanting to make sure they all stayed together as a group.

"Hey, Bry? Where exactly are you heading? We don't know where we are yet!" He called, realising they didn't have a map or anything to help them figure out their location. They only had their phones but they had discovered earlier that day that the forest seemed to have absolutely no reception.

"I've no idea! Wherever the bushes end, I suppose! There must be a clearing *somewhere!*" She shouted back, twisting round to look at him before she continued her wild exploration.

Ashley had only crawled a little way after Luke when someone tugged at his ankle urgently and he twisted round to see what was going on. When he found Robbie sprawled out on the ground behind him, he rolled his eyes and gestured for Robbie to pass him.

"Well you go first then, Rob, if it bothers you so much. Go on!" He snapped, glaring back at his little brother irritably.

Robbie shook his head.

"It's not that. It's Mitch. He doesn't want to come." He explained, pointing back at Michael, who was still cowering in the old train tunnel.

Ashley sighed, obediently rolling back onto his front and lunging forwards to grab hold of Luke's foot before he disappeared too far into the bushes.

There was an indignant shout from up ahead and Luke twisted round to stare back at Ashley, his eyebrow raised slightly in disapproval.

"Hey! What the hell was that for? Let go of me!" He demanded, a little bad-tempered from spending all day stuck in the dark tunnel.

"Hang on. Michael's not coming." Ashley muttered before he wriggled round to face his brothers again.

Luke frowned, quickly crawling through the bushes to catch up with speedy Bryony and pass the message on to wait for them.

Ashley looked up at Michael expectantly.

"Come on. It's okay." He beckoned, reaching out to his little brother with one hand and offering him an encouraging smile.

Michael shook his head.

"No. I'm not coming out until I know that beast is locked away somewhere. I'm staying right here. It can't get to me in here. I'm nice and safe." He growled, folding his arms like a stubborn child.

Robbie groaned, still sprawled out in the dirt and idly drumming his fingers on the ground as he waited for Michael to toughen up.

"Oh, pull yourself together and don't be such a baby. You might not like being *called* a baby, but you sure act like one sometimes. What are you going to do now then, Mitch? Are you just going to live in that tunnel forever? Come on, don't be an idiot." He grumbled, turning to scowl at Michael over his shoulder.

Michael pouted, looking both furious and hurt at the same time.

"You're so mean to me. You weren't *there*. That dog terrified me so much and I thought I was going to die. You don't know what that feels like. I don't want to go with you. What if the beast is still out there? I don't want to go through all that again; I'm scared." Michael mumbled, nervously.

Robbie merely gave a loud snort of derision and crawled forwards into Bryony's little green tunnel to continue their explorations. He was fed-up with Michael's silly behaviour and decided that he'd let Ashley deal with this particular tantrum. He didn't even wait to let Ashley move aside, simply flattening him into the mud and giving a wicked cackle as Ashley cursed him to the deepest pit of hell.

Ashley glared at Robbie coldly for a few moments before he turned back to consider Michael thoughtfully. His brother looked quite hurt at Robbie's mean comments and was anxiously biting his lip as he debated the situation.

Ashley beckoned to him again.

"Hey, it's alright. I promise you, Michael, that dog will not hurt you when I'm around. I met it the other night too when I was out with Tom and it wouldn't hurt me either, the same way it left Rose alone earlier today. I think it's another Morgan secret we need to learn about, so you'll be safe with me. Don't worry, I'll look after you. The dog won't get anywhere near you, I swear." He murmured and Michael studied him quietly, taking in Ashley's soft tone and big, honest eyes and suddenly feeling a lot safer with his oldest brother around to protect him. After all,

Ashley had always kept his word before whenever he spoke of looking after Michael, no matter the risk to himself.

"Okay, Ashley. I trust you." Michael whispered, looking round nervously for any sign of the dog before he crouched down amongst the bushes.

Ashley smiled, waiting until Michael had crawled past him before he turned to follow, understanding that Michael would want him at the back in case the dog decided to sneak up on them.

Up ahead, Bryony had just wriggled out into a forest clearing and stood up to survey the area curiously. She could just make out the railway track curving off down the hillside as it emerged from the tunnel, still buried deep within the undergrowth somewhere. It was only because she knew about the tunnel that she understood the significance of the trackway, but to anyone else, the route would simply look like an old road carving its way through the trees and seeming like it had been there forever.

Beside the railway track was a stone cabin, presumably an old watchman's hut or something that had survived the decades. Bryony glanced back into the undergrowth for a moment to see where the others had got to before turning her attention back to the cabin. Her first cursory glance had missed the smoke rising from the chimney and Bryony was startled.

One by one, the boys emerged from the undergrowth too and straightened up beside her to see where they were.

Ashley frowned, surprised to find a cabin here in the middle of nowhere.

"Someone lives here? Why would anyone want to live here? It's so lonely! I could never do that." He exclaimed, amazed.

Robbie shrugged, shoving his hands in his pockets as he turned to study the area, looking for some other signs of civilization. But there weren't any. The strange cabin was truly alone and hidden away deep in the forest.

"Well, we found the end of the tunnel. What do we do now? Do you want to follow the track-way further down and see where it goes? Or should we head back to the manor?" He asked, looking round at them for suggestions.

Ashley scowled at him.

"We find Rose and Jenna of course. I can't leave them out here by themselves if they're anywhere near as scared as Michael was. Maybe the owner of this lonely cabin can help? I say we go down and ask if they saw anything." He decided, gesturing down at the little house in a rather authoritative manner.

Michael cringed.

"Please don't make fun of me." He pouted, looking round at them all miserably.

As they stood there gazing down on the cabin, the door slowly opened and a black-haired man emerged, followed by a teenage girl. Bryony automatically screamed in delight and ran over to hug Jenna tightly, thankful that they had found her at last and she looked to be okay.

"Oh my God, I was so worried about you! I'm so glad you're safe!" Bryony gasped, finally releasing her sister as the others came over to see what was going on.

Jenna beamed at them, relieved to be reunited with some of her friends and staring round at them happily. Eventually, she spotted Michael half hidden behind Ashley and gave an excited squeal as she dashed over to hug him.

"I thought you were dead! Are you alright?" Jenna asked, as Michael awkwardly patted her on the back.

Luke smiled, reaching out to tousle Michael's hair fondly while Ashley sat down on a nearby log, his feet sore from wandering through the tunnel all day and spending most of the night before traipsing through the forest. His boots weren't exactly made for hiking and the aching of his feet was starting to radiate upwards to affect the rest of his body.

"Trust me, Mitch is fine. He's just worn out. He fell down another steam vent and frightened us half to death." Ashley murmured, reaching down to loosen his boots a bit more as Jenna sat down beside him, glad that they were all safe and hoping that Rose had managed to find her way back to the manor.

She introduced the stranger as Glen Morgan, brother of Dean and Enid, before turning to announce her friends in turn, leaving Ashley until last since he was a Morgan too.

Ashley eyed Glen critically while Luke gave a sudden exclamation of surprise at recognizing the name from the disgraced portrait they'd found upside-down in the attic.

Luke stepped forwards to shake Glen's hand politely while Ashley stayed stubbornly rude, refusing to give Glen his friendship until he'd proven himself trustworthy.

"So *you're* Ashley. My nephew." Glen murmured, moving over to lay one hand on Ashley's shoulder as he quietly examined the long scar down his face.

Ashley flinched uncomfortably, shrugging Glen's hand away from his shoulder and glaring at him.

"Please don't touch me." He growled and Glen cautiously pulled his hand back, studying Ashley thoughtfully as though he wasn't quite sure yet what to make of him.

"Come inside, I want to talk to you." Glen instructed, gesturing to the cabin with a smile that looked like it hadn't been worn in years.

Jenna nodded eagerly.

"He's okay. He's not one of the bad Morgans, like your dad. You can trust him." She said, recognising that Ashley was a little wary.

Ashley shook his head.

"No. I need to find my cousin." He replied, standing up and turning to head back into the forest.

Glen frowned, reaching out to grip Ashley's arm firmly and pulling him back with a surprising amount of force.

"Please, Ashley. Stay. I haven't seen you since you were a child! Now you show up at my house all grown-up and then threaten to leave after only a couple of minutes. Come on. Stay a few minutes longer at least. I would like to learn more about my only nephew." He pleaded, desperately.

Ashley looked at him for a few long moments before giving a heavy sigh and moodily shoving his hands in his pockets.

"Alright. *Five* minutes." He agreed, a huffy little scowl slowly spreading across his face that made it clear he didn't like his uncle one bit and would much rather be out looking for Rose instead.

They all followed Glen inside the small cabin, which became quite crowded with so many people now occupying the space.

Glen seated himself in his old rocking chair, looking round in amusement as the others tried to organise themselves into the remaining spaces.

Of course, selfish Robbie was quick to claim the stool next to the cosy warm fire while Bryony moved over to take the wooden dining chair and Michael and Jenna calmly seated themselves on the bed.

Grumbling, Luke and Ashley crouched down to sit on the floor at Robbie's feet and Luke looked up at Glen curiously.

"Sir, do you know anything about a great black dog that roams these parts?" He asked, politely.

Glen nodded.

"Yes, I do. There has always been a savage black hell-hound that roams these lands. It is part of the Morgan story and many people have met a gruesome end on the wild and treacherous moors from encountering the beast." He explained.

Michael and Jenna both scowled as they considered their own encounters with the creature and Robbie stared at them quietly for a few seconds before turning back to Glen.

"What do you mean, 'part of the Morgan story'?" He asked, intrigued.

"Well, the dog always appears when there's trouble afoot. It served as the perfect distraction, leaving the Morgans free to get on with whatever dirty deed was planned while the beast roamed loose, protecting them from anyone who might come snooping. Both the black dog stories and the dark Morgan family have kept these lands free from tourists for decades and so the small town in the valley below the manor is a quiet and secluded place. Of course, the town hosts plenty of markets and fairs for the community, but there is little interaction with tourists. The families who live there are ancient bloodlines, some as old as the Morgan one itself. The black dog even features on our family crest since it is so important. Obviously, it hasn't been the *same* vicious hound surviving through the centuries, but a number of great black dogs, trained to protect our lands and the secrets that lie within. The beasts are taught by the Morgan criminals to expect food and shelter from them, so they are very loyal and won't attack anyone with black hair. Honestly, don't worry about Rose. She's a Morgan, so the beast won't hurt her. If anything, it would be more likely to try and help her." Glen explained, eyeing Ashley suspiciously as a scheming grin slowly spread across his face.

"I wouldn't be so sure about the loyalty part. I think the dog's allegiance to Dean is weak and it has found a new master. It wants me instead." Ashley muttered, looking quite pleased with himself.

Michael frowned as he considered the beast he'd encountered back on the moors.

"What do you mean?" He asked and Ashley shrugged.

"Well, when the dog found me and Tom asleep in the forest, it was really happy that I treated it with kindness and respect. The poor thing looked to have suffered a lot at the hands of its real master and so it has followed me ever since, seeking my friendship and protection. It first led me and Tom back to the manor because we'd gotten hopelessly lost, then it accompanied us again last night when we went out to look for the ghost train. I could hear the creature padding through the undergrowth nearby, but it was always just out of sight. Then, today, it caught up with Michael, Rose and Jenna when they were tracing the route of the tunnel above ground while I was in the tunnel below. If I'm right and the dog has followed me ever since I met it the other night, then it should still be around here somewhere, hidden in the bushes. I showed that I would be a kind Morgan master, so I reckon it wants to leave Dean and join me instead." Ashley smirked and Michael promptly turned to stare out the window, fearful that the beast could still be lurking somewhere nearby.

Luke studied his best friend cautiously, thinking that Ashley's face had suddenly transformed into a vision of his cruel father. After meeting Dean for himself, Luke could clearly see that Dean and Ashley had the same evil, scheming grin when they chose to display it and that really scared him. There was no doubt that they were father and son and Luke found himself debating whether or not it had been a good idea to bring Ashley back to his ancestral homeland after all. He had never seen Ashley make that face before and wondered what was going through his friend's head to inspire that kind of sinister reaction.

Judging by the expression on Glen's face, it seemed that he had similar concerns and Luke was glad to see that Ashley's uncle still loved him even if his father didn't.

"Don't give me that look, Ashley. Please. That expression belongs to the dark side and I really don't want you to take that path. You're much too good for that." Glen sighed and Ashley frowned at him irritably.

"Sorry, but this is my *face*. That's just how it works. What do you want me to do; only display expressions that reflect my mother? I don't like it any more than you, *uncle*, but Dean is in my blood, so occasionally my face might look a bit like his." He scolded, hating to be reminded that he looked a lot like his wicked father. He was beginning to wonder if he should start dyeing his hair another colour so that people would finally leave him alone, but black had always been his *thing* and he really liked being dark and mysterious. He couldn't imagine himself looking any different and didn't like the idea of changing himself just to please everyone else. He never had. Grumpy, he offered Glen a final menacing glare before he turned his attention to watching the crackling flames dance about in the fireplace instead and impatiently tapping one finger against his arm as he did so.

Jenna eyed him nervously for a few moments, recognising when Ashley was in a bad mood and knowing that it always made him very difficult to talk to. He had made it perfectly clear he didn't like or trust Glen one bit at the moment, so Jenna decided it might be a good idea to do some damage control before the two fiery Morgans got the wrong idea about each other.

"Believe me, Glen; your nephew would never turn to the 'dark side' as you call it. I've known Ashley for five years now and while he might be a notorious wild child and a troublemaker, he wouldn't dream of doing anything to betray his mother's memory. And besides, Ashley has the most devoted best friend in the world, so he's well protected from his dirty Morgan blood. Luke is basically a guardian-angel. He's really intelligent and he cares about Ashley more than anything, so he'd never let him take the wrong path. Those two are absolutely inseparable. Even Luke's *names* imply that he's some kind of divine, angelic being. Both his first name and his middle name, Ray, mean 'light' so he is honestly the best person for Ashley to have by his side. Really, Glen, you don't have to worry about Ashley being led astray." She explained, peering across at Luke fondly.

Meanwhile, Bryony had spent the past few minutes staring across at Glen suspiciously as she considered the location of his cabin, right beside the old track-way, and wondered why he'd never found the train tunnel himself. He pretty much lived right next to it and yet, for some reason, the tunnel had remained untouched. She didn't think Glen was particularly stupid, so he must appreciate what the surrounding landscape meant, but she couldn't understand why he had never reported the stolen train. After all, he was a Morgan too, and a good one according to Jenna, so Glen must know the truth about where the train was hidden.

It seemed to her that he knew all about the tunnel and had chosen this lonely little cabin on purpose. But she wasn't sure yet whether that was to protect the train or for other nefarious reasons, so she thought it might be a good idea to call him out. She couldn't believe Luke hadn't already done it since he was supposed to be the observant one, but he was currently sitting with his back to the track-way and was distracted by the conversation, so Bryony supposed Luke just hadn't had chance to properly evaluate their location yet.

"Excuse me, Glen. What do you know about the old railway tunnel out there? We walked all the way through it earlier and it looks completely abandoned. Do you know why the Morgans stopped using it? I would've thought it was the perfect warehouse for their stolen goods since it offers so much space, but it looks like no-one's been there in decades." She asked, subtly highlighting the issue to her friends and frowning when a dark and angry scowl slowly spread across Glen's face.

"So, you know about the train." He sighed, peering round at them all with a look of hard warning as he considered what Bryony was really asking. "Now, you listen to me, all of you.

Stay away from that place. It's dangerous. That tunnel has caused nothing but trouble since it was built. I know the stolen train is still hiding in there; I've seen it myself. I fell down one of the old vents in my youth and then found my way out again through a secret passage. But you have to believe me when I say that it's best for *everyone* if it just stays hidden. That's why I live here, to guard it. I dread to think what my brother would do if he found out that I'd discovered the train and donated it back to the local community. You've not heard the old tales of what happens when you go up against the Morgans. But I grew up with those stories as my father and brother tried to teach me to become a criminal too, just like them. I've already been outcast from the family for refusing to do as they asked and you know well enough that my brother is capable of murder when someone betrays him. This is just the same. You don't understand the *wider picture*. If I revealed the location of the stolen train, it wouldn't just be me who suffered as a punishment, it would be everyone involved in the rescue operation. That tunnel is now Morgan territory, even if it is abandoned, so handing it over to the authorities would be like handing yourself over for execution. But at the same time, the tunnel must not fall back into Morgan hands since it is basically an enormous warehouse for stolen goods, as you say. I cannot allow it to be rediscovered and made operational once again, so I stay here to guard the train from my brother, or anyone else who might come snooping. I would advise you, in the interests of your own safety, to stay away from that tunnel." Glen warned them and Ashley gave a loud sniff of contempt. His eyes also seemed to darken slightly and he scowled up at his uncle with a look of deadly black rage on his face that sharply extinguished all the warmth from the cabin and replaced it with a feeling of icy menace.

"So, you never reported it because you're *scared* of what Dean might do to you? How could you be such a bloody coward? It's true that we stumbled across the stolen train mystery by accident, but now that we know about it, I'm telling you, I won't rest until it is safely returned to the local community. I know perfectly well what Dean is capable of; don't think you need to remind me. How could I forget that he *murdered* my mother? I think of him every damn day when I look in the mirror and see this bloody great scar that he gave me. Believe me, I know all about his ugly black temper. But I'm no coward. It is my civic duty to make sure all of the Morgan treasures are safely returned to their respective owners because it is the proper thing to do. That's how I was raised. My mother and my guardian between them taught me that I must always try to do the right thing, regardless of how hard it might be. I don't care about Dean, or anyone else, who thinks they can bully me into obeying the Morgan traditions of crime and social intimidation. They can't tell me what to do with my life, I make my own rules. And if you think it is better to sit by and let the stolen train go unreported, then you are just as much of a criminal as Dean is, no matter how much you might argue otherwise. I can't believe you've known about it all these years and not done anything about it. How could you?" Ashley raged, shocked at the dirty little secret Bryony had exposed.

"I had my reasons. Trust me. There's nothing more I can do. I've caused my family enough grief as it is so I can't risk putting another foot wrong. I don't want to be shipped halfway around the world like one poor bloke was." Glen replied, frowning to himself uncomfortably as he stared out the window at the surrounding trees.

"What do you mean? What did you do that was so bad?" Ashley demanded and Glen sighed.

"I landed my father in prison and helped your mother to escape from Dean." He admitted and Luke raised his eyebrow.

"Wow. Never saw that coming." He muttered, shocked by the scale of Glen's misdemeanours. It was no wonder he had been cast out of the family.

Ashley cocked his head to one side as he considered this intriguing piece of information. He'd never expected that the weak little man in front of him would be so brave.

"Go on." He muttered, idly shoving his hands in his jacket pockets as he fixed his uncle with a hard stare to keep talking.

"You've probably worked this out already but the Morgan attitude is still very sexist and outdated. The men are seen as superior and therefore it is them who are trained to become criminals while the women must stay behind to look after the manor and the children. That's the way it has always been. So, my sister, Enid, was largely ignored and grew up to have a normal education while my brother and I were pushed into becoming the next generation of infamous Morgan criminals. Dean was always quite inspired by the promise of freedom and adventure, so he accepted the training whereas I refused. I wanted to *'do the right thing'* instead as you say and help to make peace with the local community. I'd overheard Dean and our father discussing some of their plans, so I reported them to the police and my father ended up going to prison for a while. That's why I was cast out of the family, because I betrayed them." Glen explained, patiently.

"And Mum-?" Ashley persisted, his eyes softening a little at the idea that Glen had helped to give Heidi a better life.

Glen frowned, holding out the family photograph that he'd shown to Jenna. Ashley obediently reached over to take it and peered down at the image thoughtfully for a minute before he turned to pass it to Luke, wondering what his super-observant best friend would make of it.

"I'm so sorry. This is all my fault and I'll never forgive myself." Glen whispered, reaching out to gesture at Ashley's long scar but taking great care not to touch him since Ashley was already in a foul mood and he didn't want to make it any worse.

"How so?" Ashley demanded.

"I didn't mean for anything to happen, I swear! I only wanted you to be safe. Dean never cared about your musical interests, look! He just wanted a precious son of his own who would honour the family traditions and make our criminal ancestors proud. Even in this picture, he's trying to drag you into the Morgan lifestyle by offering you a cuddly little wolf to play with instead of the noisy rattle from Heidi that you were happy with. Dean *hated* that you wouldn't listen to him and I was worried you might get hurt. I knew Heidi wanted to run away with Ethan and start afresh, so when I heard that she'd stolen you away in the middle of the night, I offered to come down to London and help. I just had to keep my brother occupied until Heidi and Ethan had smuggled you safely out of the city and off Dean's radar. I couldn't stand by and do nothing; I had to give you a chance to grow up safe and happy away from all of this mess. Believe me; Dean was furious when he woke up to find that you weren't there anymore. Then, when I learned he'd murdered Heidi and Ethan a few years later and almost killed you and Robbie too, I was horrified. I'm so sorry, Ashley. It's my fault that Heidi and Ethan were killed, because I gave them a chance to escape and it made Dean feel angry and betrayed. So that's why I can't do anything about the stolen train. As I said, I've caused too much trouble already. I'm really sorry." Glen mumbled, gazing across at his nephew with a look of deep sadness in his eyes.

Ashley considered him for a few moments before he suddenly stood up and pulled his uncle into a tight hug, surprising all of his friends and causing Jenna to well up.

"You're not to blame for any of this. We were perfectly fine down in Cornwall, thanks to you. I even gained two little brothers. It was only because Mum and Ethan came back to visit Dean one Christmas that things got messy. Ethan wasn't my real dad after all and Mum wanted my biological one to be part of my life. If we'd stayed in Cornwall, we would have been okay. Dean couldn't find us down there. You played your part perfectly, Glen; don't beat yourself up about it. You did the right thing for us." Ashley replied, shocked by his uncle's confessions and feeling a little guilty for yelling at him.

The look of enormous relief that took over Glen's face on hearing Ashley's forgiveness was incredible and he reached out to pull Ashley closer, hugging him with such desperate need and affection that an outsider would never believe they were practically strangers.

Jenna sniffed.

"Awww." She mumbled, pleased to see that Ashley had calmed down a little and wondering what he thought of the smothering hug.

"Thank you. I'm glad to hear that you forgive me." Glen muttered, finally letting go of Ashley and reaching out to take his precious photograph back.

"You don't need my forgiveness. What you really need is to forgive *yourself*. And I'm sorry for yelling at you earlier. I'm starting to realise that things might not always be as straightforward as I'd like them to be. At least not around here." Ashley sighed, embarrassed that he had been quick to judge Glen when he'd always hated people doing the same thing to him. He was just very worried about his young cousin and it was making him quite short-tempered. "Okay, enough of this. I'm going to find Rose. I can't stay here while my cousin is out there lost and alone. Sure, the dog might not hurt her, but there are plenty of bogs and rocky cliffs that could just as easily kill you when the cold mists move in. She's not answering her phone and I'm really worried that something bad has happened to her." He declared, gesturing round at the foreboding forest as he considered that Rose couldn't be back at the manor yet because Tom and Suzy would have posted something in their group chat to say that she'd arrived. Therefore, Rose must still be on the moors somewhere and Ashley didn't like that thought one bit.

"Then I'm going with you. You shouldn't go wandering around alone. Not while Dean still poses a threat to you." Luke insisted, reaching out to give Ashley a fond pat on the back.

"I'll come too." Robbie added, taking everyone by surprise since he and Ashley usually hated to be in the same room for five minutes, let alone spending the whole day together.

Bryony stared at him.

"What's up with you? Are you feeling alright?" She asked, fixing Robbie with a suspicious look for his uncharacteristic behaviour and taking a step away from him as though worried his body had been taken over by aliens.

"What? I just want to know Rose is safe, that's all. Don't give me that look, Bry; you know I hate it." Robbie protested, staring back at her in stubborn defiance.

Ashley rolled his eyes and reached over to accept the maps that Michael was holding out before he turned to head back into the forest with Robbie calmly sauntering along behind him.

Luke was about to walk after them when Glen suddenly reached out to grab a tight hold of his arm and fixed him with a worried frown.

"It's Luke, isn't it? Ashley's best friend? Please, look after him. I couldn't bear it if anything happened to him." He pleaded and Luke nodded solemnly.

"You don't have to ask me. I'll always look out for him. That's my job." He promised, offering Glen a playful salute before he sprinted off into the gloomy trees after Ashley and Robbie.

Rose

Luke turned to look up at the dark and cloudy sky nervously as he trudged along beside Robbie while Ashley led the way a few metres ahead, pausing occasionally to compare the landscape with the crumpled maps that Michael had donated.

It looked like a bad storm was moving in and Luke didn't much fancy being caught out on the moors in a howling gale and pouring rain. But, as the second-oldest member of his friendship group, it was his responsibility to help look after the younger ones, which meant that he would have to put his own comfort aside for a while until they found out what had happened to Rose.

Eventually, Luke swivelled his calculating gaze round onto Robbie, eyeing the scruffy boy curiously as he tried to make sense of the situation.

"Why did you want to come out here with us? Regardless of whatever small friendship you and Ashley may have established during the past few days, I know you still dislike him. I'd have thought you'd be happy to be rid of each other after spending all day together, but instead you offer to come with us. What do you *want,* Robbie?" Luke asked suspiciously.

"Hey, I care about Rose too, you know! I just want to make sure that she's safe. We are kind of related after all, through Ashley, like half-cousins or something. I don't know. Besides, I could ask you the same question. You didn't have to come out either but you also volunteered. Are you genuinely worried about Rose or are you just following my brother as usual?" Robbie protested, indignantly.

Luke snorted.

"Don't give me that. You've barely spoken to Rose since we arrived! I got the impression you didn't like her very much, so it's a little odd that you would offer to come out and help look for her. It feels like you're up to something and using Rose as an excuse. Were you hoping we might bump into Dean and you could give Ashley up as a peace-offering?" He retorted, eyeing Robbie intently.

"*No.* I might not like my brother very much but I'm not that cruel." Robbie insisted, glancing round at Ashley thoughtfully before he turned his gaze back onto Luke. "Besides, you never answered my question. Why are *you* here? Why do you follow Ashley all the time? Even at school you're always trailing after him like a loyal puppy. It's creepy." He added, shuddering slightly at the idea of having someone follow him everywhere he went. Why did Ashley allow it? How did he cope with having no privacy?

"It's not *creepy!* I just see Ashley as my home. We've known each other for twelve years now and it feels weird when we're not together. It's like I'm suddenly missing half of myself and I don't know what to do. You wouldn't understand. The world just seems different when Ash isn't around and it makes me very anxious." Luke explained, shrugging slightly. "And you're wrong to say I don't care about Rose. I care about *everyone* in this group, even you. So don't think I'm here just for Ashley." He added, staring back at Robbie wearily.

Up ahead, Ashley suddenly stopped and turned to face them with a frustrated scowl as he gestured at the maps in his hand.

"Would you two quit arguing and *help* me? For goodness sake..." He snapped, shaking his head at them in disapproval before he continued onwards through the forest.

"I was multi-tasking." Robbie protested while Luke awkwardly turned to consider the dark sky again. He really hoped that the weather would hold off until they'd found Rose or it would make the task a whole lot harder.

"Why won't you answer me?" Ashley whined, shoving his phone back in his pocket as another attempt at ringing his cousin proved unresponsive. So far, he'd called Rose four times and sent her a bunch of worried texts but she hadn't replied to any of them and Ashley couldn't understand it. Why hadn't she sent them a message to say where she was? That would certainly make things a lot easier. Instead, he had to keep yelling her name and hope that eventually she would shout back.

It was only when they'd climbed up onto the bleak moors that they finally got a response. By now, all three boys were shivering against the cold winds and heavy rain that had battered them ever since they left the shelter of the dense forest. Ashley had just screamed Rose's name again as loudly as he could and was about to continue onwards when a distant cry for help answered his call. Delighted, he was about to go tearing across the moors towards her, but Luke and Robbie both reached out to grab hold of him and roughly pulled him back.

"*Don't* go rushing off like that. Remember the treacherous bogs and cliffs you mentioned back at Glen's cabin?" Robbie growled, keeping a tight grip on his brother's arm and fixing him with a look of stern warning.

"Yes, we don't want to lose you as well as Rose." Luke agreed, still with a fistful of Ashley's jacket to make sure he didn't go charging off into the mist.

"You're right, I didn't think. I was just so excited to hear some kind of response to my screams." Ashley sighed, nodding at them gratefully as they finally released him, satisfied that he wasn't going to do anything stupid.

Luke cupped his hands around his mouth and yelled Rose's name again to make sure they weren't being led astray by the howling wind. Soon after, another miserable wail of *'Help!'* floated back to them and Ashley smiled, carefully picking his way across the moorland heather towards the sound.

Eventually, Robbie spotted a small figure huddled down in the bushes and they padded over to investigate. There, curled up amongst the heather, was Rose. Cold, wet and frightened, she stared up at them for a few moments in shock before Ashley fell to his knees and hugged her tightly.

"Why didn't you call me? I was so worried! What happened?" Ashley demanded, relieved that they'd finally managed to locate her and reaching out to examine her intently. She looked like she had been through hell with scratches across her face, torn clothes and muddy skin and he felt awful. He dreaded to think what Enid would say about him bringing her daughter home in such a horrific mess.

Rose clung to him desperately, trembling from the cold, wet weather and the stress of her ordeal. Above them, Luke and Robbie exchanged a victorious high-five before they turned to consider the angry weather that was closing in.

"Oh, I'm so happy to see you! I knew you'd come to find me." Rose gasped, clinging to Ashley tightly as though worried he might suddenly disappear if she let go. "I got lost. Your brother, Michael, had taken the maps and I didn't know where I was going. I tried to find my way back to the manor but I couldn't work out how to get there. We don't normally explore this landscape much since it is part of our dark family history and Mum prefers to ignore it. I'm really sorry I couldn't contact you, Ashley. But my phone fell into a bog after I tripped over a rock and rolled all the way down a hill, so I had no means of communication. Now, my ankle really hurts and I'm cold and hungry." Rose explained, mournfully.

Ashley nodded.

"Ah, so that's why you didn't answer any of my calls. Here, let me have a look at your ankle. Maybe you sprained it or something? It doesn't look particularly swollen at the moment but we'll keep an eye on it. I don't think it's broken. Would you mind if I carried you back to the manor anyway? It'll be quicker that way and I'm sure you're keen to get home. We can't risk staying out here much longer and getting caught up in the storm. That could be really dangerous." He suggested and Rose nodded, staring up at the threatening dark sky overhead.

The wind had already picked up quite a lot over the past half hour and she didn't want to spend another minute stuck out here amongst the bleak moorland heather. She just wanted to curl up in front of the fire back home with a large meal and hear about what the others had discovered on their various adventures. But first, there was still one thing bothering her and she wondered why none of the boys had thought to mention it.

"What about Michael and Jenna? Are they okay? Did you find them?" She asked, staring up at Ashley nervously and feeling relieved when he offered her a faint smile of reassurance.

"Yes, we did. Don't worry, they're both fine. Michael fell down an old steam vent and joined us in the tunnel while Jenna ended up at a log cabin that belongs to our uncle, Glen. I don't know if you've met him. He lives in the forest." Ashley explained as he continued checking Rose over for injuries.

"Oh, thank goodness!" Rose gasped, pleased to hear that her friends were safe.

"Ash, give me the maps. We should get moving before the storm gets any worse." Robbie ordered, waiting as Ashley dug the soggy papers out of his jacket pocket before turning his attention to figuring out where they were.

He hadn't admitted it to Luke when he was being questioned for fear of sounding bossy and overconfident, but the impending storm was actually one of the reasons he had offered to come and help find Rose. His mountaineering interests meant that he had done a lot of reading and training relating to survival skills and thought his knowledge might come in useful. Ashley had been too worried and impatient to realise that he was putting himself in danger as well and so Robbie had felt obliged to accompany him to make sure everyone got back to the manor safely.

Luke helpfully moved over to illuminate the maps with his torch, alarmed that the landscape had suddenly been plunged into darkness and thinking they would have to find shelter and fast.

"We're here, I think." He muttered, reaching out to tap one finger against the map as Ashley straightened up beside them with Rose securely cradled in his arms.

"Okay, let's go." Robbie nodded, carefully leading the way back across the moor with Luke helping to light the way and Ashley following a short distance behind.

When they eventually reached the welcome shelter of the forest a few minutes later, Robbie paused to study the maps again and Luke turned to consider Rose thoughtfully for a while before he offered out his phone.

"Here. You can have my phone until we go back home. That way, you can still ring us if you need to. I'm sorry you had such an awful time today. I don't want you to ever feel lonely and abandoned like that again, so you can borrow my phone for the time being and I'll make do without." He explained as Rose cautiously reached out to accept it.

"Thank you, Luke. You must really trust me a lot. I promise I won't look at your photos or anything. And I'll do my best not to lose it. I'm usually very careful with my phone but it fell into the bog before I could snatch it up." She said and he shrugged, amused that the Morgan lands seemed to be quite a dangerous place for mobile devices seeing as Ashley had temporarily lost his too the first time he dropped into the train tunnel.

"To be honest, I don't really care if you look at my photos or not. There's nothing private on there. Normally, I have a passcode on it so my siblings can't get into my social media accounts and ruin my life, but I've taken it off for the time being so you don't have to worry about getting locked out. Just give me the phone back if my parents decide to ring me or someone sends me a message." Luke smiled and Rose nodded obediently.

"But what about you? What will you do if you get lost somewhere now that I have your phone?" She asked, staring across at him anxiously.

Luke chuckled.

"Don't worry. It's unlikely that I'd be out on my own. You've probably noticed that I go everywhere with Ashley, so I'll just share his phone instead. Honestly, don't panic about leaving me stranded. I'll be fine." He answered as Robbie gave a decisive sniff and pointed towards a faint, leafy track a few metres away that curved through the trees before vanishing into the darkness.

"I think it's this way." He announced, squinting at the map intently for a few moments before he nodded.

"You don't sound very confident." Ashley remarked, obediently following his brother through the forest and wondering if they would *ever* make it back to the manor. He was already soaked to the skin as it was, with his wet hair plastered across his face, rain dripping off his nose and his precious eye make-up smeared across his cheeks from where it had gotten washed off. He'd never felt so cold in his life and really hoped that he wouldn't get sick. That would be a disaster.

Robbie led them through the trees for a while before he stopped to examine the landscape again, surprised when he found a dark figure watching them from further down the path.

"Hey, what's this guy doing? I thought we were the only ones still foolishly wandering about in the storm." He muttered, looking round expectantly as Ashley and Luke finally caught up.

Ashley scowled, crouching down slightly to set Rose back on her feet as he considered the newcomer.

"That's my dad." He declared and Luke nodded in agreement.

"Yeah, that's Dean." He muttered, squinting through the rain that was dripping off his eyelashes.

"What does *he* want?" Ashley grumbled, protectively walking forwards to meet his father underneath a giant oak tree.

Robbie frowned, offering out his arm for Rose to lean on since Ashley had ditched her.

"So, *this* is Ashley's father? The man who murdered my parents?" He asked and Luke nodded, eyeing Robbie warily as he considered the boy's infamous hot temper.

"Wait here. And don't do anything stupid. We can handle Dean." He advised, offering Robbie a hard look before he padded over to join Ashley underneath the ancient tree.

Dean eyed them critically before he gestured round at their location.

"What are you kids doing out here?" He demanded, staring across at them suspiciously.

"Sightseeing." Ashley replied, calmly folding his arms across his chest.

"In the rain?" Dean challenged as he considered the way his son looked absolutely drenched.

"Sure, why not?" Ashley shrugged, automatically stepping back as Dean reached out to try and wipe the make-up off his face.

"What is this stuff? Take it off. It makes you look like a bloody girl for Christ's sake. I won't have any son of mine walking around like that." Dean asked, deeply offended by Ashley's appearance and feeling that it reflected very badly on him too. Maybe he shouldn't have let Ashley spend so much time with his mother when he was a baby. It had made him soft.

"Ideally, you wouldn't have me walking around at all..." Ashley muttered under his breath as he reached up to roughly scrub his face clean before pointedly reapplying his precious eyeliner twice as thick as it had been to make it absolutely clear that Dean had no power over him anymore.

Luke smirked, amused that Ashley had responded the same way that he did back home when his bullies were having a go at him. Instead of meekly backing down and doing what he was told in order to get some peace, Ashley just went bolder and invited the trouble in. He was a *Morgan* for pity's sake. He liked breaking the rules and causing chaos. It was in his blood.

"So why are *you* out here in a raging storm? And what were you doing skulking through the forest last night?" Luke asked, bravely directing Dean's attention away from Ashley in an attempt to keep things civil between them.

"That's none of your damn business, you nosy little brat." Dean growled and Ashley sighed. As much as he appreciated Luke's unwavering loyalty, he didn't want his best friend getting hurt in a fight that had nothing to do with him. This was something he had to settle with Dean on his own.

Unfortunately, it seemed that Robbie had other ideas.

"You are going to *pay* for what you did to me and my family!" He yelled, suddenly charging down into the clearing towards them with a dangerous, blazing fire in his eyes.

"I'm sorry! He's really strong!" Rose called, having ended up on the ground from her efforts in trying to restrain the angry teenager. Robbie was three years older than her after all, and a good deal taller, so she hadn't been much of an obstacle to him.

Alarmed, Ashley turned to face his deranged little brother, managing to catch Robbie around the chest and firmly pushing him back a few paces.

"No! Let go of me, Ashley! Why are you protecting him? He *deserves* to suffer!" Robbie howled, struggling furiously against Ashley's tight grip and glaring at Dean sourly across the clearing.

"I'm not protecting *him,* you idiot! I'm protecting *you.*" Ashley snapped, finally succeeding in pushing Robbie up against a nearby tree and holding him there. "What are you doing? Huh? What was that feral attack supposed to achieve? Don't be foolish. Trust me, Dean will get what he deserves soon enough. Just be patient." He murmured, watching his brother intently while Rose carefully picked herself up off the floor with a groan of pain.

Luke frowned, glancing between Dean and Ashley nervously. Robbie's actions had caused Ashley to turn his back on Dean and that made him vulnerable. Luke decided that he would have to be extra observant now, in case Dean decided to launch a surprise attack of his own while Ashley was facing the other way.

"Ah, Robbie. We meet again. And it would seem that you're just as irritating as your meddlesome father. Good riddance to him, that's what I say. The insufferable creep got exactly what he deserved." Dean muttered, eyeing Robbie curiously and causing him to fall limp in shock.

"How the *hell* do you know my name?" Robbie snarled, feeling a little vulnerable himself at this unexpected development.

Dean merely offered them a mysterious little smile and Ashley frowned.

"Come on, let's just go. It's freezing out here." He urged, worried by the news that his father somehow knew Robbie's name. Dean had also correctly identified Michael too when they first met in the forest and Ashley didn't like it one bit. It made him wonder what else Dean knew about them. He decided that he would have to be very careful about what he posted on social media from now on. He didn't want Dean to suddenly come knocking on their front door.

Offering his father a final, threatening scowl, Ashley firmly marched Robbie away down the path to safety, shaking his head slightly at his brother's angry curses. Rose hobbled after them anxiously while Luke hung back to make sure Dean wasn't planning on following them.

Thankfully, it seemed the man had more important things to do at the moment because he only watched them for a couple of seconds before he disappeared into the forest again.

Luke frowned. He really didn't like Ashley's father. The guy was so unpredictable and it made his head hurt. On the one hand, he had tried to murder Ashley as a child and continued to insult him even now, many years later. But, on the other hand, Dean had left Ashley unharmed just now when he could have taken advantage of Ashley being distracted by Robbie's rage. Luke didn't know what to make of him.

"How do we keep bumping into him so often in this huge forest? Doesn't he ever sleep? And where the hell does he even live? Has he got a tent set up out here or something? What's going on?" He wondered, turning to survey the surrounding forest critically.

Cruel Master

They followed the squelchy forest path a little further before a tentative bark floated through the trees towards them. Rose promptly gave a squeal of terror and jumped over to hide behind Robbie. She'd already had an awful day because of that satanic creature and she really didn't want to encounter it again. Her luck couldn't possibly be that bad.

"What was that?" Robbie asked, turning to stare into the trees expectantly. A few seconds later, another soft bark was heard and Ashley beamed.

"Shadow? Is that you? Where are you, boy?" He called, wondering if this might explain why Dean was sneaking around the forest in the middle of a violent storm.

A third nervous bark came back from somewhere on their right and Ashley cocked his head slightly before he turned to follow the sound, silently gesturing that his friends should do the same.

"Hey! Where are you going? And who's Shadow?" Luke hissed, rolling his eyes at Ashley's insatiable curiosity.

"Come on!" Ashley whispered back, beckoning to them urgently as he climbed through the bushes. At the moment, he didn't know if there were any of Dean's followers lurking somewhere nearby so he daren't risk making too much noise. He didn't want his father to grow suspicious and come back to investigate what they were doing.

Luke sighed, crouching down to let injured Rose hop up onto his back before he reluctantly trailed after Ashley, with Robbie bringing up the rear a few paces behind.

They caught up to Ashley at the edge of a misty hollow, where he was quietly gazing down on a dilapidated wooden cabin. The roof had collapsed at one side and the front wall was missing altogether, so it was clear the place had been abandoned for a long time.

"*That's* Shadow." Ashley muttered, reaching out to point down into the clearing with one hand.

Following his gaze, Luke was horrified to find an enormous, shaggy black dog chained up to the back wall of the cabin, curled up into a tight ball and whining softly. There was no doubt that this was the same hellish creature that had terrorised Rose, Michael and Jenna out on the moors, but now it seemed quite small and vulnerable.

"Oh my God." He gasped, appalled to witness the cruel way Dean treated his animals. The man was a true monster. Not only had he maimed his own son, but he also had no respect for the other creatures under his care.

Ashley shook his head in disgust as he carefully slithered down towards the old cabin. He'd thought Shadow's faint barks had sounded a bit strange at first but now he understood them perfectly. Shadow had obviously sensed that Ashley was nearby and wanted his soothing friendship, but barking too loudly would attract Dean's attention as well and that was bad.

"Hey boy, it's okay. I'm here." Ashley murmured, carefully padding inside the rotten shelter and crouching down beside the miserable beast.

Shadow gave a soft whine and raised his head up to stare deep into Ashley's eyes for a few moments before he affectionately curled his long tail around Ashley's waist. The boy made him feel safe and loved and that was all Shadow really wanted.

"I'm so sorry." Ashley whispered, leaning forwards to give the dog a big hug and gently scratching behind his ears. Then he turned to look round at his friends expectantly, beckoning them closer with one hand. "Come on down. Let me introduce you. We can shelter in here for a while until the storm passes. It might not be ideal, but the cabin does offer *some* protection from the pouring rain and the howling wind. What do you say?" He called and Rose's eyes widened in desperate fear. There was absolutely no way she was sharing a room with that terrifying creature. After all, the dog was the reason she was in this mess to begin with.

"No, thank-you! I'm staying right here. I'm safe here. There's a nice, wide tree I can shelter under instead. It looks like it's been here for hundreds of years and protected many people from the elements so I should be fine." She protested, sliding down off Luke's back and hobbling over to lean against the ancient tree trunk.

Luke eyed her thoughtfully for a moment as he considered her previous encounter with Shadow before he obediently slithered down to join Ashley in the dark little hollow.

"Alright. *I* trust you, Ash, even if these two don't." He nodded, gesturing round at Robbie and Rose briefly and then slowly taking a few steps towards the cabin.

Shadow promptly let out a threatening low growl and Luke paused, not wanting to alarm the creature by invading its territory without permission.

Ashley reached out to gently stroke one hand through Shadow's thick, matted fur to help calm him.

"It's okay, buddy; don't worry. Luke's my best friend. He won't hurt you." He murmured, first taking a moment to reassure the nervous beast before he turned his gaze on Luke. "Same for you. I *promise* Shadow won't hurt you while I'm around. As Glen explained, Shadow has been trained to serve black-haired Morgans, so he'll do whatever I say. Just take it slow and introduce yourself." He added and Luke smiled, carefully stepping inside the old cabin and kneeling down beside Ashley.

"Hello Shadow. Would you like to be friends with me?" He asked, nervously reaching out towards the great dog with one hand.

Shadow gave another suspicious low growl and Ashley frowned, thinking it sounded like the beast was asking for proof that Luke was trustworthy. So, he calmly reached out to drape one arm around Luke's shoulders and patted him a few times to show that everything was fine.

"There, you see? I like him. Come on, Shadow, there's nothing to be scared of." Ashley smiled as the dog leaned a bit closer to give Luke a tentative sniff. Then, satisfied that the new boy was friendly, Shadow laid a heavy paw on Luke's knee and nuzzled into his chest contentedly.

Luke petted the dog for a while before he twisted round to beckon at Robbie, who was currently watching them from outside with his hands shoved in his pockets for warmth.

"What about you, Rob? Would you like a furry new friend?" He asked, thinking this might be a good way to distract the boy and cool his temper.

Robbie considered the dog for a while before he obediently padded inside, glad to be out of the rain. The storm had been getting a bit dangerous so he'd been very happy when Ashley suggested they shelter inside Shadow's decrepit cabin. It was much better than recklessly plodding on towards the manor and risking being struck by a falling branch or trampled to death by frightened deer.

Unfortunately, it seemed that Shadow did *not* want to be friends with Robbie at all, something Ashley found highly amusing. It was like Shadow could sense that they didn't get on very well. No matter how gentle or friendly Robbie was, the beast just growled and snapped at him until he eventually gave up.

"Alright, *fine*. Be like that. See if I care. I didn't really want to be friends with you anyway. You bloody stink." Robbie huffed, wriggling backwards to sit against the cabin wall and folding his arms across his chest.

"Ruff." Shadow barked, pressing a little closer to Ashley with a victorious look on his face.

"Good boy! You're very wise, aren't you, Shadow? I don't really want to be friends with Robbie either. I'm only pally with him because I *have* to be as his brother. But most of the time he's not very nice to me." Ashley cooed, rubbing Shadow's belly for a few moments before he peered round at the dog's appalling abode. "How about you come home with us, eh? We can give you a lovely big meal and a proper bed to sleep in. How does that sound? Would you like that?" He asked and Shadow gave an excited bark to show that he thought this was a great idea.

Luke and Robbie however, were a lot less enthusiastic. Luke simply muttered under his breath that Ashley had gone insane while Robbie urgently shook his head and pointed outside at the gloomy forest.

"*No.* You can't do that! It's one thing to befriend Dean's savage black dog for protection in future, but he would definitely notice if it went missing. And then he'd be mad as hell." He protested, eyeing the massive creature doubtfully.

"Well, we can't just leave him here either! Look at this place! We'd be just as cruel as Dean if we left Shadow tied up like this. Come on, what do you say? Will you help me free him?" Ashley argued, gesturing round at the run-down little shack.

Meanwhile, the rest of their friends had already arrived safely back at the manor, with Glen accompanying them through the forest in case the black dog showed up again since there was no-one else of Morgan blood amongst the group. On the way, Bryony had insisted they return to the tunnel entrance to haul their rope ladder back up and stuff it in the bushes to prevent Dean and his gang from using it to access the lost train below. They didn't want to make things easy for the criminals.

Now, they were all gathered together around the banquet table with some sandwiches and juice as they waited for Ashley, Luke and Robbie to return with Rose. Thankfully, Enid was still out at work for a few more hours, so she had no idea about their perilous adventures and Jenna was quite grateful. She didn't like to think what their host would make of their holiday activities. Even Tom and Suzy seemed to have had quite an exciting day despite spending all their time inside the manor as they hunted for the elusive secret passage that linked up to the old train tunnel.

However, for the time being, the mood was tense and quiet as they waited for their friends to return. Michael was particularly anxious since he had encountered the savage Morgan hellhound himself and he couldn't bear to think of Ashley, Robbie, Luke and Rose lying out there in the wet, badly injured and unable to call for help.

If his brothers *had* been killed by the dog, then Michael would be the only one left in his family and this terrifying thought was clearly stamped across his face. This was already the second time in one day that he'd had to deal with the possibility that he may never see his siblings again and he hated it. Even though Robbie teased him all the time, he was still family and Michael couldn't stand the thought of losing him.

At one point, Suzy leaned over to give him a sympathetic little hug but he flinched away and turned to her with big, scared eyes.

"Don't make it worse." Michael muttered, shaking his head firmly and shuffling his chair closer to Tom. They had chosen to sit together since they both had relatives lost out in the storm and were feeling equally worried. Tom didn't know what he'd do if Luke never came back. He *needed* his crazy young cousin around.

They ate in silence for half an hour until the sound of the outside gates creaking open caused everyone's heads to snap round in eager anticipation. Soon after, the front door was pushed open and Rose limped out from the entrance hall.

Jenna was on her feet so fast that she knocked her chair over, running over and hugging Rose so tightly that the younger girl looked amazed.

"Oh, thank goodness! I'm so glad you're safe! Are you okay? I was so worried about you! Here, sit down and have something to eat. You must be famished!" She gasped, stepping back to eye her friend critically and frowning when she spotted Rose's swollen ankle.

Tom and Michael had also jumped to their feet in expectation and Tom quickly crossed the room to peer down into the entrance hall, wondering what was keeping Ashley, Luke and Robbie from coming into the building.

"Luke-? Are you alright? What's going on out there? Do you need any help?" He called, eyeing the open gates outside but unable to see any of the boys.

"Oh, hey Tom! Don't worry, we're all fine. Is Enid home yet?" Luke shouted back, sounding a little nervous as though he was hoping their host was still out.

"Not yet. Why? What are you guys doing?" Tom answered, wondering what kind of mischief his friends had gotten themselves into this time.

"Blame Ash! This was *his* idea!" Robbie shouted back and Tom raised his eyebrow, thinking the whole thing sounded very ominous.

He was about to wander outside to investigate when a loud Ashley-ish howl stopped him in his tracks. A few moments later, Ashley staggered into view with a disgusted look on his face and Tom eyed him suspiciously.

"What's going on?" He asked, watching as Ashley padded down the entrance hall past him and snatched up a tea-towel from the banquet table.

"Eww, dog saliva, gross." Ashley moaned, furiously scrubbing his face clean and completely ignoring his friends' curious looks as he tended to himself.

Michael flinched.

"D...dog?" He asked, glancing round fearfully as a violent, Robbie-like yell was heard from outside, along with a few soft curses that belonged to Luke.

"Watch out, Ashley! He's loose!" Luke's voice called and Tom gaped as a familiar shaggy black dog suddenly bounded into the entrance hall and dodged past him.

"Whoa!" He muttered, spinning round to stare at the beast in shock as it made a beeline for Ashley, who was still cleaning himself up in the banquet hall next to the old fireplace.

"Aaargh!" Ashley gasped, forcefully knocked off his feet as Shadow jumped up at him excitedly. There was a loud thud as they landed on the floor together and Suzy looked around nervously as the various antiques displayed in the hall wobbled a bit.

Horrified, Michael turned to flee halfway up the stairs to safety, peering down at the demonic creature through the bannisters and praying that he would go unnoticed.

Down below, Ashley gave a pained gasp as the dog flopped down heavily on top of him with a contented bark. Then it began licking his face again, delighted to be free at last and thinking Ashley was the most wonderful person in the entire world.

"Oh my God, get him off! I can't breathe! He's so freaking heavy!" Ashley protested, feeling like his lungs were being slowly crushed from the weight of the enormous beast.

"Sorry, Ash!" Luke called as he finally padded inside with muddy, ripped jeans and a dirty face. "Come here, you big menace. Stop squishing my best friend. That's not very nice." He added, coming over to try and haul Shadow out of the way while Robbie firmly pushed the front door closed with a deep thud.

Ashley howled, crossing both arms over his face to try and protect himself a bit from the beast's smothering affections.

"Hey, stop licking me all the time, I don't like it! Seriously, Shadow, we'll have to do something about your breath; it properly stinks! I swear, if you lick me *one* more time, I'll...I'll...I don't know! Just stop it, okay?" He moaned, reaching round to pinch his nose with one hand as Shadow nuzzled into him happily.

Between them, Luke and Robbie eventually managed to haul the great dog off Ashley and Luke quickly sat astride Shadow's back before he could cause any more trouble. Then he turned to fix his best friend with an apologetic look.

"I'm sorry I let go of him, Ashley. I couldn't help it! He's just so excited at being free that it's difficult to control him. It's quite cute. Shadow must really love you a lot already. When he noticed that you'd gone inside, he gave a miserable little whine and then bounded after you, so Rob and I got pulled forwards onto the chippings and the leash flew out of my grip. I promise it won't happen again." He muttered, leaning forwards slightly to give the dog a few friendly pats. Shadow growled in protest and Luke frowned. "Hey. Stop it. Calm down." He warned, adopting the same threatening tone that had always worked on his young siblings when they misbehaved.

Robbie smiled to himself as he padded over to pick up Shadow's leash. Since Ashley was still nearby, he was hopeful the dog would settle down and behave for a while. Things would only turn messy again if Ashley wandered off into another room.

"He's very strong, isn't he? I wonder how the Morgan criminals train their guard-dogs. And where do they even find such enormous creatures?" He remarked, glancing round at his friends curiously.

Tom folded his arms and fixed them with a hard look.

"I will ask again; what is going on?" He demanded, a little insulted that they had completely ignored him the first time he asked.

"Disgusting." Ashley muttered as he picked himself up off the floor and glared at Shadow irritably. He gave his face a final wipe with the tea-towel before he turned to explain things to his friends, knowing that Tom didn't like to be kept waiting any longer than necessary.

His friends weren't wholly on board with the idea of taking care of Shadow but agreed that it would have been equally cruel for Ashley to leave Shadow behind in the dilapidated old hut. Even so, Tom couldn't help wondering how Enid would feel about their new guest when she eventually arrived back from work. He didn't think she'd be particularly happy about having such a large dog bounding around the manor since it was full of valuable antiques and irreplaceable history. But they'd deal with that problem later. For now, they had to make sure Shadow was clean, healthy and fed.

Once the discussions were done with, Tom sauntered over to join Luke and Robbie beside their furry new friend and eyed Luke's dirty jeans critically.

"Are you okay?" He asked, worriedly. Long ago, he'd been instructed by his parents to take good care of his cousin and took his job very seriously. He didn't want to get into trouble with Luke's mother for bringing her son home injured.

"I'm *fine,* stop fussing. It's only a grazed knee, nothing major. Come on, Tom. I'm not a little kid anymore. You don't have to keep looking after me all the time. It just makes things weird. You're only a few months older than me, you overprotective little pest." Luke grumbled and Tom frowned, stubbornly reaching out to examine Luke's knee anyway.

"It's no weirder than you freaking out every time Ashley falls over, or him tending to his little brothers whenever they hurt themselves." He muttered, shaking his head slightly in weary exasperation. Why did he have to be cursed with such a troublesome and adventurous cousin? Why couldn't he have someone calm and neat instead? He was forever giving Luke plasters for his injuries and it was getting a bit ridiculous.

Bryony eyed them fondly for a few moments before she gestured round towards their shared bathroom.

"Come on, Shadow. I think it's about time we gave you a bath. We can't have you stinking up the banquet hall. We have to *eat* in here you know!" She called and Shadow gave a low growl of protest.

Ashley chuckled.

"Here, let me try." He offered, calmly sauntering over to join her by the door and giving a sharp whistle with his fingers.

Sure enough, Shadow was delighted to answer Ashley's call and Luke gave a startled yell as the dog firmly hauled itself up off the floor and carried him across the room.

Bryony tutted as Ashley turned to offer her a smug little grin.

"Yes, alright, very good. But now you have *two* devoted fans to deal with. You'd better hope they don't start fighting over your affections." She grumbled, pointing down at Luke mischievously.

Shadow stared up at Ashley expectantly and he nodded.

"Right, you monster. Bath-time." He ordered, turning to lead the way towards their private wing of the manor and gesturing for Shadow to follow.

Luke smiled to himself as Shadow obediently carried him down the long, wood-panelled hallway after Ashley.

"You know, when you get past the smell and the dirty fur, he's actually pretty comfy." He told them, calmly folding his arms across the dog's back and crossing his feet over in the air behind him. Shadow was by far the biggest dog he'd ever met and he couldn't help wondering what kind of breed the great beast was.

One by one, the rest of their friends turned to traipse after Ashley too, with Michael firmly planting himself at the back where he was safely out of the way and there was less risk of being viciously mauled.

Shadow obediently followed Ashley into the bathroom before he paused, eyeing the old tub and giving a sharp bark of protest. But, when he turned to flee back out into the corridor, he found Tom and Robbie already blocking the doorway and peered up at them darkly. It took Luke, Tom, Robbie and Bryony together to keep the great dog under control while Suzy walked over to run a deep, warm bath.

Eventually, the water was ready and Ashley whistled at Shadow, trying to tempt him into the water by sitting on the edge of the bath himself.

"Come on, boy. It's not that bad!" He called, reaching down to swish one hand back and forth through the water.

Shadow turned to fix him with a look of mournful betrayal before he quietly padded over to join Ashley and considered the bathwater. Then, with another rude bark, Shadow roughly flung

Luke off his back, pitching him straight into the tub with a loud yell and causing Ashley to be knocked off his perch too as Luke crashed into him.

The others all screamed in protest as Luke's giant splash showered them in soapy water and flooded the bathroom floor.

"Hey, this wasn't supposed to be *my* bath, you monster!" Ashley shouted, finding himself to be painfully stuck in the tub and unable to get out. His body wasn't meant to be folded in half this way and he glared at Shadow irritably as the beast made a beeline for the exit.

Michael promptly fled down the corridor in terror and shut himself in the boys' room while Robbie and Bryony both grabbed the dog and sternly hauled him back.

"Get in the tub right now, you *naughty* dog. Look, you made me all wet." Bryony scolded, gesturing at her damp clothes.

"Me too." Luke grumbled as he finally resurfaced and set about shaking the water out of his hair.

"Help!" Ashley muttered from somewhere behind him, still awkwardly sat in the tub with his legs hooked over the edge.

Jenna smiled to herself in amusement before she padded over to take his outstretched hand.

"I've got you, don't worry." She said, placing one foot on the edge of the bath and leaning back to try and pull Ashley out while Bryony, Robbie and Tom dealt with Shadow. They were treated to a few indignant barks and growls first but eventually managed to haul the dog into the bath with Luke and began carefully scrubbing Shadow's fur clean.

Luke frowned, suddenly trapped in-between Ashley and Shadow and thinking he might need another bath himself afterwards, as Shadow's was only making him dirtier. Since he was already in the water underneath the dog, he decided that he might as well make himself useful and set about washing Shadow's belly.

A few moments later, Jenna finally managed to haul Ashley up out of the tub and he nodded at her gratefully before padding over to wash his hair in the sink. He'd never expected that this holiday would be so grungy, but that was what you got from exploring a dusty tunnel, wandering around in a wild storm and befriending a smelly dog. Adventuring wasn't supposed to be easy.

Bryony and Suzy prepared themselves beside the bath, waiting with a few large towels and ready to pounce on the dog before he could send water everywhere a second time.

Meanwhile, Jenna decided it would probably be a good idea to hunt down some suitable dog-food for their unexpected guest and turned to head back towards the kitchen with Michael and Rose in tow. Their previous encounter with Shadow out on the wild and lonely moors meant that none of them were particularly comfortable around the beast just yet, with Michael looking as though he'd much rather be in a different county altogether. Besides, the bathroom was already pretty crowded with so many people inside, so Jenna thought it was quite sensible to free up some space and make themselves useful another way.

Then, once they'd taken care of Shadow and cleaned themselves up, they sat down in their private living room to hear what Tom and Suzy had discovered during their exploration of the manor.

The Morgan Gallery

Tom was really excited to share what they had found.

While the others had been traipsing through the forest and getting covered in mud, he and Suzy had come across the most incredible secret room. As it turned out, they'd been living right next to it for days and Tom knew that he'd never be able to view stately homes the same way again. Now, whenever he accompanied his family on a daytrip to visit one of the country's grand old houses, he'd be looking at it very closely to find out what secrets it held. Was that bookcase really just a bookcase or a doorway to a private study? And what about that big, fancy statue in the corner? Maybe it was hiding the way down to a secret wine cellar or dungeon.

Rose frowned. She had lived at the manor all her life and knew of a few secret passages but not a hidden *room*. How on earth had she missed that? And how had Tom and Suzy managed to find it so quickly?

"Come on. It's down this way." Suzy announced, reaching down to help pull Ashley up off the floor before she led the way back towards the banquet hall.

Wondering what was going on, Shadow obediently padded after them, finally catching up with Ashley at the end of the corridor and rubbing against him gently as he gave a soft, enquiring bark.

"I don't know, Shadow. They didn't say where the secret room is. They didn't even say *what* it is. We'll just have to wait and see, okay? And please don't knock anything over. Some of this stuff is pretty valuable." Ashley replied, idly reaching down to scratch in-between the dog's ears and gesturing round at the nearby cabinets.

"Here we are. So, where do you think the secret room is?" Tom asked, stopping in the banquet hall itself and peering round at them curiously.

Rose bit her lip, eyeing the familiar room in surprise.

"Wait, it's in *here?* I thought we were just passing through!" She gasped and Tom nodded.

"Yep, this is it." He confirmed and Rose blinked. She'd never expected to find the secret room in the banquet hall of all places. How very odd. She'd spent a lot of time in this room over the years since it was the main communal area and couldn't believe she'd been sitting next to a mysterious hidden room.

Robbie turned to study the banquet hall critically.

"Is it behind the old tapestry?" He asked, thinking that seemed like a fairly logical place for a secret room.

Tom shook his head.

"Nope." He answered, his eyes glinting with mischief as he watched them spread out to examine the walls.

"Is there like a fake panel or something here then?" Ashley asked as he walked around the edge of the room giving each wooden panel a few sharp knocks.

"How about behind the suit of armour?" Jenna asked from where she was busy examining it for a hidden lever or anything that might indicate it concealed a secret door.

"Both wrong." Tom called and they stepped back, disappointed. "Luke's in the right area if you want a clue." He added, pointing over to where his cousin was standing beside the grand piano.

Luke promptly spun on his heels to consider his location before he stepped forwards to investigate the old fireplace, thinking there must be some kind of button hidden amongst the intricate carvings. Clearly, the fireplace hadn't been properly used in a long time as it now housed a small electric heater instead of the original wood-burning grate.

"Try looking inside it." Suzy advised and Luke twisted round to squint at her in confusion before he obediently crouched down and ducked into the fireplace.

"Whoa! That is a really weird place for a trapdoor!" He called, his head and torso disappearing from view as he straightened up inside the chimney.

"What-?" Ashley frowned, dashing over to see for himself, along with Bryony, Rose and Michael.

Tom smiled to himself in amusement.

"Yeah, it's a fake fireplace. Since it looks exactly like the other one across the hall, I'm guessing that both fireplaces must have worked properly during the manor's heyday. But as the family got smaller, this one wasn't needed as much and so it was put out of action and the chimney was blocked up." He explained and Suzy nodded in agreement.

"I've got to see where this goes…" Luke's voice muttered, eagerly hoisting himself up onto the metal rungs of a ladder that was hidden inside the old chimney. Of course, it didn't stretch all the way to the ground as that would give away the secret trapdoor, so the first part was a bit difficult as you had to pull yourself up by the arms. Thankfully, Luke was quite strong, so he was able to climb up fairly easily and wondered what he might find in this peculiar secret room. He couldn't imagine why it needed such a complicated entrance and hoped everything would make sense once he opened the trapdoor.

"Hey! Wait for me!" Bryony called, quickly chasing Luke up the chimney before anyone else had chance to claim second place.

Confused, Shadow gave a soft whine and pawed at Ashley's leg a few times, hoping his young master would stay behind and keep him company since he obviously couldn't climb up the chimney with them.

"Oh! I'm sorry, Shadow, but you'll have to stay down here. We won't be long, I promise." Ashley muttered, crouching down to pet the beast's head while Robbie disappeared up the chimney behind him.

Up above, Luke had finally managed to push the trapdoor open and climbed into a beautiful wood-panelled room filled with old portraits and family treasures. He gazed round in wonder for a few moments before he padded over to flick the light-switch on, revealing the true elegance of the place.

He was surprised to find the top-half of a magnificent, two-storey stained-glass window staring back at him from the opposite end of the room and frowned to himself in confusion. He'd not expected that the secret room would be spread across two different levels and wondered why they had entered from the top one. Hopefully Tom and Suzy would have some answers.

"Hey, Ash-? Get your butt up here right now. You *have* to see this!" He called, helping to pull Bryony and Robbie out of the chimney and smiling as they both displayed the same look of awe and disbelief on their faces that he had.

"I'm coming! Just give me a minute!" Ashley shouted back, offering Shadow an apologetic look before he disappeared up the ladder after Jenna, leaving Tom to help Suzy, Michael and Rose, all of whom were too short to reach the bottom rung and didn't have much upper-body strength either to pull themselves up.

When Ashley eventually poked his head through the trapdoor, he stared round at the exquisite paintings in amazement for a few moments before he realised Luke was holding a hand out towards him. "Wow, what is this place?" He asked, allowing Luke to help him up before stepping out of the way to let Suzy escape the chimney as well.

"We think this is the Morgan Gallery." She replied as she brushed herself off. "This seems to be a visual record of your ancestors right back to when they lived in the nearby castle. It's extraordinary! *Every* generation of your family has been documented and there are helpful numbers engraved onto each frame so you can work out the timeline. You can also see what people did, as they have been painted holding certain objects or have something pictured in the background next to them. And the Morgan family crest is included in the top corner of each painting too; do you see? I think it's really interesting to see how it has changed over time. It's a lot more elaborate now than it used to be." She continued and Robbie frowned.

"So why's this one empty then? It doesn't even have any names engraved on the plaque." He asked, pointing up at a fancy golden frame hanging on the wall nearby that didn't have any occupants.

Suzy smiled.

"I believe that one is waiting for a portrait of Ashley and Rose since they are the latest generation of the family. So the plaque remains blank in case any more children were born. When we found the room earlier this afternoon, we discovered that the portraits are arranged in chronological order and the one beside the empty frame belongs to Dean, Glen and Enid, so it makes sense that Ashley and Rose would be next." She answered and Ashley wrinkled his nose.

"Ugh, no, thank-you. I don't want to be put into a portrait. I don't want everyone thinking I'm a criminal like the rest of my ancestors." He complained, clearly disgusted by the idea.

Luke chuckled.

"I would imagine you can choose how you want to be portrayed. Or at least *nowadays* you can. So if you don't want to be associated with your ancestors then make that clear. That way, in years to come, people will be able to look at your frame and see that you were different; that you wanted to make things better and heal the wounds of the past." He suggested as Jenna wandered over to examine the portraits of the criminals who had stolen the old steam locomotive.

"I suppose." Ashley agreed, a little annoyed that Luke seemed to think the portrait was a good idea. "So, why do you think this room would be hidden, Suzy? That seems really odd. I'd have thought the Morgans would like their proud criminal heritage out on display but it's actually been shut away." He asked, turning back to her curiously as he considered the peculiar way they had arrived.

"I don't know if this is true or not but I think your aunt, Enid, was the one who sealed this place up. Some of the paintings look to have been damaged quite badly over the years so I think this room was once used as a kind of school, to teach young Morgan children about their ancestors. Therefore, the damaged paintings, where people have scratched-out faces or insulting graffiti written over them, show the angelic ancestors; the ones children were *not* supposed to follow. But, as you can see, Glen's portrait looks to have been attacked with a lot more venom than any of the others. That makes me think it must have been Dean who defiled it since he would have been *particularly* offended by Glen's betrayal as his brother. Then, when Enid inherited the house, so to speak, she had the old gallery hidden away in order to protect the paintings and make sure all of the family history was preserved. Originally, you would have entered this place through a door like normal and there *is* one downstairs that is sealed shut. It links up to our private wing of the manor, so we think that must have been the criminal headquarters or something in days gone by. Our rooms feel a bit distant from the rest of the manor, which is probably why Enid assigned them to us since we are all teenagers and like our space. But I think at one time that area would have instead housed a study and perhaps a storeroom for stolen goods. The secluded nature of that area meant there was less chance of being overheard. Now, there's a tapestry hanging over the gallery-door to help conceal it. We've been walking past it for days and not realised! It's that lovely medieval woodland scene between the girls' room and the banquet hall." She explained and Rose nodded, finally appearing through the trapdoor behind them.

"Yes, that makes sense. My mum has done a lot of courses on art history over the years so it's understandable she would want to protect these old paintings. She once said that she was always fascinated by the various antiques on display around the manor as a child and she wanted to learn how to look after them and what their stories were. It's her passion. So now she works at a local art gallery by day and then comes home to care for our private family collection." She announced, having been listening to their conversation as she climbed up the chimney.

Luke smiled, impressed by Enid's efforts to protect the family history whilst also keeping it locked away so she didn't have to be reminded about it all the time.

"How did you even *find* this place?" He asked, padding round to examine the nearby portraits intently. He couldn't believe Ashley had such an interesting background and wondered what would happen to the manor in years to come. After all, Enid had explained that she was merely a caretaker, so who would take over her job of maintaining the building and all the treasures that lay within? Was that something Ashley was supposed to do when he was old enough? Somehow, Luke didn't think Ashley would agree to that, or that Dean would be willing to gift him the house in the first place.

Suzy also glanced round at Ashley curiously before she gestured at the impressive stained-glass window.

"Well, after we split off from you this morning, Tom and I went for a walk around the manor to see what it looked like from outside. It has the most peculiar architecture I've ever seen with extensions and mismatched windows everywhere. We easily identified the long windows of the banquet hall and I pointed out the window of the girls' room to Tom. But we were confused by the strange, tall window in-between the two. Clearly, there was another large room hiding in that space so we set about trying to find it. First, we went back into our wing to look for a secret door somewhere and eventually found it behind the tapestry, but it was locked and so we had to find another way in. We spent absolutely ages looking for this place, believe me. We didn't know if it was connected to the secret link-up tunnel Dean is trying to find seeing as he was snooping around the boys' room the other day. I went up to examine the rooms above ours while Tom stayed downstairs to search the banquet hall. Eventually, he found the entrance hidden inside the fireplace when he was standing next to it and realised he couldn't feel a draught coming down the chimney. We didn't spend much time exploring the lower level though. It's not very nice down there." She said and Robbie grinned.

"Let me see." He insisted, excited at the chance to explore something *first* for once. Usually, bossy old Ashley always took that job, arguing that he should go ahead as the big brother to make sure the place wasn't dangerous. But this was just a *room;* there wasn't likely to be anything threatening in here, right? Surely Ashley would let him take the lead on this particular adventure?

Just as he'd expected, Ashley remained silent and Robbie eagerly descended down the spiral stairs, wondering what he might find once he reached the bottom. He was a bit surprised to discover a small table set up by the stained-glass window that housed various framed photographs, including a beautiful one of his parents on their wedding day.

He reached out to pick it up, tracing his thumb over the image sadly for a few moments before he turned to examine the other pictures. Next to the precious wedding photograph, he found one of himself and Michael as small children and smiled to himself faintly, pleased to see that they had been included in this room too since they were also connected to the manor through Ashley. In the photograph, Robbie could see his podgy young self sitting on a sandy beach and holding a crab up in front of his face while tiny Michael was attempting to build a sandcastle next to him. Ashley was also present in the background as he angrily chased after a seagull and Robbie chuckled, gently setting the picture back down on the table and turning to investigate what else was stored on this lower-level.

He came face-to-face with another terrifying, great black dog looming out of the darkness and automatically jumped backwards with a loud yell of shock. He ended up accidentally knocking over the table of special photographs behind him and gave another howl of misery as he fell down with it.

"Rob-? Are you okay? What are you *doing* down there?" Ashley called, alarmed by his brother's panicked cries and the almighty crash that had followed.

Thankfully, as Robbie lay sprawled out amongst the debris of smashed photo-frames and splintered wood, the satanic creature didn't move and he exhaled in relief when he realised that it was dead and stuffed. The beast's eyes may be glazed and motionless but it still had a really menacing, bloodthirsty look about it with its sharp teeth bared in a final, hungry snarl as it jumped out from the gloom. Robbie had thought that Shadow had quite a wild and savage appearance when they first met, but he was actually really small, tame and cute compared to this massive, nightmarish monster hidden away in the dark depths of the manor.

"Oh God." Robbie gasped, reaching up to press one hand over his heart as Ashley leaned over the railings above to peer down at him suspiciously.

"What's up?" He asked, having never heard Robbie scream like that before. What could possibly be hiding downstairs that would scare his tough little brother?

"Where is he?" Luke's voice called as he rushed down the spiral stairs with Bryony and Jenna to see what was going on.

"By the window." Ashley replied, leaning a little further over the railing as he tried to see what had frightened Robbie in the room below.

"Ah, there you are. What are you doing down there?" Luke asked, finally reaching the bottom of the stairs and eyeing Robbie critically.

"Bloody hell; I thought I was gonna die for a few seconds then." Robbie mumbled, accepting Luke's proffered hand and allowing the older boy to pull him back to his feet.

"Why? What happened?" Bryony demanded, padding over to lay a concerned hand on his shoulder.

"Turn round." Robbie instructed, a mischievous little smile slowly spreading across his face as he considered where the demonic creature had been displayed. It was obvious that someone in the Morgan family had developed the same kind of sadistic humour as him and Robbie was quite impressed by their evil genius. They had taken great care to place the beast in such a way that it remained cruelly hidden from view until you reached the bottom of the stairs and turned into the room properly, where you would suddenly find yourself confronted by a terrifying set of sharp teeth. Judging by the height of the creature, Robbie got the impression that it's eyes would also glint at you through the steps on your way back up too as a final creepy joke.

Jenna eyed him suspiciously for a moment before she turned to see what he found so amusing. On seeing the monstrous creature lurking behind the corner, she promptly screamed and turned to flee back up the spiral staircase while Luke and Bryony gasped and reached out to clutch at each other in shock.

Robbie couldn't help the wicked cackle that jumped into his throat as he watched their reaction and Luke turned to scowl at him in obvious disapproval.

"I worry about you sometimes." He muttered, shaking his head slightly before he turned to follow Bryony back upstairs, clearly keen to be away from the freaky dog.

"You say that a lot." Robbie commented, crouching down to tidy up the mess he'd made when he jumped backwards into the table.

Then, he padded over to examine the stuffed creature curiously, wondering which part of the Morgan history it belonged to. When had this evil beast roamed the landscape? He couldn't help thinking how Michael might have reacted if he'd encountered this demon out on the moors instead of Shadow. Most likely, his little brother would have just died on the spot in fright.

Glen had mentioned that Shadow was the latest in a long line of huge black dogs trained to serve the Morgans and this beast was clearly their favourite pet since they had chosen to preserve it after it died. The thing had the same kind of long, shaggy black fur as Shadow, but it was a *lot* bigger and had a very sinister aura even now. Shadow was only threatening in appearance and quite friendly when you got to know him, but this beast was obviously a terror in both looks and nature.

"You scared the life out of me. But you'll never manage it again; I know you're hiding down here now." Robbie hissed, giving the beast's plinth a firm kick in retaliation and feeling a bit stupid that he'd been completely petrified of a dead dog. He'd never been so scared in all his life, turning to find himself face-to-face with the creature and wondered if anyone had actually perished upon meeting it.

"Seriously, what's going on down there, Rob? Who are you talking to?" Ashley called, his curiosity obviously getting the better of him as his footsteps padded over towards the spiral stairs.

Robbie grinned, shrinking further back into the dingy old room as he waited to see how Ashley would react to the unpleasant surprise waiting for him at the bottom of the stairs.

Sure enough, Ashley gave an automatic howl of shock when he found the beast before he doubled over beside it, swearing softly as he tried to compose himself. Unfortunately for him, Shadow chose that moment to give a menacing growl at a spider that had emerged from the skirting board in the banquet hall, where he was still waiting beside the fireplace for them to return. His threatening growl seemed to boom through the wall towards Ashley and Robbie and also echoed up the chimney so that it sounded to be coming from all around.

Ashley screamed, turning to stare at the stuffed monster beside him before he fled back up the spiral stairs, tripping over himself slightly in his terror. Robbie, meanwhile, burst out laughing at his brother's misfortune and was unable to move for a few moments until he had calmed down a bit.

"Oh, thank-you, Shadow. That was fantastic. I've not laughed that much in years." He gasped, reaching up to wipe the tears off his face and weakly staggering back up to join the others on the floor above.

Luke had apparently collared Ashley at the top of the stairs because Robbie found him gripping Ashley's arms tightly and staring deep into his eyes with a rather protective look on his face.

"*Ashley,* it's okay. That was Shadow. Alright? *Shadow.* There's nothing to be scared of. Don't worry; you're safe." Luke murmured solemnly.

"Yeah, I *promise* you that thing's dead." Robbie muttered, feeling a little guilty now as he considered Ashley's fearful, wide eyes.

Ashley glanced between them a few times before he exhaled in relief and sank down to sit on the floor next to an old globe.

"Oh, Shadow, you bad boy. Don't you ever scare me like that again, please! Now I'm going to have nightmares for weeks. Well, *new* nightmares at least." Ashley complained, shaking his head in awkward embarrassment.

Michael frowned.

"I'm not sure I want to know what's downstairs if it managed to scare both you and Robbie. Normally you're pretty tough." He muttered, staring across at the spiral staircase anxiously.

Suzy offered Michael a friendly smile and reached out to wrap one arm around his shoulders.

"Hey, you don't have to go down there if you don't want to. I wouldn't blame you. It is quite scary. I went down with Tom too when we first found the room and I ended up fleeing in terror as well, just like Ashley did. Don't worry; I wouldn't say you're missing anything really important." She explained, thinking that Michael had been traumatised enough from his encounter with Shadow and that it wouldn't be at all healthy for him to venture downstairs and meet the other hellish beast.

Ashley nodded in agreement.

"Yeah, there's no way I'm letting you go down there. That would make me a really terrible sibling. And I'm not Robbie. I don't take pleasure in other people's misery." He muttered, looking a little calmer as he picked himself up off the floor and stretched.

Suzy reached out to pat him on the shoulder sympathetically before she turned to gesture round at the nearby displays.

"Come on. Let's see what else we can find up here. I can't believe your family has so many ancient portraits, Ashley; it's amazing! It must have cost an awful lot to have all these made, so they must have been very successful in their criminal adventures." She suggested and he nodded, awkwardly padding over to investigate the one of his father, uncle and aunt.

Clearly, this must have been painted shortly before Glen was cast out of the family because the portrait seemed to capture a lot of tension between the three siblings and Ashley thought that was really interesting. The portrait showed Dean and Glen seated together on a wooden bench and dressed in smart suits with matching green ties while Enid stood behind them in a beautiful green evening gown. But Dean and Glen looked to be seated as far apart as the bench would allow while Enid had a gentle hand placed on their shoulders as though silently warning them to behave. The three siblings may be smiling for their portrait but the atmosphere between them was definitely frosty to say the least.

Honourable Ancestors

It was Luke who eventually solved the mystery of Ashley's offensive middle names. He'd been idly wandering round the portrait gallery with Tom when a name engraved on one of the small plaques caught his eye and he leaned closer to squint at the lettering critically.

Just as he'd suspected, the man's name was 'Seth' and Luke frowned to himself as he turned to study his best friend across the room, who was currently peering into a so-called 'cabinet of curiosities' with Suzy and Rose.

"Hey, Ash-? Come over here a sec." Luke called, as Tom gave a faint gasp of shock beside him, having finally noticed why Luke found this particular portrait more fascinating than the others. "Look at this." Luke muttered, reaching out to show Ashley the names listed on the gilt frame.

"Oh my God. He has my name!" Ashley exclaimed and Tom gave a faint chuckle of amusement.

"I think it's more likely that you have his." He corrected and Luke nodded.

"Yeah, I don't think that's a coincidence. I reckon your mother decided to name you after some of your more honourable Morgan ancestors. See? If you match up the names to the people in the painting, the guy who should be Seth has been quite badly damaged, meaning he was one of the people who tried to make things better. So, if my theory is correct, there must be someone in this room called 'Hunter' as well to link up with your other middle name." He explained, pausing as he considered the way their friends were dotted around the room. "YO! ANYONE FOUND A 'HUNTER' AMONGST THESE OLD PICTURES?" He yelled, causing them all to jump slightly in fright.

"Yeah, he's over here." Robbie called back and Ashley's eyes widened.

"I don't understand. Why would Mum do that? Why would she name me after the honourable Morgan men? Surely she must have known that Dean would find her choices inappropriate." He mumbled and Luke smiled to himself.

"I imagine Heidi probably chose those names in the hope they might offer you some protection. She knew you were destined to join the Morgan family after all and that Dean would expect you to fall in line and follow the dark, criminal traditions. He must have brought Heidi up to the manor once while she was pregnant in order to try and impress her with the manor's grandeur and to demonstrate that he could provide for the baby. If that's true, it was probably before Enid had the portrait gallery sealed up. I can't picture Heidi climbing up that ladder while you were still growing in her belly." He replied, frowning slightly as he turned to eye the trapdoor they had used to access the room.

Tom laughed.

"No, but I *can* picture your father proudly gesturing round at all of his wicked relatives as he told Heidi their stories." He agreed, peering round at the grand room thoughtfully. "Of course, with your mother being the kind soul that she was, I expect she was more inspired to see the scratched-out portraits of the Morgans who tried to challenge the system. She must have asked Enid about them in order to avoid making Dean suspicious but, of course, seeing as Enid never received the same criminal schooling as her brothers she wouldn't have known the tales. So she probably had to collect them from Glen first before passing them on to Heidi. Maybe that was what kickstarted all of this research?" He theorised, watching as Ashley reached out to pick up the folder that lay on the sideboard directly underneath Seth.

"I guess it's time to find out what Mum found so impressive about these guys that meant she was willing to betray Dean and cut her own beloved father out of my name." He muttered, glancing round nervously as his friends all padded over to listen to Seth's grand tale as well.

Ashley was startled to learn that it had been Seth who paid for the locomotive they had found and paused to eye the man's damaged portrait admiringly. Enid had discovered the information in another local newspaper, along with a grainy photograph of her ancestor posing in front of the gleaming engine.

Seth had felt that it was time the dirty Morgan wealth was put to good use and hoped that the locomotive would help to give the local townsfolk a better life since it meant that coal from the new mine could be shipped out more quickly and in bigger quantities. He had even stipulated in writing when the engine was handed over to the mine officials that the labourers had to be paid a higher wage and given safer working conditions in exchange since the site wouldn't even function without them. But apparently, this wasn't good enough for Seth as he had gone on to help fund a new public library as well so that people could continue to better themselves and discover their own interests.

Understandably, the criminals had been absolutely livid when they found out what he had done with their money and so Seth had been cruelly stripped of all his belongings and sent to start a new life in America with nothing but his name, where he couldn't cause the family any more trouble. Then, the gang had begun plotting to reclaim the locomotive while Seth spent the next few years trying to survive in a wholly unfamiliar land.

The final page of Enid's research revealed that, sadly, Seth had been one of the men who died in the first world war and had been buried with his comrades at a cemetery in France. Enid had even managed to track down his grave and Ashley was rather lost for words as he stared down at the image. It seemed that Seth had been training as a doctor when the war broke out and felt so deeply compelled to help his fellow countrymen back home that he had volunteered his services at the earliest opportunity. He'd ended up being dispatched to the trenches and had dealt with a wide range of gruesome injuries and diseases and witnessed a tragic amount of death. But, thanks to his medical knowledge, determination and courage, a lot of the men he treated went on to survive and return home. Seth, however, hadn't been so lucky as he was killed in the summer of 1918, leaving his American wife to raise their young daughter all by herself.

It was Suzy who voiced what they were all thinking.

"I think you should be really proud to have been named after him." She remarked and Ashley gave a stiff little nod, taking a few deep breaths to compose himself before he raised one hand to give Seth's portrait a solemn salute.

"I'll come and find you one day, I swear. You deserve to be remembered with pride and not just for being a thorn in your relatives' lives. And on that note, I promise to finish what you started and return that locomotive to the community. Your struggles won't have been in vain." He declared and his friends turned to eye each other curiously as they considered his bold speech. Maybe Ashley *would* be the one to finally end the Morgans' reign of terror. He'd certainly been given the right motivation now at least.

Ashley could easily understand why his mother had chosen to name him after the man. The message he got from Seth was that you should never give up and that you must always help people if you can. It was a really powerful idea and Ashley knew he would never forget it.

Inspired, he wandered over to locate the other person he had been named after, eventually locating Hunter in a portrait that dated to the fourteenth century. Apparently, he'd been the youngest of five siblings and had once been a very important member of the family since he was positioned in the middle of the painting. Hunter was standing with a longbow held horizontally in front of his waist and was even pulling back slightly on the arrow he had fitted onto the bowstring. His two sisters were positioned on either side of him while his two brothers stood at opposite ends of the canvas, meaning all five siblings were protected behind Hunter's bow.

The three men had a sword fixed at their side too while the two women were adorned in expensive jewellery and looked as though they could rival any royal princess. Even now, after seven hundred years, the message was easy to understand. The portrait was designed to show that the Morgans were well defended and shouldn't be messed with. Ashley found it rather distasteful. He didn't like to think of his ancestors lording themselves over people but you couldn't just sweep history under a rug and pretend it had never happened. The whole point of history was about learning where you had come from and making sure past mistakes were never repeated.

He couldn't believe that his ancestors had once lived in a castle and been considered part of the nobility. He was even more surprised to read that his family had acquired their lands following a heroic victory in battle and that the castle's first residents had been very kind and respectful. Unfortunately, that ended when one lord died without leaving any heirs and the castle had fallen into the hands of his greedy brother instead. Emyr was the one credited with causing the Morgans' spiral down into darkness and, as yet, no-one had successfully managed to haul them back up into the light.

Enid's research folder on Hunter revealed that, just as his name implied, the man had been tasked with providing the Morgans with meat and using his fearsome archery skills to defend them when necessary. Therefore, Hunter had spent most of his time roaming the landscape and had developed a deep appreciation for the ancient forest and the changing seasons. He knew every plant and tree and how to use them, both for good and for evil and had fought hard to keep the old pagan festivals alive, which had caused a great deal of consternation. Hunter had been the first member of the family to challenge the system and was still commemorated in a local nursery rhyme, except the locals seemed to have forgotten the fact that he was a Morgan.

Hunter had seen the hardships people faced thanks to his wicked relatives and had vowed to do everything in his power to help them. He'd been horrified to witness people being forced in starvation as the Morgans demanded they pay their respects, literally, by handing over everything they owned. Hunter couldn't stand it. He thought it was absolutely disgusting that he came home to a feast every night while the people in the surrounding villages barely had enough food for one person, let alone a whole family.

Therefore, Hunter had begun to teach the locals everything he knew about the forest so that they would be able to support themselves a little better and wouldn't have to rely so heavily on their cattle and the yearly harvest, both of which would later be claimed by his greedy relatives anyway. In those days, the woods were still considered a wild and terrifying place full of savage beasts, but Hunter wanted to show people that wasn't the case. The only 'beasts' that he knew of lived in the Morgan castle. Hunter had been rather amused when the people who had relentlessly mocked him for following 'the old ways' were now praising him for helping to save their lives.

He had also begun to leave the villagers gifts from his various hunting trips in a secret place which was still known as 'Archer's Cave' to this day. This little arrangement had continued for three glorious years, with Hunter calmly fobbing his relatives off by telling them that the colder weather was making it harder to secure food as the animals changed their grazing patterns, bushes produced fewer berries and storms wreaked havoc with the harvest.

Eventually though, the Morgans had grown tired of their 'measly' rations and Hunter had been enraged to discover that his relatives planned on demanding higher taxes from the local population in exchange for their ongoing protection, just so they could enjoy the same grand feasts as before.

Therefore, he spent the next few weeks quietly stealing weapons from the castle stores and depositing them in his secret cave for the locals to collect before he led a dangerous revolt against his abusive family that caused one of the keep towers to go up in flames.

Unfortunately, Hunter had been captured when his four siblings cornered him in the castle's grand old reception hall. Of course, being the family's best archer and swordsman, Hunter had given his brothers and sisters quite the run for their money, but they had eventually succeeded in overpowering him and Hunter had been thrown in the castle's underground prison.

His family had been equally enraged to learn that, as well as stealing most of their weapons, Hunter had also managed to half-empty the castle treasury without them noticing and spent the next couple of weeks questioning him on where the money was now. But Hunter had never answered them directly, merely repeating the same cryptic riddle each time they came to torture him. He had even carved the message onto the wall of his cell and took great delight in the fact that his relatives couldn't work it out.

He wasn't stupid. He'd known that his family was strong and tough and that there was a chance his revolt might not go the way he wanted. So, the treasure had been his insurance policy. Therefore, if things did go horribly wrong and he lost the battle, he would have still won the war in the sense that his family would be left much poorer and less able to defend themselves. But, if the revolt had been successful and Hunter had managed to dispatch his wicked relatives and install himself as the castle's new lord, then the money would be distributed fairly amongst the villagers.

Eventually, seeing as he refused to co-operate, Hunter's relatives had had him executed for his treacherous behaviour and his body was dumped in an unmarked grave outside the castle walls. He had died in flames as his family had thought it would be quite poetic for him to meet the same fate as the keep tower that had been set alight during his revolt. They also hoped the fire would cleanse Hunter's soul and prevent his angelic madness from spreading to anyone else.

Unfortunately, Hunter had returned to haunt them since his treasure remained undiscovered and Enid had written in her notes that the man was still armed with a sword, longbow and arrows in the afterlife since those objects had been such an important part of his life. He was also permanently encased in smoke and glowing embers and accompanied by a sharp crackling noise that represented the way he died. Furthermore, since Hunter's portrait had been so badly damaged, his ghost now had no visible face either, only a suffocating mass of shadows in the space between his shoulder-length black hair, ears and neck.

Even now, seven hundred years later, he continued to repeat the same infuriating message to anyone who came seeking his treasure and Ashley smiled to himself as he considered the man's stubborn defiance. He thought that Hunter's story was absolutely extraordinary and was fascinated by the way his ancestor was still honoured in a local nursery rhyme. He was also really excited to learn that he might actually be able to meet the heroic figure he'd been named after and wondered what the man would make of him. Would he be proud or would he just think that Ashley was a big disappointment?

According to Enid's research, it had taken the Morgans a long time to recover from the damage Hunter had caused and his legacy was one of the reasons why the castle had been abandoned, in addition to it becoming rather old-fashioned. After all, Hunter had not only let the building go up in flames, but he had also taken away the money needed to repair it and continued to haunt the site from the afterlife, so his family did not like him one bit.

Ashley, meanwhile, was very proud. He could see now why his mother had chosen to give him the name 'Hunter' and also understood why his father had taken such a violent disliking to his birth certificate. He was amazed that Hunter's treasure still hadn't been found after seven hundred years and understood that the ghostly archer obviously felt that anyone seeking his goods must first prove themselves worthy of it. Instead of just hoarding the goods, they would be more likely to finish his mission and Ashley really hoped that he would be the one to finally uncover the goods. First though, he had to honour Seth's memory by protecting the stolen train from Dean.

Recognising the grim look on Ashley's face, Tom padded over to lay a gentle hand on his arm.

"There is one more thing we should tell you." He began, waiting until he had Ashley's full attention. "We found the secret passage to the train tunnel that Dean has been looking for." He announced and Ashley's eyes widened.

"Are you serious?" He gasped and Tom nodded.

"Yep. Oh, and get this. We've been walking over it for days. So I think Suzy is right about our wing of the manor once being the criminals' headquarters." He grinned and Ashley turned to frown at him in confusion as he tried to imagine where the tunnel could possibly be hiding.

"Show me." He insisted, annoyed when Tom shook his head.

"I think it's better we save that for tomorrow now. We've all had a pretty long day, so I vote we get some rest first and explore the tunnel properly in the morning. I don't think Dean has found it yet so we can afford a little break. To be quite frank, Ash, I don't know how you're still standing after spending the past two nights wandering through the forest. Besides, I'm still not quite sure what to do about the tunnel seeing as the police didn't believe me when we tried to report it. I'd imagine we would need an *actual adult* to explain what we've found but Glen seemed to think the place should stay hidden and I don't imagine Enid would be too happy to learn what we've been doing the past few days. For now, I'm thinking we should sleep on the problem and attack it with fresh minds tomorrow." He argued and Ashley huffed.

Mad Runaway

It was almost two a.m. when Luke stirred, roused from his sleep by the soft click of the bedroom door as it was pulled shut. This was now the third night in a row that he'd lost sleep and he was quite surprised he'd actually woken up at all.

Yawning slightly, he sat up and gazed around the room to try and figure out what had woken him. For a few moments, everything was just a dark and confusing blur until his eyes managed to focus properly and revealed Tom still fast asleep in his bed by the window. Across the room, Luke could also make out Robbie and Michael still buried under the covers in their own bunks and smiled to himself as Michael gave a cute little snuffle of contentment. Shadow, their new canine friend, was curled up on the floor by the old fireplace with his great shaggy black tail flicked over his body like a blanket, which meant there was just Ashley to check on before all the boys were accounted for.

Luke wearily hauled himself out of bed and turned to climb up the narrow ladder that led to Ashley's bunk. When he reached the top, he discovered that it was completely empty and frowned to himself suspiciously. Ashley's nightclothes were neatly folded up on his pillow, along with a piece of paper that had obviously been torn out of his precious journal.

"What are you up to now, Ashley, you maniac?" Luke muttered, leaning over to snatch up the handwritten note and eyeing it critically:

Hey Guys,

I'm going out into the forest to look for my father because we really need to talk. I've learnt a great deal about my past these last few days and it has left me feeling quite confused and angry. There are a lot of things I still don't understand, so I want to find Dean and get some answers.

Don't worry about me; I can take care of myself. And please don't follow me, LUKE. This is something I have to do on my own. It's family business and likely to become pretty heated, so I don't want to risk anyone getting hurt by letting you tag along with me. I'd never forgive myself.

See you soon,

Ashley

Alarmed, Luke jumped down off the bed and set about quickly pulling on his boots, not caring at all if he woke up the other guys in the process. Ashley may have ordered Luke not to follow him this time, but he didn't seem to be in his right mind at the moment, so Luke decided he should probably go and rescue his foolish best friend before things got really dangerous. How could Ashley possibly think going off in the middle of the night alone to look for his murderous father was a *good* idea?

Thankfully, seeing as Ashley had accidentally woken him up on his way out, he couldn't have gone very far, so Luke was confident he'd be able to catch up in no time. He reached out to grab a thick hoodie from the end of his bed before he roughly flung the door open and sprinted off down the hallway.

He was so focused on chasing Ashley down that he never noticed the girls' bedroom door open a crack as Bryony poked her head out to investigate who was making all the noise. Seeing the look of grim determination plastered across Luke's face as he passed, she decided to head out as well to find out what was happening.

By the time she'd fastened her boots and pulled on her jacket, Luke was already gone and Bryony hurried out into the night after him, pausing to pull the front door closed again since he'd just left it wide open in his panicked haste.

"Ashley-! Where are you going? Come back!" Luke's angry voice yelled from somewhere in the distance. Judging from the direction it had come from, it seemed like he had taken the narrow forest path that led up towards the old mine and Bryony rushed to follow him, startled by the news that Ashley was apparently out here as well.

Eventually, she spotted Luke's dark figure up ahead and put on a burst of speed to try and catch up, not wanting to get lost out here on her own.

"Hey, wait up! What's this all about?" She called, completely bewildered by their peculiar behaviour. Almost immediately, a surprised howl floated back from further up the trail as Ashley twisted round to investigate the noise and discovered he was being followed. He promptly turned to flee deeper into the forest with Luke hot on his heels and Bryony frowned in silent confusion.

"Get back here right now, Ashley, you idiot!" Luke roared, his torchlight bouncing around all over the place as he ran and making it quite difficult for Bryony to figure out where she was going since he kept accidentally blinding her.

"God-dammit, Luke, I told you not to come! Why can't you just leave me alone for once? I'm not that much younger than you! Stop treating me like a baby!" Ashley shouted back, skilfully vaulting over a fallen branch and giving a wicked cackle as Luke had to slow down to climb around it instead.

Unfortunately for him, Luke wasn't about to give up that easily. Ashley may be a lot more flexible and agile, but Luke had always been superior when it came to speed so it didn't take him long to catch up again.

"What's going on with you tonight? Have you gone insane?" He demanded, roughly tackling Ashley round the waist and bringing them both crashing down onto the dirty forest floor.

Ashley groaned, struggling against Luke furiously as he tried to free himself. Why did his best friend have to be so damn strong?

"Let go of me!" He howled, getting absolutely covered in mud and damp leaves as they rolled around together.

Bryony stared at them in shock. She'd never seen Luke and Ashley fight like this before and wondered what could have provoked such a violent reaction. She couldn't decide whether she should step in and try to separate the two boys or leave them alone to work through their issues, so she ended up hovering uncertainly nearby while she debated the situation.

Eventually, following a pained grunt and leafy thud, she looked up to find Luke sprawled out on the ground and gently rubbing his stomach while Ashley sprinted off into the forest.

"Oh no you don't." Luke growled, angrily picking himself up out of the dirt and chasing after him again. Obviously, he would have to be a lot more cunning and unpredictable if he wanted to get Ashley safely back to the manor without attracting Dean's attention in the process from all the noise they were making.

This time, instead of simply launching himself at his mad friend, Luke reached out to grab hold of Ashley's wrist, causing him to give another loud yell of surprise as he was roughly hauled back round to face Luke. He barely had time to register this new development before Luke lifted him off the ground with ease, simply crouching down and pulling Ashley forwards across his shoulders like a firefighter.

Ashley gasped, shocked that Luke had managed to immobilise him so quickly and reaching out to smack him a few times with his spare hand. Now, with one leg and one wrist firmly trapped in Luke's iron grip, it was a lot harder to fight back and Ashley eventually had to admit defeat.

"LUKE MATTHEWS, YOU PUT ME DOWN RIGHT NOW." He howled, giving his best friend a few angry kicks as a punishment for kidnapping him like this as though he were a disobedient child.

Luke shook his head, taking a moment to adjust Ashley's weight across his shoulders before he turned to head back the way they had come.

"No, Ashley. You're a mess. I'm taking you back to the manor and we're going to have a long chat about all of this. What made you decide to go looking for Dean? Why not talk to your aunt and uncle instead? I'm sure they could answer your questions too." Luke scolded, peering round at Ashley worriedly as the boy continued to mutter and swear under his breath, clearly furious at having his plans ruined. "Come on, buddy, talk to me. I just want to help." He pleaded, adopting a gentler tone of voice in the hope that it might make Ashley feel more comfortable.

"What's going on? Why have you fallen out?" Bryony asked as they finally re-joined her in the muddy little clearing where they'd first fought.

Luke sighed.

"Hey Bry. Sorry you had to see that. Ashley thought it was a good idea to go looking for his father all by himself in the middle of the night. He just left a note behind to explain his absence and then scarpered." He explained and Ashley meekly curled over a little further on Luke's shoulders to try and hide himself.

"Why would you do that? Are you mad? You could have been killed!" Bryony demanded, staring up at Ashley in horror.

"Ugh..." Ashley grumbled, hating to be lectured like this and feeling even more embarrassed at being stuck up on Luke's shoulders now that Bryony was around too. "Please, Luke, just put me down! You're hurting me! I *promise* not to run away again. Really, I won't." He begged, squirming slightly as he tried to free himself.

Luke merely huffed.

"No, I'm not putting you down. Not until you tell me what's going on. And you hurt *me* too when you kneed me in the stomach, so I'd say we're even." He answered, sharply turning his head away from Ashley to make his displeasure a little more venomous.

"Okay, *fine,* I'll talk. I went looking for Dean because I'm really confused. I've spent my entire life believing that he tried to kill me that night but then we found a whole album full of pictures up in the attic that showed him taking care of me. Then, yesterday, we found out that my middle names are *also* connected to this stupid place. Now I don't know what to think and it's driving me crazy. I just feel like a pawn in a giant game of chess or something, like my whole life has been planned out from the moment I was born. I need to know the truth of what happened that night. Over the past few days, I've begun to wonder if Dean was actually aiming for Robbie under the bed and I got hurt by mistake. Did he not know I was under there too? Tom did say that I would have blended into the shadows quite well with my black hair. Was Dean just trying to steal me back from Heidi so that I could be raised *properly*, like all the other Morgan kids? Nothing makes sense anymore, so I wanted to find my father to try and get some answers because he's the only one who knows the truth. I *need* to know if I was supposed to die too that night, or whether my facial injury was just a horrible accident. I get now why Dean is so offended by my middle names but maybe he hoped to disrespect Hunter and Seth even further by raising me to be a criminal despite Mum's efforts to try and protect me. Perhaps Dean saw her betrayal as an opportunity to slander their legacies even further; I don't know. Besides, if the family really is as thin now as Enid claims, then why would Dean even want me dead? That would just push the Morgans even closer to extinction and I can't see that *his* father would be too pleased with that. It's all just so complicated and I don't know what to make of it." Ashley muttered, staring down at Luke's feet as he talked to avoid seeing the judgemental expressions on his friends' faces.

Bryony turned to share a look of silent concern with Luke before she reached out to affectionately tousle Ashley's hair.

"I don't think it matters whether Dean meant to hurt you that night or not. You shouldn't start visualising him as a good person just because your scar *might* have been an accident. Dean still killed your mother and stepfather and wounded your little brother, so I'd focus more on that if I were you. Don't let your guard down now by deciding that Dean's not a threat to you. For all we know, he *did* try to kill you that night and that makes him really dangerous. Don't forget he also hit you in the face last night as well. That definitely wasn't an accident. And I'd say the photos in that album are more abusive than caring. The few that I saw anyway. Just because Dean held you occasionally and spent time with you doesn't make him trustworthy. Have you forgotten why your mother ran away from him? You said that she caught Dean smacking you quite violently and that you were terrified of him. I can certainly imagine that progressing to attempted murder." She scolded and

Luke nodded, giving the back of Ashley's captive leg a few gentle pats to show that he understood Ashley's confusion and wanted to help.

"I agree. Besides, how would you even *know* if Dean was telling you the truth? You were really small when Heidi and Ethan were murdered, so Dean could spin whatever story he likes to suit his current purpose. If he wants you out of the way, then he'd say yes; you were supposed to die too that night. But if he's still interested in trying to make you the next generation of Morgan criminals, then of course he would say no; you weren't meant to get hurt. I reckon his answer would depend on what he wants now, rather than what actually happened back then, so it's not worth the hassle. He'd only end up breaking your heart again if his answer wasn't the one you wanted to hear. Don't put yourself through that." Luke reasoned, awkwardly carrying Ashley back over the fallen branch and taking great care not to whack his head on anything.

"Yeah! What if you *had* managed to locate your father out here in the forest and ended up getting attacked again? Maybe Dean's just been biding his time until he could finally get you alone. We don't know. You could have been waiting in pain for hours before anyone woke up and discovered your note and then it would have taken a while until we actually found you. Please, Ashley, don't ever run away like that again. Just talk to us, like Luke said. Even if we can't give you the answers you need, you'd surely feel a lot better by voicing your concerns than keeping them bottled up inside. You might have been named after Hunter and Seth and have their blood flowing through your veins but that doesn't make you invincible." Bryony added and he rolled his eyes.

"Oh, please. I can take care of myself." He grumbled and Luke snorted.

"Really? Then how come you're currently trapped up there on my shoulders if you can take care of yourself so well?" He retorted, shaking his head slightly at the way Ashley thought he was really powerful.

"That's because you're a sneaky little rat." Ashley complained, sourly.

"And Dean isn't?" Luke challenged, raising his eyebrow slightly at Ashley's delusional ideas.

Bryony eyed them curiously for a moment, amazed at Luke's strength since he was obviously capable of carrying tall Ashley round for a long time without it hurting very much.

"Well, I'm glad Luke is a 'sneaky little rat' or we might still be chasing you through the forest, you bad boy! Seriously, Luke, how are you even doing that?" She replied, staring up at Ashley in wonder as Luke carried him further down the moonlit path.

Luke smirked, obviously quite proud of his kidnapping abilities.

"Ashley may be the tallest member of our group, but he's actually really light. It's weird." He answered, peering round at his friend anxiously for a few moments as he tried to understand Ashley's shocking behaviour. "I reckon you just need some rest. I know you didn't get much sleep before the holiday seeing as you were worrying about it so much and then you've spent the past few nights roaming the forest and napping outside in the cold air. It's not good for you. Obviously, I'm no doctor, but I think you'll be able to make sense of things more once you've had a really nice, long sleep. At the moment, you're like a totally different person and I don't know how this new Ashley works." He added, pausing as a deep, menacing growl echoed through the trees towards them.

Ashley frowned, raising his head up off Luke's shoulder to examine their surroundings.

"Was that Shadow? What's *he* doing out here? Has everyone come to watch my humiliation now? That's just what I need." He asked and Luke chuckled.

"Well, you do seem to be his new Master so it's only logical that he would keep following you around." He muttered, wondering if Shadow's threatening growl had been a demand for him to release Ashley. "It's alright, boy. I'm not going to hurt him, I promise! Where are you anyway? Come out and join us." He called, alarmed when a series of hostile, angry barks floated back a few moments later.

Confused, Bryony turned to survey the area with her torch, expecting to find Shadow hunched down in the bushes somewhere and frowning when she discovered that everything looked normal.

"But...how did he even get out? I closed the front door behind me when I left!" She protested and Luke shrugged.

"I don't know. He was still fast asleep in the boys' room when I ran out. Maybe someone else found Ashley's mad note and brought Shadow out to help look for him? Actually, why didn't I think of doing that? Shadow would have made things a lot easier." He muttered, shaking his head slightly at his stupidity.

Bryony smiled to herself before she reached out towards Luke expectantly.

"Luke, where's your phone? If someone else *is* out here looking for Ashley, then we should probably let them know he's safe. There's no point anyone getting unnecessarily cold and wet when we're already on our way back. But I left in such a hurry that I accidentally left my phone behind on the nightstand so I can't send anyone a message." She asked and he frowned.

"Don't look at me. My phone's still back at the manor as well. I loaned it to Rose when hers fell into a bog." He answered and Bryony sighed.

"Oh, for heavens' sake..." She muttered, boldly reaching out to pluck Ashley's phone from his pocket instead and quickly typing in his passcode.

"Hey-!" Ashley protested, glaring at her indignantly and reaching out to try and snatch his phone back. Luke had already stolen his dignity by forcefully carrying him through the forest, so there was no need for Bryony to add to his misery by nicking his phone as well. That was just *mean*.

"All done." Bryony announced as she calmly posted a message on their group-chat before turning to place the phone in Ashley's outstretched hand.

"Thank-you." He snapped, eyeing her suspiciously as he shoved the device back in his pocket. He was quite shocked to learn that Bryony somehow knew his passcode and decided that he would have to change it pronto. He didn't want anyone else rudely breaking into his phone.

They continued in awkward silence for a few minutes before they finally arrived back at the manor, where Bryony helpfully rushed ahead to open the front door seeing as Luke didn't have any free hands and Ashley was clearly feeling uncooperative.

"Thanks." Luke muttered, carefully carrying his grumpy best friend through into the banquet hall before turning to continue onwards into their gloomy wing of the manor. He was so busy making sure he didn't whack Ashley's head on anything that he never noticed the rug outside their bedrooms was now slightly loose.

"Here, let me get that for you." Bryony whispered, quietly dodging past them to open the boys' bedroom door and gasping when she found *all* of her friends gathered together in the room and looking somewhat moody and defeated. "Hello, what's going on here? And where's Shadow?" She asked, padding over to sit beside Tom and staring round at them expectantly. Since they'd heard Shadow barking outside in the forest, she was quite surprised to find all of her friends accounted for and wondered what she had missed.

"Where the hell have you been?" Tom demanded and she blinked.

"Didn't you get my message? Well, *Ashley's* message since I sent it from his phone. I told you that we were outside in the forest and we'd be back soon." She replied and he promptly leaned over to snatch his own phone up from the windowsill. Sure enough, there was a message from Ashley on the screen and he frowned slightly as he read through it.

"Right, so I see. Sorry, Bry. It's been a bit chaotic around here." He mumbled, looking up in quiet concern as Luke finally appeared in the doorway with Ashley slung across his shoulders.

"Bloody hell, Luke; just put me down already, will you? This is embarrassing!" Ashley whined, scowling as his friends all turned to eye him in concern, with Jenna even rushing over to examine him for wounds.

"Oh! What happened to you? Did you get hurt?" She asked and Ashley sniffed.

"No, only my pride. Luke seems to think I'm a bloody baby." He complained as Luke carried him across the room before crouching down to set him back on his feet beside their bunk-bed.

"I didn't say you were a *baby*. I said you were an *idiot.*" Luke corrected, offering Ashley a stern look before he reached up to pluck the discarded note off Ashley's bed where he'd left it. "This stupid fool decided to go traipsing off into the forest all by himself to look for his wicked father. So I kidnapped him before he could get into trouble." He explained and Jenna gasped, turning to stare at Ashley in horror.

"Why would you do that? Are you mad? You could have been killed!" She exclaimed and Bryony smiled to herself slightly.

"That's what *I* said." She muttered, amused that her sister had given the exact same reply since they didn't normally have much of a special, twin-like bond.

"Ugh, leave me alone." Ashley grumbled, climbing up to perch on the edge of his bed and glaring round at them all.

Robbie eyed his big brother critically for a moment before he gestured out into the hallway.

"Funnily enough, you just missed Dean. He was here with the rest of his gang. That's why we're all awake." He explained and Ashley promptly let out a furious howl.

"Are you kidding me? Of course he'd come snooping around *here* just when I decide to go out *there* to look for him. Bloody typical!" He muttered, shaking his head in disgust as he considered his pointless midnight adventure. He should have just stayed put.

Missing Key

"What do you mean 'Dean was just here'? I didn't see anyone on my way in." Luke asked, peering back out into the hallway expectantly.

Robbie sighed, one arm wrapped protectively around Michael's shoulders as he sat on the bed beside his little brother.

"No, he's already gone. As it happens, the secret passage to the train tunnel is just out there in the hallway under that long rug. Tom and Suzy found it yesterday but then we found out about Ashley's middle names and Tom decided to wait until this morning instead to show us where it was. But Dean must also have discovered the secret passage at some point because he came back with his entire gang to go and investigate the tunnel now, while we were all asleep. Unfortunately, as you know, the floorboards out there are really creaky, so we got woken up by them and Shadow went berserk when he realised that Ashley was missing and Dean was just outside the room." He began, giving Michael a gentle hug.

Ashley frowned, noticing for the first time that Michael looked to be trembling slightly while Robbie was clearly trying to comfort him.

"What happened?" He growled, staring across at them intently and feeling his blood starting to boil again at the thought of Dean coming in to harm his siblings while he was off exploring the forest. How could he have left them unprotected like that? He must be the worst big brother in the world.

Michael sniffed.

"Obviously, when Dean heard Shadow barking and snarling, he came in here to investigate and was absolutely furious when he discovered that we'd stolen his precious guard-dog. Shadow was dragged off outside by one of Dean's henchmen while he stomped around looking for you. He was really angry and called you all kinds of horrible names. Eventually, when he couldn't find you, he turned on me instead, roughly hauling me out of bed and screaming insults in my face. I still don't understand how he knows my name. Dean only stopped yelling at me when Robbie dived on him from the top bunk. Honestly, I've never seen Robbie look so dangerous; it was amazing how he saved me! I would never have had the courage to tackle Dean like that, but *he* did." He explained and Robbie shrugged.

"Yes, well. *No-one* hurts my little brother and gets away with it. Especially not Dean." He declared, fondly tapping Michael on the nose.

Ashley cringed, feeling immensely guilty as he padded over to join them.

"I'm sorry. I should have been here to protect you." He mumbled, dropping to his knees in front of them and reaching out to pull them both into a tight hug. Robbie automatically pulled a face before he seemed to reconsider and awkwardly reached round to pat Ashley on the back.

"Actually, I'm kind of glad you weren't around. You could have been seriously hurt." He admitted and Ashley frowned.

"Wait; is that *affection* I hear in your voice?" He asked, thinking he must have misheard somehow. Robbie wasn't often nice to him like this and even when he was it usually meant that he was up to something.

"Don't get used to it." Robbie muttered, reaching out to give Ashley a fond tap on the nose too before pushing him away.

Luke smiled.

"I get it now. We heard Shadow growling and barking outside in the forest on our way back and wondered what was going on. I just assumed he was mad at me for kidnapping his beloved master, but he must have been struggling against Dean's mate instead." He muttered, glancing round at Bryony as she threw her hands up into the air in disbelief.

"So, what-? Are you just going to sit back and let Dean win? After all our hard work? I don't think so. Come on Robbie, there must be *something* you can think of to help us protect that old train. You're the one who's always dreaming up all those nasty tricks and stuff; surely you can't be so easily defeated this time?" She pleaded, staring round at them in dismay.

"Hey, don't blame me! I don't do spontaneous. All of my tricks take devious planning and even then half of them don't work or Ashley sees straight through them. I can't just come up with a master-plan to outwit Dean off the top of my head, you know! Why do you think I'm tearing my hair out here? Of course I don't want Dean to win, but I don't see how we can stop him. He's probably already in the train tunnel by now." Robbie argued, glaring back at her indignantly.

Tom sighed, padding over to plant himself in the doorway and spreading his arms out to stop them from leaving.

"Don't you think this has gone too far? Dean is a *criminal* and we could get badly hurt or worse if we keep going after him like this. Don't you think that *our lives* are worth more than the entire value of that stolen locomotive and its coal wagons?" He asked and Robbie raised his eyebrow.

"You're not *that* valuable, Tom. Come on! Who do you think you are, the Prime Minister? Get over yourself, man." He scoffed, amused that Tom seemed to think he was really important.

"No, I'm saying that we are irreplaceable so we should be careful. There's only *one* Tom Hayes, *one* Robbie Slater, *one* Ashley Morgan and so on. We're all unique and that makes us valuable. What would happen if you died? It's not like your guardian could just go out and buy another one of you from the shops. If you die, that's it, game over. You can't just reset and try again. As far as the locals are concerned, the stolen train is already gone, so it's not like we've lost much if Dean reclaims the tunnel." Tom argued, reasonably.

Ashley considered this for a few moments before he stood up, a look of fiery determination in his eyes as he gazed round at them.

"Nope. Sorry, Tom, but I disagree. You can stay here if you like but I will *not* let my father get away with another evil crime. It's about time he was made to face the music in my opinion." He declared, causing Luke to peer round at him curiously since it sounded like Ashley had finally come to his senses. "Look, I admit this is dangerous. I don't think we fully realised what we were getting into when we first stumbled across this lost treasure-hoard and learned there were others seeking it too. Back then it was just an exciting adventure. But we're in this too deep now to just turn around and give up. We'd be no better than Dean if we just sat idly by and *let* him take control of the train tunnel. Wouldn't that make us accomplices in the eyes of the law? I certainly don't want to be associated with my father that way and have everyone thinking I'm wicked and selfish too. So I'm going to do everything in my power to make sure he never succeeds. Come on, who's with me?" Ashley finished, looking round at them expectantly.

Luke nodded, eyeing his best friend proudly.

"I'm in. But you know that already." He smiled, padding over to join Ashley in the middle of the room.

Robbie frowned, staring across at them incredulously.

"Seriously, Luke? You were literally *just* complaining about Ashley going out to look for Dean and fretting that he might get hurt. Yet now, when he suggested doing the exact same thing, you were supportive of the idea instead. I swear, some days you make no sense at all." He exclaimed and Luke rolled his eyes.

"Yes, Ashley going out *by himself* to look for Dean was a bad idea. But this is different. We actually know where Dean is going to be, so there's less chance of him sneaking up on us. That was the dangerous aspect of Ashley's solo mission. Plus, if we tackle him as a team, then we can look after each other and we have a much broader range of skills available." He pointed out, watching Robbie quietly as he waited for the boy's answer.

"Alright then. Count me in. I've also got a score to settle with Ashley's father, remember?" Robbie muttered, tapping his scarred forearm darkly.

One by one, the others all voiced their support too and Ashley looked round at them in silent admiration. He couldn't believe they were willing to help him fight against Dean and decided they must be a lot braver than he'd ever realised.

Bryony turned to Tom and Suzy intently.

"So where is this secret passage? I'd really like to see it." She asked and Suzy obediently stood up to lead her out into the gloomy hallway, with Ashley, Luke, Michael and Rose also following behind for a curious nosy.

"It's right here." Suzy announced, pausing beside an old chest and gesturing down at the long, patterned rug that lay in front of it. "I've been tripping over this thing all week since it curls up slightly at one corner. So, when I was exploring the manor earlier with Tom, I thought I'd kneel down and see if there was a way to flatten it a bit more and make it less of a hazard. That's when I discovered *another* trapdoor hidden underneath it. Honestly, this old house is obsessed with trapdoors. That's four we've found now since we arrived! So, as you can see, we both had quite a productive day. Tom found the secret entrance to the Morgan gallery while I found this one that leads to the train tunnel." She explained, gazing round at them proudly.

Bryony crouched down to examine the rug for a few moments before she pushed it back out of the way.

"Are you sure this goes to the train tunnel?" She asked and Suzy nodded.

"Yes. Tom climbed down with a torch to find out where it went and saw you guys walk past through a narrow grate in the wall. He said that he tried to open the passage door so he could call out to you, but it wouldn't budge." She replied as Luke and Ashley also dropped down beside Bryony to investigate the worn old trapdoor.

"Interesting." Luke mumbled, wondering how successful the criminals would be in accessing the tunnel.

"So, are Dean and his mates still down there?" Ashley asked and Tom nodded, having sauntered out from the boys' room to supervise their activities seeing as he was the eldest.

"Yeah, they are. But don't worry. I think we've got a bit of time yet before the gang return from the tunnel. They need to investigate the place first before they can come back with vans and retrieve the stolen goods. Plus our rope ladder isn't down yet and they don't know about the door you found at the other end, so they would *have* to come back this way. We just pulled the rug back over to make it harder for them to escape since it's quite heavy. I think Dean must have done the same thing as me when Suzy and I found the tunnel. He probably found it by himself and went down to check it out. As Suzy said, there's a small air-vent in the tunnel wall and you can see through it to the old locomotive, so Dean wouldn't have had to go all the way down the passage to find out it was the one he needed. And now, he's come back at night to explore it further with his gang, just like we were waiting to share it with you guys." He answered, grimly.

"Yes, well, now he's going to wish he'd never found it." Ashley muttered, frowning as he reached out to curl his fingers through the trapdoor handle before roughly hauling it open.

Bryony wrinkled her nose in disgust as she peered down into the gloomy shaft. She reckoned it must be at least twenty feet deep and couldn't believe she'd been happily walking over it the past few days. Access was provided by a rusty ladder that was partly hanging off the wall, while the other side of the hole hosted a series of sharp metal hooks. Bryony supposed these must have been installed as lantern-holders at some point to make the climb a bit easier.

"That does not look at all safe." She remarked, cautiously reaching down to tug on the ladder with one hand. "Did you really climb down that, Tom? What were you thinking? You're supposed to be the sensible one!" She exclaimed, looking round expectantly as Ashley reached over to grab her hand and pulled it back.

"Hey, don't go and make it worse!" He scolded while Tom gave a small shrug.

"I did, but I was very careful." He argued and Bryony huffed.

"Stupid, more like." She grumbled, shaking her head at him in disbelief.

"What's that sticking out of the wall halfway down?" Luke asked, reaching down to point at something with one hand and squinting slightly as he tried to make out what it was.

Ashley obediently reached round to dig his phone out of his pocket and switched on the torch function before shining the light down the hole to see what Luke had spotted.

"How on earth did you notice that in the dark?" He asked, turning to stare at his best friend critically.

"Help me down will you, Tom? I really want to know what that thing is." Luke asked and Bryony gasped.

"*No.* Don't be silly, Luke. That ladder is way too dangerous! You shouldn't risk it." She protested and Luke grinned.

"I never said I was planning on using the ladder. We can just adopt the same method we used to access the attic but the other way around. Come on Tom; give me a hand." He pointed out, twisting round to face away from the hole and staring up at his cousin expectantly.

Tom frowned, glancing over at Bryony nervously for a moment before he reached out to take a firm hold of Luke's wrist and set about carefully lowering him down the hole.

"Wow, Luke, you got heavy!" He gasped and Suzy smiled to herself at the indignant shout that floated back in reply.

Tom merely rolled his eyes, silently cursing his cousin's insatiable curiosity as he was forced to lie down across the floorboards with his torso halfway upended inside the old shaft.

Alarmed, Bryony quickly crawled over to sit astride Tom's legs, hoping to anchor him in place a little more and counter-balance Luke.

"Oh my God, please don't fall!" She begged, pleased that Ashley seemed to be behaving himself for once and she didn't have to try and restrain him as well. He'd just shuffled over to join Suzy on the other side of the corridor and was reaching out with one hand to illuminate the hole more with his phone so that Luke and Tom could see what they were doing. It didn't *look* like he wanted to join in with their intrepid adventure but after witnessing his mad runaway stunt, Bryony wasn't taking any chances.

"What can you see down there?" Ashley called, cautiously leaning further over the hole to peer down at his best friend.

"Not much. It's mostly just rusty metalwork and a load of old cobwebs. I accidentally put my foot through one a minute ago so now I've got a spider crawling up my leg." Luke replied, calmly.

Rose pulled a face, looking round as the others emerged from the boys' room too, their curiosity having gotten the better of them.

"What's he found now?" Robbie asked, carefully peering over Bryony's shoulder to find out what was going on.

"Hey, guys? Any chance you could lower me down a bit further? I think I've found some kind of key, but I can't quite reach it." Luke shouted, hopefully.

"You've got to be kidding me..." Tom groaned, glaring down at Luke while Robbie and Bryony moved to grab hold of his ankles instead and set about carefully lowering him further into the shaft.

"Almost there!" Luke called back, stretching out his spare hand towards the rusty old key tucked into a crack in the wall. He batted it a few times before he eventually managed to pull it free and curled his fingers around it tightly.

"Stop swinging about so much! You're just making yourself heavier!" Tom scolded, now almost entirely suspended in the hole too and feeling a little dizzy.

"Shut up!" Luke hissed, cocking his head to one side slightly before a look of panic spread across his face. "Oh no! Guys, we've got a problem! Dean's coming back!" He yelled, having heard voices approaching from further down the tunnel.

Bryony frowned.

"I knew something like this would happen…" She muttered, shaking her head in disapproval as she set about hauling Tom back up with Robbie's help.

Down below, there was a sudden howl of rage and Ashley flinched.

"I knew you kids were up to no good! Come back here, boy, with that key! It doesn't belong to you!" Dean shouted, quickly scrambling up the old ladder to swipe at Luke's ankles.

"PULL ME UP!" Luke yelled, furiously kicking at Dean's hands while Tom desperately tried to hang onto him.

Horrified, Ashley turned to face his youngest brother, knowing that Tom was going to need some help if they stood any chance of keeping Luke safe.

"Mitch, hold me up." He ordered, carelessly dumping his phone on the floorboards and gesturing down at the gloomy tunnel entrance.

"What-? No way! I can't do that! You're too big! You're almost seventeen for goodness sake!" Michael protested, staring back at Ashley incredulously.

"I'll help." Jenna offered, kneeling down beside Michael and giving Ashley a firm nod.

"Hang on, Luke!" Ashley called, bravely slithering into the dirty hole beside Tom while Jenna and Michael reached out to grab his legs.

"Gotcha!" Dean crowed, finally catching Luke's foot and roughly yanking him downwards.

"Ahhh!" Luke gasped, staring up at Tom anxiously as he felt their connection begin to weaken.

"Come back here, you little brat!" Dean snarled, angrily tugging at Luke and narrowing his eyes suspiciously as he recognised that this kid had been the one to stand up for Ashley at the abandoned mine.

"Let go of me!" Luke howled, swinging his free leg around desperately as he tried to free himself.

"Leave him alone, you monster!" Suzy called back, quickly snatching up Ashley's discarded phone and shining the torchlight down the shaft in the hope that Dean might let go of Luke to shield his eyes instead.

"I can't do this…" Tom gasped, caught up in an agonising tug-of-war between Dean and Luke below and Robbie and Bryony above. His hands were getting really sweaty from the intensity of their midnight adventure and he wasn't at all sure how long he could hang onto his cousin.

"Almost there!" Ashley grunted, urgently clawing his way past Tom and reaching out towards Luke. Unfortunately, he was a second too late and stared down in dismay as Luke's hand finally slipped out of Tom's grip and he fell out of reach.

"Dammit!" Ashley yelled, smacking the wall with one hand in frustration as Luke and Dean landed in a chaotic heap on the tunnel floor with matching groans of pain.

"Luke, watch out!" Tom gasped as the rusty old ladder broke away from the wall and dropped down into the darkness as well from the stress of Luke and Dean's fight.

Luke cried out in shock as the ladder landed in the soft soil beside his head like a spear and eyed the jagged metalwork fearfully. He was lucky it hadn't taken his eye out and decided he would have to be a lot more careful in the future.

Paranormal Assistance

Up above, the mood was tense.

Jenna and Michael had barely hauled Ashley up out of the hole before he was off down the corridor like a rocket. He didn't really care all that much about himself anymore. He *had* to protect his best friend from getting hurt by his wicked father, no matter the cost. Dean was going to pay for ever laying a finger on Luke.

"Ashley, wait-!" Jenna called, turning to stare after him in alarm while Michael quickly rushed to swap his slippers for outdoor shoes instead.

Seeing as Bryony was already wearing her boots thanks to chasing Luke and Ashley through the forest only an hour before, she was the second one out. She knew that Ashley was heading for their hidden rope-ladder and hoped they might be able to access the train tunnel before Dean got to it.

Shocked at how things had turned out, Robbie turned to follow Michael into the bedroom, simply snatching up the first two items of his scattered footwear that he found and charging back out into the corridor without a care for whether they matched or not.

"Come on you lot, hurry up! No-one cares what you're wearing, *Jenna;* just grab some shoes and a torch and get out!" He yelled, dodging past Suzy as she re-emerged from the girls' room and sprinting off down the corridor after Ashley and Bryony.

"Alright, I'm coming! Keep your hair on!" Michael grumbled, awkwardly hopping around as he tried to pull on a very uncooperative trainer.

Rose frowned, biting her lip anxiously as she considered the situation. She didn't think it very wise for them to be chasing after Dean and his gang like this and was very worried someone might get hurt. But since she was the youngest member of the group, she wasn't sure they would listen to her concerns and half of her new friends had already charged off into the forest anyway. That left her with only one option. She had to tell her mother what was going on. For once, they actually knew where Dean was going to be and Rose decided it was about time her wicked uncle was put behind bars for his crimes.

"Come on, Rose; what are you waiting for?" Jenna called as she hastily pulled a hoodie and a pair of jeans on over her pyjamas.

"I'll meet you there." Rose mumbled, taking a deep breath to compose herself before she rushed off to wake Enid.

Jenna stared after her curiously for a few moments before she turned to sprint after the others, pausing briefly to haul Michael up off the chippings on her way out after he'd tripped over the doormat in his haste.

By the time they arrived at the train tunnel, Ashley had already dropped their secret rope into the vent and slithered down it while the others tried to catch their breath amongst the damp ferns.

Not wanting to leave his mad friend alone for too long, Tom was the next one to climb down into the train tunnel and eyed Ashley critically.

"What are you thinking?" He asked as Ashley turned to consider the nearby coal wagons.

"I'm *thinking* Dean cannot be allowed to get the upper hand. We need to find a way of trapping him somehow. And I'm willing to offer myself as bait if it will help save Luke." Ashley replied solemnly.

"There's no way I'm letting you do that. Don't be stupid! Now that Dean knows you've been meddling with his plans, he'll make sure to punish you harshly. And I really don't want to witness your death. Come on, there must be something else we can do instead." Tom protested, horrified that Ashley was so quick to sacrifice himself for the people he loved.

"I wasn't asking for permission." Ashley muttered, turning back to fix Tom with a hard look as Robbie set about making his way down to join them in the tunnel. He'd barely made it halfway when the rope suddenly came loose and he fell back into the dirt with a loud yell of shock.

"Owww…" He groaned, creasing his eyes up in pain as he reached round to carefully nurse his back.

"Oh God. Rob, are you okay? Where does it hurt?" Ashley gasped, quickly side-stepping around Tom and kneeling down beside his little brother.

"Why do these things always happen to me?" Robbie complained, glaring up at the overhead vent sourly while Ashley continued to paw at him.

Tom helpfully reached down to pull the knotted rope away from Robbie before he offered the younger boy a hand.

"Are you alright? Can you stand?" He asked and Robbie nodded.

"I think so." He muttered, allowing Ashley to gently lift him halfway up before he reached out to accept Tom's outstretched hand. "Yeah, I'm fine. It doesn't hurt that much." He insisted, even though he felt like he could hardly breathe.

Ashley raised his eyebrow and reached out to carefully lift up the back of Robbie's top to examine him a little better.

"You don't *look* hurt." He muttered, gently pushing his fingers into Robbie's spine to try and find out where the pain was coming from.

"I said I'm fine, Ashley! Leave me alone!" Robbie snapped, reaching round to push his brother away and grimacing slightly.

"Okay, this jump is much harder in the dark..." Bryony mumbled, understanding that she would now have to drop straight down into the tunnel since their handy little rope had somehow unknotted itself from around the bush. "Well, move over then, boys! I don't want to squish you!" She called, waiting until they'd shifted themselves out of the way before she wriggled into the vent and came down to join them in the tunnel, landing neatly on her feet and sinking down to break her fall.

Soon, Michael, Jenna and Suzy had safely arrived in the gloomy tunnel as well and Ashley padded over to lay a few torches on the ground by the bricked-up entrance to help illuminate the area. Once he was satisfied, he wandered off to find the half-buried skeleton of the train driver and placed another torch on the ground beside him, wanting to know where the bones were located in the darkness so they didn't get damaged. He didn't want the man's spirit to think that he was disrespectful.

"Do you think Dean is scared of ghosts?" Suzy asked, having traipsed after Ashley along with the rest of his friends to find out what he was planning.

"Well, he grew up in the Morgan manor, so I'd say probably not. That place has all kinds of creepy things so I doubt if anything could scare him now. Why do you ask?" Ashley replied, peering round at her curiously.

"I just wondered if there was a way of spooking up the tunnel a bit to try and freak him out. I know if it was me coming to look for the old train and it seemed to be alive and working, I'd be pretty scared and confused." She explained and Jenna nodded in agreement.

"I wouldn't be surprised if Dean is scared of ghosts. I mean, he can't exactly fight the dead, can he? From what I've heard, Dean doesn't like to feel powerless so it would make sense for him to dislike the supernatural. It's certainly worth a try. But how do you suggest we make the tunnel all weird and spooky in the first place? We don't have a lot of time before the criminals unlock the passage door." She asked, looking round at the locomotive thoughtfully.

"Maybe our friend here could help with that?" Ashley muttered, gesturing down at the bones in front of him as he remembered the way his phone had ended up in the man's hand when they first discovered the place. "What do you say, mate? Are you up for a little mischief?" He asked, peering round the dark tunnel expectantly.

They waited a few moments before Robbie suddenly turned to point up at the locomotive's cab behind him.

"Do you hear that?" He asked and Ashley nodded, smiling to himself as he considered the crackling noise that had taken over the tunnel. He could only assume that it was meant to be the sound of the locomotive's roaring firebox and wondered what other tricks the ghost was capable of pulling off.

Nearby, Jenna pulled a face and reached up to pinch her nose with one hand as she glared round the tunnel irritably.

"Ew, no! Stop it! I hate that smell!" She complained, gagging slightly as an oily scent slowly drifted past her.

"Nice. This is really setting the scene." Ashley murmured, looking round in approval while Robbie set about studying his torch intently.

"Don't these usually have a flash setting somewhere too? That would be a lot spookier than just leaving them on a constant beam." He suggested, finally locating the right function and holding it out to demonstrate. Then, he turned it round to illuminate his face before pulling a different expression with each flash.

Michael snorted.

"Cut that out. We're stuck in the middle of this dangerous night-time adventure and you're still playing the fool." He scolded, trying to give Robbie a stern frown before he broke down into helpless laughter a few seconds later.

Robbie smiled to himself proudly as he wandered over to place the torch inside one of the old coal wagons. Then he turned to consider the rusty locomotive for a few moments while Ashley climbed up into the cab to find some more hiding spots for their torches.

"I wonder if it would still move." Robbie muttered, thinking that it would be a great shame if their grand discovery was just left to rot after all their hard work.

Tom bit his lip.

"It *has* to move. It's got to come out of the tunnel at some point, right? I'm hoping a local museum will take care of it since the train is such an important and exciting part of the area's history. But they can't begin to restore it properly and put it on display until it's out of the tunnel. I doubt the locomotive would steam on its own though after being neglected for over a century, so it would need a modern one to drag it out and maybe some assistance from the ghost train as well to power the wheels and keep everything intact. That's the whole point of the ghost train, isn't it? To help people find and rescue the real one? I reckon, with a strong new engine pulling on the front end of our stolen locomotive and the ghost train pushing it from behind, we could get it safely out of the tunnel. Then, once the old engine emerges into daylight, the ghostly one would probably fade away now that its unfinished business is completed." He explained and Ashley nodded in agreement.

"Wouldn't that be a magnificent sight?" He muttered, gazing round the tunnel thoughtfully as his imagination conjured up magical visions of the rescue operation Tom had just described. After all, they'd already discovered that the ghost train was somehow able to power the whistle in the locomotive cab, so he saw no reason why the spooky engine wouldn't be able to use its supernatural abilities to help push its decrepit twin down the tunnel and out into daylight again by Glen's cabin.

The Battle for the Locomotive

Meanwhile, in the secret passage, Luke was not having a good time. Dean had him in such a tight stranglehold that he could hardly move and Luke didn't like feeling so powerless.

"Remind me, why do we need the boy still?" A woman asked, turning to offer Luke a suspicious glare through the dim torchlight. From what Luke had seen, she was the only female member of Dean's gang and seemed to really admire the criminal, for she kept batting her eyelashes at Dean and biting her lip seductively whenever he looked round in her direction.

"We need him because he's close to my son. Trust me, Lilith. You should have seen the way they looked at each other in the forest. I don't know what kind of relationship they have, but this boy is our guarantee that Ashley will do as he is told. Okay-?" Dean replied, forcefully shunting Luke a bit further down the passage.

The woman gave a reluctant shrug of obedience and Dean nodded in quiet satisfaction.

"I still can't believe you chose to name your kid 'Ashley' of all things. What made you pick that? It doesn't seem very appropriate for a Morgan son at all. The first time I heard the name I thought you had a daughter instead so it's very confusing for people. I'm surprised your father even allowed it. I certainly wouldn't have." Lilith protested, wrinkling her nose in disapproval.

"I had my reasons." Dean growled, sounding as though he'd been asked this question hundreds of times over the years and was getting sick of it.

Luke smiled to himself as he considered the various schoolteachers Ashley had confused over the years when they were calling out the names on the register and a boy answered instead of a girl. It was no secret that Ashley had always loved his name, but it was definitely associated more with girls and Luke couldn't help agreeing with Lilith that it seemed quite odd for Dean to give his much-desired baby boy a unisex name.

"I can't believe anyone would actually fall in love with you. Seriously, how does Ashley even *exist?* You're the most repulsive man I've ever met." He muttered before grunting in pain as Lilith turned to roughly shove him up against the wall and punched him in the ribs.

"You don't *know* him." She argued, inspired by Dean's exciting, adventurous lifestyle and wishing more guys were like that. She thought it was very sexy and thrilling to exist outside the law and have the freedom to do whatever you wanted and felt a little jealous that Dean had grown up with such a supportive and badass family.

"I know enough, lady. You must be out of your god-damn mind to find this guy attractive. Didn't you hear what happened to his ex? You'd better tread lightly now if you don't want to meet the same fate." Luke snapped, angrily pushing Lilith away from him and causing her to trip over herself and end up sprawled out in the dirt at Dean's feet.

"That lying cow got exactly what she deserved." Lilith replied, blushing slightly as Dean reached down to lift her back up and helpfully dusted her off.

"Watch your mouth, boy, or you'll be the one who gets hurt. You must be a proper delight for your parents. Maybe I should do them a favour and arrange for you to disappear. I'm sure they'd be grateful. Who knows; they might even pay me for taking care of their problem!" Dean growled, stepping closer to hiss the threat directly into Luke's face in the hope it might scare him into submission.

Luke automatically gagged at the overwhelming scent of alcohol on Dean's breath before he offered the villain a wicked grin.

"My parents are your worst nightmare; lawyers. Oh, and they also treat Ashley like an extra son, so I'd think very carefully about what you do next. You might not care about Ashley anymore but there are a lot of other people who still do, including your brother and sister." He pointed out and Dean glared at him irritably.

"Ashley is no-one's business but mine…" He insisted, pausing as a loud whistle suddenly echoed round the passageway.

"What was that?" Lilith asked, confused by the unexpected noise and turning to see if any of her fellow gang members had caused it by accidentally leaning against an old lever or something.

Luke grinned, understanding that the sound had come from the old steam locomotive and that his friends must be somewhere nearby in the main tunnel. He'd always known that they would never abandon him and hoped that hearing the train whistle meant they had come up with a clever plan to help protect the stolen goods.

"What the hell-?" Dean muttered, turning to roughly drag Luke down the rest of the passageway before he set about searching through the boy's pockets for the key he'd discovered.

"Hey!" Luke protested, feeling a little violated at being patted down so thoroughly and grimacing when Dean finally located the old key in a hidden section of his jacket. The man eyed him threateningly for a few seconds at this deception before he reached out to give Luke a violent back-handed slap.

"Don't try and hide things from me, boy. It doesn't work." Dean scolded, smiling to himself cruelly as he considered the small cut he'd carved into Luke's cheek from having the key still gripped in-between his fingers.

"Nice one, babe. That should teach him not to interfere in other people's business." Lilith commented, offering Dean a bright smile as he turned to unlock the passage door and stepped out into the main tunnel.

"What the-?" He muttered, pausing in shock when he found the stolen train already illuminated by flashing lights. Some came from inside the old coal wagons while others lit up the locomotive's cab, giant wheels and distinctive funnel.

"Wow." Luke smiled, staring round at the impressive theatrics in awe before he reached up to pinch his nose as a strong, oily scent wafted over towards them. In addition to the flashing lights, his friends had also set up a few torches on a constant beam and placed them in the locomotive's disused lanterns, but Luke couldn't work out how they'd managed to achieve the loud crackling sound that was coming from the engine's cab. That was very weird.

At the far end of the tunnel, a lone figure was waiting for them by the last coal wagon, silhouetted against the torchlight behind them. Luke only needed a quick glance to recognise that this person was Ashley and wondered why his friend looked to be alone. Surely he hadn't decided to try and challenge Dean all by himself again? Hadn't he learnt anything?

"Is that him-?" Lilith asked, reaching up to point at the figure suspiciously and seeming a lot less confident than she had been a minute ago.

"Yeah, that's my boy." Dean growled, forcefully shunting Luke further up the tunnel towards his troublesome teenage son.

"He's taller than I expected. Aren't you two about the same height already? How are you supposed to beat him if you're evenly matched?" Lilith continued and Dean frowned.

"He must get that from *my* father. Myles is pretty tall as well. And besides, who said I was planning on fighting fair? Don't you know me, Lil? Trust me, Ashley is going down." He remarked, annoyed that his partner suddenly didn't seem to have much faith in him.

He had just hauled Luke past a rotten workbench when another shrill whistle blasted down the tunnel and he twisted round to see where it had come from. He was alarmed to discover that the way back was now blocked as Ashley's friends slowly crawled out from various coal wagons and storage crates, looking a bit like hungry, apocalyptic zombies out for his demise with their dirty clothes and messy hair.

Luke smiled to himself, thinking his friends had been clever to use Ashley as bait to lure Dean and his gang closer before cutting off their exit. Now, with the criminals totally surrounded, they had the advantage and Luke planned to make the most of it.

"Get off me, you lunatic." He snapped, roughly stamping on Dean's foot and elbowing him hard in the chest before dodging out of the man's grip and moving over to stand in-between Tom and Bryony instead.

"Back off. These goods don't belong to you." Ashley's voice growled as he finally stepped forwards into the light and glanced round at Luke worriedly. Luke offered him a faint smile to show that he was okay and gestured for Ashley to focus his attention on his wicked father instead.

Dean chuckled.

"Oooh, I'm scared. What are you going to do now, Ashley? *Fight* me? Bring it on; I dare you." He replied beckoning to his son with both hands and quirking one eyebrow up as a bold challenge.

"Are you sure you want to go down that road? You have no idea what I'm capable of." Ashley warned, understanding that since Rose had gone to explain the situation to Enid, they only had to delay Dean's gang for long enough to give the police time to catch up.

"Please. You're nothing special." Dean scoffed, eyeing Ashley critically while the rest of his gang spread out to choose their own opponents.

Obviously, since Luke and Lilith were Ashley and Dean's most loyal friends, they ended up being paired together again and Luke frowned to himself irritably.

"Come on then. I've already knocked you down on your ass once, lady. Do you really want me to do it again? I wouldn't think you'd appreciate that kind of humiliation in front of your *boyfriend.* But what do I know?" He teased, skilfully dodging underneath Lilith's angry punch and grinning at her mischievously.

Nearby, Suzy quickly climbed back up into one of the old coal wagons for safety, alarmed that the situation had broken down so quickly and wondering how she could make herself useful. She didn't really approve of violence and decided that she wouldn't be much help anyway since she was quite small and weak.

Therefore, she settled for lobbing lumps of coal into the mess occasionally to try and distract her friends' opponents. This turned out to be quite a good strategy until one of her missiles hit Robbie in the head by accident and caused him to look round expectantly when he should have been focused on the dangerous incoming kick. Suzy cringed in awkward shame at the loud howl of pain that echoed round the tunnel a few moments later and cautiously raised her head up over the edge of the wagon to offer Robbie an apologetic little smile.

Meanwhile, on the other side of the tunnel, Tom had ended up battling against the biggest member of Dean's gang and was not having much success. His attacks didn't seem to hurt the man at all, but Tom was already in quite a lot of pain from being thrown against the wall three times.

"Come on, man! That's not fair!" He whined, reaching up to rub his head as he landed in the dirt by the train driver's bones.

"Maybe you should work out more." The man advised, roughly hauling Tom back to his feet before looking round in alarm when an agonised yell suddenly echoed round the tunnel.

It turned out that Lilith had pulled Luke back against her by the hair and Luke was *not* happy about it. Tom, however, was very appreciative of the distraction and took the opportunity to dodge back into the shadows, ready to launch a surprise assault on his monstrous opponent when he turned round again.

Unfortunately, Luke's desperate cry of pain hadn't been very beneficial for Ashley. He'd been busy trying to avoid the small knife in Dean's hand when Luke was attacked and had automatically turned to see what had happened to his best friend. This momentary lack of concentration had caused him to end up with a deep gash in one side from Dean's rage and a violent kick to the abdomen that knocked him off his feet.

"Ooof..." Ashley groaned, a little winded as he reached down to gently examine his bleeding wound. It stung like crazy, but from what he could see, he didn't appear to be *seriously* hurt which was a relief.

"Ha! Serves you right." Dean sneered, delighted to have Ashley sprawled out in the dirt at his feet where he belonged. Unfortunately, he didn't get chance to punish Ashley any further because Robbie suddenly leapt up onto his back with a furious howl and pushed him off balance.

"Leave my brother alone!" Robbie snapped, causing Dean to stagger sideways in shock at the unexpected ambush while Jenna boldly moved forwards to try and prise the weapon out of Dean's hand.

The three of them struggled against each other for a while until Jenna finally succeeded in batting the knife away, accidentally sending it spinning dangerously through the air in the process and giving Ashley a nasty fright when it suddenly landed in-between his legs.

"Oh my God…" He gasped, automatically jumping back in horror before he reached up to press one hand over his heart to try and calm himself down.

"I'm so sorry! I didn't mean for that to happen, I swear! Are you alright?" Jenna called, rushing across to fuss over Ashley worriedly as she tried to make up for her mistake. He eyed her critically for a moment before he reached out to pull the scarf away from her neck and set about trying to fashion it into a makeshift bandage around his waist instead, hoping it would protect his injury a bit until he could get it seen to.

"Don't worry, it doesn't hurt that much." He insisted, offering Jenna a brave smile as he allowed her to carefully help him back to his feet. She merely fixed him with a stern look that showed she knew he was lying before she bent over to examine him properly, shocked that Ashley had now been knifed by his father not once but twice.

Behind them, Robbie gave a loud grunt of pain as he and Dean suddenly fell over together and ended up fighting on the floor instead for a few seconds until Michael stepped forwards to roughly push the criminal away with his foot.

"Thanks…" Robbie muttered, accepting Michael's proffered hand before frowning to himself darkly as two of Dean's henchmen moved over to harass them, leaving their leader free to crawl away to safety.

"Anytime." Michael nodded, finding himself now back-to-back with his older brother as the villains circled around them.

"What are you gonna do now, little boy? Have we trapped you in a corner? You can't fight back if you've no space, right?" One of the men laughed, boldly stepping closer until he was practically in Michael's face.

"That's what *you* think." Robbie growled, reaching round to forcefully lock arms with his sibling before he doubled over to sharply lift Michael off his feet.

"Take that!" Michael crowed, obediently rolling backwards over Robbie's spine and extending one leg out to kick the man in front of him. Then, as he was flipped upside-down, he gave Robbie's aggressor the same treatment, leaving both men sprawled out in the dirt and allowing himself a smug little smile as he landed safely on his feet in front of his brother.

"Nice." Robbie grinned, nodding at Michael proudly as he considered what they had just accomplished.

Satisfied that their own threat had been taken care of, Robbie turned to look around the tunnel to see if any of their friends needed assistance. So far, it seemed like Bryony was managing quite well on her own, but Luke had somehow found himself laid out on the ground with Lilith knelt astride him and reaching down to press one arm into his throat.

"We should help him." Michael declared, feeling a lot braver now that he had Robbie around to protect him. At the moment, Robbie was one of the few people who didn't have a scratch on them and Michael was quite impressed.

However, they'd barely taken three steps towards Luke when disaster struck and Robbie frowned to himself awkwardly as he realised they'd been watching over the wrong person.

"ALRIGHT, THAT'S ENOUGH! STOP IT!" Dean yelled, causing everyone to abruptly halt what they were doing and turn to face him expectantly. They found Ashley on his knees in front of Dean with another knife held up to his throat and his arms painfully twisted round behind him leaving his injured side exposed and vulnerable.

Jenna groaned, ashamed that she'd only managed to protect her bandmate from one of Dean's weapons. She couldn't imagine where he'd gotten the second one from.

"No! Please! Don't do this!" She begged, quickly turning to scan the tunnel as she looked to see if there was a way of rescuing Ashley from his current peril.

Luke, meanwhile, took advantage of Lilith's distraction to throw a handful of dirt up into her face before wriggling out from underneath her as she gave an angry cry of protest.

"Let him go." He insisted, staring across at Dean darkly as his hands curled up into threatening fists. There was absolutely no way he was just going to stand by and watch his best friend get his throat slit.

"Luke, please don't do anything stupid. It's okay. I've got this. Trust me." Ashley muttered and Luke paused, understanding from the burning fire in Ashley's eyes that he hadn't given up just yet. Somehow, Ashley still had an ace up his sleeve.

Dean laughed, roughly tipping Ashley's head back to stare at him incredulously as he considered his son's peculiar remark.

"Don't be ridiculous. You've got nothing. Your time is up, Ashley. You've had your fun." He scoffed, cruelly raising the knife up a little further to press it against Ashley's long facial scar and causing him to freeze as the blade came really close to his eyeball. "Do you have anything you'd like to say to your friends before I send you down to join your mother in hell?" Dean growled, leaning closer to hiss in Ashley's ear as he moved the knife back down to hover in front of his son's throat again, making it absolutely clear that he *had* intended to kill Ashley back at the manor all those years ago.

Ashley nodded, slowly swivelling his gaze round to fix Dean with a look of intense loathing before he opened his mouth and began to loudly sing Heidi's favourite song, his voice still really clean and professional despite being in a very dangerous situation.

He'd always been quite inspired by the lyrics of this piece as they spoke of using your voice to make a difference and not fighting with people all the time. His guardian had once told him that Heidi thought the song suited her own life really well as she struggled against Dean and would hum it to herself as she looked for strength and courage. Growing up, Ashley had also taken to singing the lyrics to himself for motivation, except seeing as he associated the tune with his mother, it had felt like Heidi was the one offering him guidance instead of the original songwriters.

"What the heck?" Lilith gasped, staring across at Ashley in obvious confusion while Dean merely froze, recognising the song instantly and finding himself transported back to a happier time when he would come home to Heidi singing away to herself as she planned out floral arrangements for her clients.

Of course, Dean had always known that Ashley liked music too, for his son had really enjoyed wailing along to the radio as an infant and playing with noisy toys, but he hadn't expected that Ashley would develop such an incredible, strong voice and wasn't quite sure how to react. The boy had obviously spent years perfecting his craft and Dean was shocked at the way Ashley had absolute control over every tiny note that left his mouth and the power coming from his lungs. It was extraordinary. He'd not anticipated that Ashley might randomly start *singing* at him and peered round at his son incredulously, too surprised and captivated by this bizarre development to realise that he was wasting the opportunity to execute the troublesome brat.

Jenna beamed, staring across at her bandmate proudly as she considered the way Ashley's strongest weapon didn't involve violence.

"Yes Ashley! You show him!" She exclaimed, feeling like her heart might burst with joy as she considered the way Ashley's voice totally filled the tunnel and caused the other criminals to glance round at each other anxiously as they wondered how to deal with this astonishing reaction.

Jenna eyed Ashley intently for a few moments before she opened her mouth to sing the words too, fully aware that he had asked his friends never to interfere with this special song but thinking that it was important, in this moment, to show her support.

"What are you doing?" Bryony hissed, not wanting to make Ashley mad by disrespecting his wishes.

Jenna merely turned to gesture at them urgently, hoping they would understand her intentions and not leave her looking really foolish.

Thankfully, Luke at least seemed to be on the same wavelength and Jenna smiled at him gratefully across the tunnel as he also began to sing the motivating lyrics, his voice sounding a little scratchy from being half-strangled but determined to help empower Ashley and spook the criminals.

One by one, the rest of their friends nervously added their voices into the mix as well, creating a wonderful backing chorus to Ashley's lead vocals and showing Dean that they would always be united in their actions. It didn't matter that some people were terrible singers; they had put their self-consciousness and lack of talent aside to support their friend and Jenna thought that was really magical.

Ashley stared round at his mates in amazement, startled by their involvement in his song but touched by their unwavering devotion. They really were the best group of people in the entire world and he felt very lucky to have them. Before, he'd always imagined that his friends would ruin the special significance of Heidi's favourite song if they tried to sing the lyrics with him. But now, he couldn't help feeling that they had actually improved it and given it a much deeper meaning.

His friends had wasted no time in adding the tune's strong beat into the mix as well through a combination of clapping, stamping their feet and banging on nearby objects and the noise was absolutely deafening. As they progressed through the lyrics, the ghostly whistle of the locomotive had also started blasting down the tunnel too at appropriate moments, as the phantom driver began to learn the rhythm and tried to show his support.

Ashley thought it was the most exhilarating moment in his life. This was his friends showing that they were one unit and that if Dean wanted to mess with Ashley, he would have to deal with them too. And they were a force to be reckoned with. This was undeniable proof that Dean was wrong. Ashley *was* loved and his friends would follow him to the ends of the earth.

What they hadn't considered was that their ear-splitting racket had also made it a lot easier for Rose, Enid and the police to find them in the darkness. That was just a happy accident. At the time, they'd been too focused on their own supportive little bubble to appreciate the wider landscape and Suzy couldn't help giving a loud squeal of shock when Enid's voice suddenly echoed round them from the steam vent above.

"Dean Morgan, get your hands off my nephew this instant!" She snapped, horrified to find her relatives engaged in another violent fight and causing Dean to flinch in shock.

"How many times? Ashley is *my* son! I will deal with him as I see fit!" Dean yelled, his short temper flaring up again as he glared up at her sourly. Thankfully, he didn't get another opportunity to try and 'deal with' Ashley as they were interrupted by a low, menacing growl from further down the tunnel before Shadow padded into the light.

Luke figured the beast must have managed to break free of Dean's gang-mate somehow and jumped down one of the other open vents as he tried to follow Ashley's scent and sounds. The boy had been the first person to show him any kindness and it was clear that the dog was now utterly devoted to him.

On seeing Dean with a knife in his hand and Ashley with bloody fingers, Shadow gave another threatening snarl before he suddenly bounded forwards, barking and snapping at Dean aggressively as he tried to separate them.

"Nobody move!" A police officer shouted from above as a rolled-up metal ladder was dropped into the tunnel to help the authorities access the scene.

Dean, of course, took no notice since he was too busy trying to fend off the savage creature in front of him. It didn't matter how many times he yelled at Shadow to stop; the stupid animal just wouldn't listen to him.

"Oh, you two bloody deserve each other! What a fine pair of failures!" He exclaimed, reaching up to roughly tug a long, golden chain out from underneath his top and carelessly dumping it over Ashley's head before he fled up the tunnel in a wild panic with Shadow angrily chasing after him and barking incessantly.

Lilith promptly turned to run after her boyfriend while Tom and Bryony reached out to collar another one of Dean's gang members, determined that *someone* should be punished for the attempted theft.

"Shadow, you silly boy! You scared him off! We were *this* close to getting him arrested!" Robbie scolded as the great dog padded back down the tunnel towards them with a rather victorious wag in his tail.

Shadow merely stared back at him blankly for a few seconds before he turned to wander across the tunnel to examine Ashley instead, who was still knelt somewhat haphazardly on the ground and clutching his side with one hand.

"Woof!" He barked, trying to reassure his young master that the threat had been taken care of. He gave Ashley a fond lick before he flopped down beside him and leaned closer to cautiously sniff the bloody scarf that was wrapped around his waist. Then, realising that his favourite human was hurt, he let out a mournful little whine and curled himself around Ashley a bit more to try and prop him up.

"Thanks, buddy." Ashley muttered, weakly reaching out to pet Shadow as the dog gave a few more insistent barks up at the steam vent in an effort to get him some help. He didn't particularly care about Dean's bizarre gift at the moment. He was in too much pain, both physically and mentally.

An Offensive Gift

The sun was just beginning to pierce through the trees as the group gathered around an ambulance Enid had called up to the manor entrance when Rose came to explain what her friends had gotten involved with. The woman had been horrified to learn that they had crossed paths with Dean and had spent the past few minutes furiously lecturing them on their irresponsibility.

Luke peered round at Ashley worriedly as he stepped down from being examined by the paramedics, his top still a little blood-stained from where Dean had carved an ugly wound into his side.

"Are you okay?" He asked, upset that his cry of pain had caused his best friend to get injured.

Ashley wrinkled his nose slightly, one hand still gently pressed over his injury as he turned to glance round at the forest.

"Don't worry about me; I'll be fine. It looks worse than it is. I just lost a concerning amount of blood because I couldn't treat it properly for a while. Apparently, Jenna's scarf wasn't a very good bandage. Who'd have thought?" He explained, forcing a small smile onto his face as he tried to reassure Luke.

"Does it hurt?" Luke asked, noting that Ashley's skin looked a lot paler than usual and wondering if his friend was secretly feeling a bit faint.

"Yes." Ashley admitted, carefully lifting his top up a bit to show Luke the medical pad that was stuck to his torso.

"I'm really sorry. I feel terrible that you got injured because of me. I hope it doesn't turn into another scar. That would be awful. I'd never forgive myself if that happened." Luke mumbled, staring down at his best friend's wounded side for a few moments before he focused his gaze back on Ashley's face. "By the way, I wanted to say that I was very impressed by your non-violent takedown of Dean back there. That was really smart. I don't think he ever imagined that you would start singing and it totally disarmed him. You should have seen his face! He didn't have a clue what to do with himself at all. It was fantastic." He added and Ashley smiled faintly.

"I guess my love of hanging out in an abandoned theatre back home finally paid off then. Practising my skills in that place helped me learn how to take control of a room and use its design to my advantage, such as the echoes produced by the train tunnel. That effect meant that it sounded to Dean as though there were four of me lecturing him from all sides so it was no wonder he got very lost and confused." He murmured, reaching over to lay one hand on Luke's shoulder to help balance himself since he felt like he was about to pass out.

Bryony eyed him worriedly for a couple of seconds before she walked over to place a hand on his back, thinking that he should really be resting inside the manor if he was hurt. But, having known Ashley for five years, she also understood that he really didn't like being told what to do. She expected that if Ashley did collapse, it would only take Luke half a second to catch him and smiled to herself wistfully as she considered their extraordinary friendship.

"So, does this mean we're going to be sent back home again now? That would be a real shame since we've only been here a few days. I feel like there's a lot more we could learn about this place, but I don't think Enid would be happy to let us stay any longer after what happened. She looked really upset back at the tunnel when she saw Ashley and Dean having another huge fight." She sighed and Michael nodded, sadly.

"Yeah. I overheard her on the phone to our guardian a few minutes ago. She was apologising a lot so I think she blames herself for what happened seeing as she invited us up here but we're definitely going home. Enid said that she wanted to make sure Ashley was safe but now I just feel really bad because I know Pamela was looking forward to some peace and quiet. I hope she's not too mad." He confirmed, biting his lip in awkward guilt.

Luke cringed as he imagined the massive lecture his parents would dish out on his return before he twisted round to peer at Ashley curiously over his shoulder.

"What did Dean give you before he ran off?" He asked, remembering how confused he'd been on seeing Dean give

Ashley a present after trying to murder him only a few minutes before.

"I don't know. I'd almost forgotten about that..." Ashley muttered, reaching down to investigate the necklace curiously, which was still loosely hanging down against his top. When he realised what it was, his eyes widened in shock and he seemed to get even paler, something Rose hadn't thought possible. "Get it off..." Ashley snapped, so offended by Dean's gift that he could hardly bear to touch it.

Alarmed, Jenna reached over to lift the necklace over Ashley's head, wondering why he suddenly looked as though his blood was boiling in anger.

"What's wrong?" She asked, gently spreading the necklace out across her hand and raising it up in front of her eyes. The silver chain housed a large, flat disc that had a swirly letter 'H' engraved in the middle and a neat pattern of leaves around the edge and Jenna bit her lip anxiously as she realised that obviously it must once have belonged to Ashley, Robbie and Michael's mother, Heidi.

Curious, she flipped the disc over to see if there was anything engraved on the back, smiling when she found the name 'Ashley' at the top followed by his birthday, then 'Robbie' underneath with a second date and finally 'Michael' at the bottom with his arrival into the world. Jenna couldn't help noticing that Heidi had also left a gap at the bottom in case she had any more children and thought it was really sweet how the woman had paid to have her sons' names engraved onto the necklace so that they would always be close to her heart.

Luke gasped.

"So *that's* how Dean knew your names!" He exclaimed, turning to stare round at Robbie and Michael with a look of great relief on his face since he'd been trying to work that out for ages.

Beside him, Ashley gave a mournful little whine of heartbroken grief as he slowly sank down to his knees and pressed both hands over his face.

"Oh God..." Tom muttered as he considered where the necklace had come from. "Mate, I'm so sorry." He added, crouching down to envelope Ashley in a tight hug and frowning to himself when he heard the younger boy give a quiet sob.

Robbie eyed the offensive necklace thoughtfully for a few moments before he dropped down to wrap his arms around Ashley too, something which took the rest of their friends completely by surprise.

Michael, however, remained standing.

"That used to belong to our mother. I've seen it before on old photographs that we have displayed around the house. It obviously meant a lot to her because she seems to be wearing it in every image. I always wondered what had happened to it. I just assumed that Pamela must have inherited it and that she was waiting for the right time to pass it on to us." He explained, his face creasing as Ashley gave another violent howl of distress.

"*He* took it! I can't believe it. I thought it had been lost! But he took it as a bloody souvenir! All this time, he's been gloating over her death. Why can't he just let her go? Why can't he let us both go? Even in death, he still has to own her! I don't understand. Why would he give me this? What's it supposed to mean?" Ashley wailed, sounding so overwhelmed that the rest of his friends promptly crouched down to help comfort him as well.

Luke suspected that Dean had given Ashley the necklace as a way to silently win the fight and scowled to himself darkly at the criminal's cruelty. One small gift had hurt Ashley more than any gunshot or knife blade could and Luke was furious.

"Hey…" He muttered, reaching out to gently turn Ashley's tear-stained face towards him and pausing when his heart immediately shattered into tiny pieces. "At least the necklace is safe now, right? Dean may have intended the gift to be malicious, but you don't have to interpret it that way. Don't let him hurt you like this, please. Instead of thinking about where the necklace has been all these years and why, you could focus on the idea that you have another piece of your mother's life back. Michael said that she used to wear it all the time so it must be full of love and positive energies since she had your names carved on the back. But if it's too painful, you can always give the necklace to your guardian for safekeeping. I bet she'd really like that." He murmured, offering Ashley what he hoped was a bright smile.

Ashley sniffed.

"Could you maybe hang onto it for now?" He asked and Luke nodded, reaching out to carefully rescue the jewellery from Jenna's fingers and draping it around his neck.

Michael nodded in quiet satisfaction, knowing that Luke would keep the necklace safe until Ashley was ready to deal with it. Luke wouldn't care if that was three days from now or three decades. He would accept the responsibility happily if it meant Ashley could have a cool head for a while.

"Thank you." He mumbled, flashing the older boy a solemn smile through the chaotic pile of bodies and hearing Robbie give a muffled grunt of agreement.

"No problem." Luke replied, gently tucking the necklace under his top so Ashley didn't have to look at it. His best friend sounded a lot calmer now from the effects of Jenna stroking his head, Robbie and Tom hugging him tightly, Rose holding his hand and Michael lightly rubbing one hand up and down his spine and Luke was pleased.

He'd never expected to see Ashley cry during the holiday and felt that the moment would be forever burned into his heart. It had been the worst thing he'd ever witnessed and he hoped never to see it again. Ashley didn't deserve to suffer so much. He just wanted to get on with his life for pity's sake! But, for some reason, people just insisted on trying to put him down all the time which wasn't very kind or fair.

He just hoped that this adventure would reassure Ashley that he didn't have to endure things on his own anymore. After all, he was currently buried under a pile of concerned friends trying to take his pain away and Luke thought it was really cosy. They might be a complicated mix of heights, ages and genders but they cared about each other an awful lot and would go out of their way to help cheer somebody up. They were friends for life.

"Sorry." Ashley mumbled as he reached out to gently push them away. "I didn't mean to break down like that. Dad's gift just stabbed me right in the heart." He added, wincing as Tom carefully lifted him back to his feet.

Jenna stared at him incredulously.

"Oh, hun; you don't have to apologise! It's fine! We all get upset sometimes. Don't be embarrassed!" She exclaimed, reaching up to gently flick a stray eyelash away from Ashley's cheek.

Robbie nodded.

"Yeah, I think you'd have to be pretty cold not to react to a gift like that. I don't blame you at all. That was brutal." He agreed, silently pleased that he didn't have to deal with the idea of Dean's blood flowing through his veins.

"I do feel sorry for him sometimes. I mean, Dean has spent his entire life being forcefully pushed into obeying the Morgan way of life and I can't help wondering if he even knows himself. Take me for example. You know that I like to sing and dance and sketch but I get the impression Dean doesn't have any of that. It's like he can't even think for himself anymore. He's just been *programmed* to cause trouble and he doesn't know anything else. I can't help wondering what my father would be like if he'd been allowed to speak his own mind and find something he really enjoyed. Ultimately, I don't think he's to blame for any of this. He was pushed into it by his father and crumbled against the pressure. Glen was the one who broke the rules after all and got kicked out while Enid had the responsibility of looking after the manor. So Dean was left to be dragged down into the darkness seeing as he was the family's last hope. It's quite sad really." Ashley muttered, his eyes now a very aggressive shade of blue from his tears.

Tom helpfully offered out a tissue from his pocket before he draped his arm back around Ashley's shoulders.

"That's true. But you've got a much better situation. Your mother knew that you'd be expected to honour the family traditions as well, so she went to great lengths to try and protect you. I think she sounds amazing. Heidi not only ran away from Dean to give you a happier upbringing, but she also betrayed him by using your middle names to honour some of the respectable Morgan ancestors instead. She clearly wanted you to know that you are free to choose your own path in life. As a result, you grew up outside the Morgan way-of-life and therefore I think you're in a really good position to challenge it.

You might have bad blood but it doesn't have to dictate who you are. You certainly showed us that tonight! Dean only gave you that necklace because it became clear that he'd lost and he didn't know what else to do. So, if you think about it, Heidi's jewellery coming back to you is a sign that you're doing what she wanted and I bet she'd be really proud." He explained, looking round as a group of police officers emerged from the trees nearby, having been sent back to their van with a few boxes of evidence.

"You kids are in big trouble. I hope you realise that. This place was condemned years ago, so by entering it tonight you were actually trespassing which is against the law." A young man commented, seeming quite smug.

Robbie rolled his eyes.

"Is it trespassing though, if no-one even knew this tunnel existed? Until we turned up, it had pretty much been lost to history. And besides, the place was only ever 'condemned' thanks to a lie and some clever theatrics. If anything, we should be suing them for not investigating more and leaving the landscape littered with dangerous holes." He grumbled once the group had moved further away and couldn't overhear what they were saying.

Tom nodded in agreement.

"Also, we *tried* to notify the police when we first discovered the tunnel, but they just sent us away. If they'd just come to explore the place when we reported it then we wouldn't have needed to fight the criminals to begin with." He pointed out, still quite resentful at being treated like a child when he was just trying to do the right thing.

Thankfully, seeing as Enid had now reported both a murder and a stolen train to the police, it seemed that they trusted her a great deal and had agreed to let the teenagers off with a warning, something they had been quite relieved about. Ashley had thought it very unfair for him to get punished for trying to protect the old locomotive while Dean had escaped justice again because he ran away like a coward.

Suzy yawned, reaching up to politely cover her mouth with one hand before she padded over to rest her head against Luke's arm.

"Oh gosh, sorry! I think I'd better head inside and start packing if we're going to be shipped off back home again. If I leave it any longer, I'll be too tired." She mumbled, the dreamy expression on her face making it clear that she thought Luke made a really good pillow.

Ashley smiled to himself faintly as he turned to face the manor, which was now beautifully illuminated by the sunrise. He stopped to admire it for a few moments before he obediently followed his friends inside the building, secretly pleased that they were being sent back down to Cornwall. The past few days had totally drained him of energy and he couldn't wait to be reunited with his own bed. He'd never wanted anything more in his life.

"I hate to say it, but I fear this is just the start. Dean won't forget that we tried to interfere with his plans and he'll be sure to make us pay. I reckon we've a long road ahead yet before we're finally rid of him. And even though we got told off by the authorities tonight, I still think that uncovering the Morgans' stolen wealth and returning stuff to the local community is the right thing to do. It's about time their dirty criminal empire was brought down as you say. Maybe the other people only failed because they tried to tackle the problem alone. But I have you guys to help me. You're the real heroes, in my opinion. I'm just the one with the Morgan surname. I've learnt a lot the past few days about myself and my past but the biggest shock has been seeing your bravery and loyalty. I always imagined that sharing my dirty heritage with you would send you running for the hills and I'd be left all alone. But it's actually brought us a lot closer and I'll be forever grateful. Thank you, honestly, for being the best group of friends anyone could wish for." He admitted, reaching out to wrap his arms around Michael and Jenna and flashing Rose the most genuine smile she had seen since he arrived.

www.ingramcontent.com/pod-product-compliance
Lightning Source LLC
Chambersburg PA
CBHW052012070526
44584CB00016B/1723